C000192891

Capabilities for strategic advantage

Capabilities for strategic advantage
Leading through technological innovation

David Birchall
and
George Tovstiga

© David Birchall and George Tovstiga 2005

All rights reserved. No reproduction, copy or transmission of this publication
may be made without written permission.

No paragraph of this publication may be reproduced, copied or transmitted save
with written permission or in accordance with the provisions of the Copyright,
Designs and Patents Act 1988, or under the terms of any licence permitting
limited copying issued by the Copyright Licensing Agency, 90 Tottenham Court
Road, London W1T 4LP.

Any person who does any unauthorised act in relation to this publication may
be liable to criminal prosecution and civil claims for damages.

The authors have asserted their rights to be identified as the authors of this
work in accordance with the Copyright, Designs and Patents Act 1988.

First published 2005 by
PALGRAVE MACMILLAN
Houndmills, Basingstoke, Hampshire RG21 6XS and
175 Fifth Avenue, New York, N.Y. 10010
Companies and representatives throughout the world

PALGRAVE MACMILLAN is the global academic imprint of the Palgrave
Macmillan division of St. Martin's Press, LLC and of Palgrave Macmillan Ltd.
Macmillan® is a registered trademark in the United States, United Kingdom and
other countries. Palgrave is a registered trademark in the European Union and
other countries.

ISBN 1–4039–4502–0

This book is printed on paper suitable for recycling and made from fully
managed and sustained forest sources.

A catalogue record for this book is available from the British Library.

A catalog record for this book is available from the Library of Congress.

Editing and origination by
Curran Publishing Services, Norwich

10 9 8 7 6 5 4 3 2 1
14 13 12 11 10 09 08 07 06 05

Printed and bound in Great Britain by
Creative Print & Design (Wales) Ebbw Vale

CONTENTS

Figures

TABLES

PREFACE

We are living in times of great opportunities; we are living in times of great challenges. We are experiencing an age in which revolutionary technological advances in fields such as nanotechnology, biotechnology and digitization are presenting unprecedented opportunities for business growth in a wide variety of industries. This is happening against a backdrop of disruption and discontinuity in the global competitive environment, in which deregulation, globalization, connectivity and new modes of knowledge production are driving the emergence of a new economic order. It would appear that the potential for innovation is greater than it ever has been.

Competition, on the other hand, is more intense than it ever has been. Increasingly, firms are under overwhelming pressure to create better value while their profit margins are shrinking. Traditional cost reduction measures that have been deployed to the hilt in the recent post-dot.com period have failed to help firms go much beyond simply holding their competitive ground. Cost reduction has not helped firms to break into the exciting opportunities that are presenting themselves in the new and emerging markets. Firms are struggling to find new ways to create competitive advantage. Creation of better value is proving to be the principal means for achieving this.

Value creation leading to profitable growth, most management thinkers and practitioners agree, can come only from innovation. Innovation is the solution, but not innovation as we have known it in the past. Converging industries, discontinuities in the global economy, and new and accelerated modes of knowledge production in an increasingly networked, global community are calling into question our basic conception of value and the processes that lead to its creation. This is transforming our paradigm of competitive advantage, and our understanding of the roles and contributions of value creation and innovation.

This book draws on almost a decade of collaborative research work that has focused on various aspects of the strategic management of capabilities and innovation. Concepts based on emerging theory in capabilities-based competition are used to explore the processes by which firms might enhance their ability to manage their innovation capabilities more effectively. Important in this context are the organization's processes both for strategic learning and for creating and deploying new strategic knowledge. The search for competitive advantage is also challenging firms to become more effective in leveraging their existing stock of strategic knowledge. The firm's portfolio of core capabilities is probably the most important manifestation of its strategically relevant knowledge. Increasingly, firms are seeking new approaches to breaking away from competitors by leveraging their strategic capabilities in competitive and cooperative interactions between organizations.

The chapters in this book are broadly organized into two parts. The first part defines and discusses the concept of "core capability" in relation to concepts in the field of capabilities-based competition. This part develops the concepts and the basic notion of competitive advantage from the perspective of core capabilities and their impact on innovation. Practical tools, approaches, and frameworks that have been developed by the authors for analyzing the strategic impact of the firm's core capabilities are presented in this part as well.

Innovation and capabilities are shown to be intimately linked through organizational learning and the organization's propensity for change in response to changes in its competitive environment. The authors show how emerging market opportunities are demanding new approaches to capabilities management and new innovation strategies. First, firms are recognizing the importance of secondary capabilities such as strategic partnering and networking to provide access to new sources of knowledge and innovation. Second, firms are experimenting with new forms of innovation strategy that range from the predictable institutional innovation to potentially disruptive revolutionary innovation. A strategy based on only traditional *institutional* innovation alone, the authors argue, is inadequate for breaking into new market opportunities that hold the potential for real business growth. An innovation strategy focusing only on disruptive or *revolutional* innovation bears a high element of risk and therefore is also unsuitable for all but a relatively small number of high-technology start-ups. *Evolutional* innovation, an innovation strategy that seeks to leverage the competitive potential of both institutional and revolutionary innovation, is most suitable for reaping emerging market opportunities for profitable growth. Evolutional innovation strategy demands deliberate deployment of the firm's secondary capabilities. Thus, we see that more and more the competition for strategic advantage is shifting towards the strategic management of the firm's secondary capabilities.

The second part of the book explores this premise in more detail. No firm can out-innovate all potential competitors. Hence firms are seeking new ways to break away from their competitors by moving beyond the traditional company-centric and product-and-service focused concept of innovation and capabilities deployment towards a new market orientation that is opening the firm to its environment. The book explains how firms are developing core capabilities around secondary activities that enhance the deployment of the firm's primary capabilities by exposing these to new knowledge through strategic partnering. These firms are discovering the competitive potential of their secondary capabilities in building, maintaining and leveraging strategic networks. Secondary capabilities in many ways are providing firms with unique opportunities for competitive differentiation.

The second part of the book ends with a chapter on innovation performance measurement. This chapter addresses the dilemma faced by many innovation practitioners in defining appropriate and meaningful measures of their innovation performance. It pulls together current thinking on the subject and provides guidance on how to approach the measurement of innovation performance. The book closes with two appendices. In Appendix A, the authors present a methodology for systematically analyzing the firm's strategic portfolio of capabilities. Appendix B presents a short case write-up of BP Amoco's efforts to institutionalize advanced approaches to capabilities development and organizational learning.

The book draws on our own research, consulting and teaching experiences at Henley Management College (UK), the University of Twente (Netherlands), ABB (Switzerland) and Arthur D. Little (Switzerland). The book is meant to engage and challenge practitioners of innovation and those managers of organizations in which innovation is important in the debate on the strategic capabilities and innovation management. In particular, the book is written with the needs of executives of companies, operational managers of innovation, and students of innovation management in mind. Toward that end, we have included key questions throughout the book that address the important issues dealt with in the specific chapters.

Acknowledgments

We would like to acknowledge the contributions of all the executives from around the world who we have consulted in the preparation of the book and those who assisted with the survey of innovation performance measurement.

Also we would like to thank colleagues who have worked with us over the years and contributed to our knowledge and understanding.

We particularly thank Professor Jean-Jacques Chanaron with support for the survey of innovation performance measurement, June Marshall and Jeni Giambona for their tireless help with the manuscript preparation, and Liz Birchall for assistance with data processing for the survey. We are grateful to the following sources for kind permission to reproduce diagrams and illustrations as follows:

Arthur D. Little, Inc. for its Innovation Process Model (Chapter 11).

Gruner, K. E. and Homburg, C., for the table 'The attractiveness of customers and impact on success in the NPD process' from "Does customer interaction enhance new product success?" in *Journal of Business Research* (2000) **49** (1), pp. 1–14.

Kauffman, P., Ricks, W., and Schockcor, J., for the table 'Three pillars and ten goals of NASA research' from "Research portfolio analysis using extensions of quality function deployment" in *Engineering Management Journal* (1999) **11** (2), pp. 3–9.

Martinelli, R. and Waddell, J., for Figures 3 and 4 from their article "Program risk management" in *Project Management World Today*, Sept–Oct 2004.

Partovi, F. Y. and Corredoira, R. A., for the figure 'The basic elements of the house of quality' from "Quality function deployment for the good of soccer" in *European Journal of Operational Research* (2002) **137** (3), pp. 642–57.

Sony Corporation for kindly letting us reproduce the drawing found at the following weblink:
http://www.sony.net/SonyInfo/procurementinfo/partnership.html

Lastly, but not least, we thank our families, Catherine, Tom, Liz and Heidi, Nicki, Matthew and Neal – for their support, encouragement, and patience throughout.

David Birchall and
George Tovstiga

CHAPTER 1

Capabilities and competitive advantage in continually changing contexts

Introduction

We are living in a time of broad and sweeping change. Knowledge frontiers are moving forward more quickly than they ever have. It has been pointed out that in almost every major discipline up to 90 percent of relevant knowledge has appeared in the past 15 years. Terabytes of data (for comparison purposes, one terabyte approximates the entire scope of Shakespeare's collected works) are added to the every discipline's database every day (Quinn 2002: 96). This trend is set to continue. The situation challenges our very conception of strategic advantage and what firms need to do in order to achieve a position of competitive advantage.

> In this chapter, we:
>
> - examine the changing face of competition in the post-dot.com era
> - explore the drivers and characteristics of the emerging techno-economic order
> - broadly scope some of the implications for the strategic management of capabilities and innovation in this emerging context.

Changing patterns of competition

Increasingly, companies are being called to rethink their notion of the firm as a self-sufficient enterprise. Indeed, firms are being recognized for what they really are: nodes in a larger network of emerging and evolving ideas and opportunities that the more successful succeed in transforming into profitable business transactions through a deliberate and strategic deployment of capabilities. We call this transformation *innovation*. Leading *innovating* firms focus on evolving patterns of change in their environment and opportunities that emerge from them; these they monitor, reinforce, and exploit for competitive advantage. In this book, we explore the notion of creating strategic advantage through the deliberate and effective management of capabilities. Invariably, innovation is probably the most important capability firms have today for driving profitable growth. Hence, in developing the notion of capabilities for strategic growth, we will in fact be talking about the innovation capability.

Recent economic and geopolitical developments have left the world as we know it irrevocably changed. The ongoing technological revolution has had no less of an impact. No one can escape the influence of technology. Where it once emerged and progressed on the peripheries of society, it is now penetrating our very lives in ways not thought possible only a short time ago. It is as much changing the way we are doing things today as it is showing how it might impact our lives in the future.

While the jury may yet be out on the question concerning the emergence of a new 'techno-economic' order—that is, a new economic order driven primarily by technological parameters—firms are finding themselves caught in a maelstrom of rapid change in their competitive playing fields. Capabilities that served these firms well in the past are very rapidly eroding into legacy liabilities. Tried and proven paradigms are rapidly becoming obsolete. Entirely new sets of capabilities, more often defined and introduced by new entrants, are introducing new rules to the competitive game. The new rules of the game appear to favour the flexible, nimble and adaptable organization. "Imperfectly seizing the unknown" is rapidly gaining precedence over "perfecting the known" (Kelly 1998).

This mantra of the newly emerging competitive order has immense implications for the ways in which organizations are managing their capabilities. As we move into the knowledge-based economy, knowledge in its many forms has replaced traditional tangible assets as the primary source of competitive advantage for firms. A firm's strategically relevant knowledge invariably manifests itself in its capabilities. These determine the boundaries of the firm's competitive potential; that is, they define both the firm's competitive opportunities and its limitations. The new competitive playing field is redefining the ways in which firms are thinking about, and ultimately managing, their capabilities.

What are these changes and what are the implications for the strategic management of capabilities? We will address the first question by taking a high-level look at some of the changes occurring in the competitive land-scape. Change in the competitive environment is occurring along a variety of dimensions: technological, economic, political, and social. Moreover, change in all four dimensions is occurring interchangeably. The resulting pattern of change is a complex product of all change in all four dimensions.

Scientific and technological change

Scientific and technological changes are being driven by the accelerated pace and nature of technological development per se. New technologies are emerging and propagating at the interfaces of scientific disciplines that in the past were staunchly divided. Revolutionary new science and technology is emerging in areas such as nanotechnology, stem-cell research, and communications and information technology. These developments are ushering in a new era of cross-disciplinary discovery. The new technologies, it has been argued (Brand 2000), differ fundamentally from technologies that preceded them. They are self-accelerating. That is to say, the products of these new technologies' own processes enable them to develop ever more rapidly; much as a computer can design a computer that computes even faster, or new computer chips are immediately put to use for developing the next generation of even more powerful chips.

This development may ultimately have a destabilizing effect on society. And indeed, recent years have seen major upheavals in the technology world. Jobs in manufacturing, software development, and traditional R&D have experienced a migration from the industrialized countries to the developing part of the world: to India, China, and other countries. Advanced automation, on the other hand, is radically changing the way the technologist works. More than anything else, new emerging technology has had, and will continue to have, an enormous impact on how we live and do business.

Third-world biotechnology

Jawaharlal Nehru, India's first prime minister, is said to have remarked, "The future belongs to science and those who make friends with science." Advanced scientific and technological research has traditionally been seen as the preserve of Europe and America, not something one would expect in developing countries such as India and China. This is changing rapidly. India, China, and some other developing countries are showing that they can move beyond imitating western science and technology. They have already staked their claim to innovation in fields such as telecommunications and information technology. Biotechnology is the next big area, as a recently published University of Toronto report argues. The report, published in *Nature Biotechnology*, examines the state of medical biotechnology in six developing countries—Brazil, China, Cuba, Egypt, India, and South Africa—and South Korea as a recently industrialized country. Many of these countries started investing in biotechnology in the 1980s. These efforts are beginning to pay off, by any number of measures.

Research output in China, for example, measured in terms of the number of scientific paper publications in the field of health biotechnology, grew sevenfold in the period between 1991 and 2002. Much of the research is highly advanced, with China making a name for itself in the fields of genomics, gene therapy, and stem-cell research. The changing research environment in China is luring back emigré researchers with promises of funding and facilities—and fewer qualms about research in these controversial scientific frontier areas than America and Europe.

China and India are also increasingly showing success at patenting the outcomes of their biotech research in America. This is another measure of how far the innovative and commercial potential of advanced research in these countries has progressed since the early 1990s, when patents from these regions in America were essentially nonexistent.

Source: *Economist* (2004a).

A new economic order

There has been much talk about an emerging information technology-driven new economy based on the Web that is separate and distinct from the previous economy. We do not believe there is sufficient basis to make the claim for an entirely new economy. There have of course been significant technological revolutions in the past. Often, these have ushered in new economic orders. For example, Schumpeter's (1939) notion of "creative destruction" tracks revolutionary cycles of technological and economic change over several centuries. Each cycle was driven primarily by technological innovation, but ultimately ushered in social, economic, and often political change.

However, we do see a number of irrevocable and significant trends and changes to the way we think about and do business today. Perhaps it would suffice to talk about an emerging new *economic order*. Even in this post-bubble period, we find creation and distribution of wealth being reshaped in this new economic order, and it has its own distinct opportunities and risks—its own new rules, which are even now emerging.

The new economic order has four distinguishing features. Each of these has significant implications for managing capabilities:

1 **The new economic order is deregulated and global.** This feature manifests itself in a variety of ways. Almost daily, we are confronted in the media by some facet or another of *deregulation* and the globalized economy, implying increasingly intense global competition in an increasingly borderless world.

2 **New and disruptive technologies.** These are rewriting the rules of competition as they transform value chains, usher in new business models, and create new sources of value. Incumbents are left vulnerable as new players redefine competitive advantage that is often short-lived.

3 **The new economic order favours intangibles.** It is driven by the economics of information rather than the economics of physical things. Intangibles include ideas, knowledge and relationships.

4 **The new economic order is interconnected.** The new economic order is driven by a distinctive logic of networks (Kelly 1998). In information technology, we have moved beyond computing power and are focusing on connectivity. Networks have already now penetrate our lives to the extent that the metaphor "networking" has come to epitomize our way of thinking and the way in which our economy is being organized.

The combination of these economic factors and the technological developments of recent years have no precedence. *Globalization*, the focus on *intangibles* and *connectivity* are driving *technological* development as no other factors have in the past. The factors are inextricably intertwined. The evolving competitive landscape has become largely obscure even to those intimately involved in its development, unpredictable and highly dynamic. Traditional approaches have become outdated; new thinking is only now emerging. Business leaders are being challenged with keeping pace in today's rapidly changing environment while being charged with laying the foundation for tomorrow's competitiveness in an increasingly uncertain world.

But there are other more subtle and intrinsic changes that, in our view, justify rethinking our understanding of technology and its management. These changes affect the way we think about, approach, and ultimately go about doing business in our organizations. These are having every bit as much impact on the way we manage technology.

Scale, scope, and mode of new knowledge production

The first of these subtle changes has to do the scale, scope, and mode of new knowledge production. Knowledge has irrevocably replaced other more traditional, physical assets as the single most important factor in the creation of wealth. We are seeing changes in the way it is being created, diffused, and ultimately exploited. Knowledge frontiers are moving faster than they have ever before. It has been pointed out that in almost every major discipline up to 90 percent of relevant knowledge has appeared in the last 15 years. Traditional means of gathering and validating information have become hopelessly inappropriate. Organizations are rapidly evolving into becoming parts of larger matrices of merging and evolving ideas and opportunities. Increasingly, the loci of these knowledge matrices are located outside the actual firm; companies access these through links that extend beyond the boundaries of the firm. As a result, companies are rethinking the traditional notion of positioning, and are instead focusing more on patterns of alliances and networks involving people and institutions they work with (Quinn 2002: 96).

Other changes are occurring in the knowledge landscape. Knowledge is increasingly being created in broader, trans-disciplinary social and economic contexts. Gibbons et al (1994) identify three emerging characteristics about the emerging, so-called *Mode 2* knowledge production.

First, knowledge in its many possible forms is increasingly being produced by closer interaction between scientific, technological, and industrial modes of knowledge production. There is a growing trend in which this is happening by the weakening of disciplinary and institutional boundaries. Second, knowledge production is increasingly being driven by the growth of niche markets that demand specialized knowledge. Increasingly sophisticated user needs are demanding the production of correspondingly complex and sophisticated knowledge, which in turn is putting a higher demand on research-related activities. Third, the diffusion of knowledge increasingly is going hand in hand with market differentiation in business environments marked by an intensification of international competition. New knowledge created provides the basis for the next set of advances in ever-shortening commercial and technological lifecycles.

Knowledge production on a worldwide basis is exploding. The *Economist* recently estimated (2004b) that there are currently over 2000 publishers in the STM (scientific, technological and medical) field alone. Together, these publish 1.2 million articles a year in about 16,000 periodical journals. In an interesting intellectual property development, governments in a number of the major industrialized nations around the world are increasingly demanding that publicly funded research be made freely available online. The implications for the scientific and technical publishing community are immense.

Nanotechnology

Nanotechnology is a good example of how the technology revolution is being driven by new modes of knowledge production. Nanotechnology does not have origins in any single scientific discipline, although it is probably now most closely aligned with materials science. This new field of technology represents an unprecedented convergence of multiple discrete technologies, and now attracts scientists and engineers from many different disciplines. It has recently been estimated that about 20,000 people are currently working in nanotechnology, though the exact boundaries of the new technology remain fuzzy thanks to the hype that has emerged around anything that carries the prefix "nano." Small-scale research work areas such as optics and biotechnology are now being called "nanooptics" and "nanobiotechnology," although one might well challenge the relabelling.

Nanotechnology is interesting in that it demonstrates the importance of path dependence in the development of technology trajectories. Scientists had thought about manipulating matter at the nanoscale (generally agreed to cover objects measuring from 1 to 100 nanometres) as long ago as the late 1950s. But they had to wait until the invention of the scanning tunnelling microscope (STM) to make this a reality. The STM, for the first time, allowed scientists to "see" atoms and molecules at the hitherto almost unimaginable minuscule nanometre scale, and thereby launched an entirely new arena of scientific and technological opportunity.

Source: *Economist* (2005a).

A new organizational order

A second trend we are observing has to do with changes in the way in which organizations are structuring themselves, in the way they operate, and in the way are made up.

Generation tech workers

Beginning with the last item, a subtle yet irreversible change in the makeup of the work force is taking place in today's firms. We are referring to an emerging new breed of employees in companies all over the globe that goes by various names: for example "generation tech" employees and "digital natives" have been used to label this group. The "generation tech" group is made up of a new generation of young technology-literate people who are collectively engaging in harnessing both new technology and new behavioural skills (Prensky 2004). Its members share a number of common features:

- The average digital native draws on a formidable wealth of digital experience, with an average of close to 10,000 hours playing video games, more than 200,000 e-mails and instant messages sent and received, nearly 10,000 hours of talking and using data on cell phones, more than 20,000 hours watching television, and almost 500,000 commercials seen—all before college. No less notable, though more sobering, this average digital native will have logged only about 5,000 hours of book reading.
- They exhibit natural organizational activist tendencies; they do not respond well to traditional command-and-control management systems and have been observed to initiate transformation of the organization from the bottom up.
- Generation tech workers typically show more loyalty to their professional peer group than to their employers.
- They process information differently and they are much less reluctant to experiment with new ideas and approaches.
- Incentives and rewards take on a different meaning with this group; generally, recognition and reputation supersede material rewards. Generation tech workers demand new and different modes of motivation; professional and personal fulfillment are highly ranked amongst these.
- It has been observed that digital natives naturally adapt to fit into the

agile, flat, team-based organizations many older colleagues tend to struggle with.

The influence of the generation tech employees on many organizations has already been substantial. Traditional managers must learn to recognise these new workers for the unique capabilities they bring to the organization of the today.

Flexible organizational structures and firm boundaries

More and more, the fast pace of technological change and the emerging knowledge-based economy are forcing pioneering and traditional companies alike to experiment with flexible organizational structures, peripheries, and organizational boundaries. Firms are moving away from monolithic and rigid organizational designs geared for repetitive action transactions and routine activities, toward flexible and agile organizational forms that can accommodate novelty and innovation (Bahrami 1996). Maira (1998) describes the fluid-network organization that connects across the traditional boundaries of the organization and draws on new capabilities, one of which is the capability continually to learn. Fluid firm boundaries enable firms to collaborate on innovation; that is, to co-innovate across networks of strategic partners, reducing risk while gaining access to new knowledge (Odenthal et al 2004).

Ambidextrous, learning organizations

Change and the need to learn are rapidly becoming imperatives for succeeding in the competitive environment facing firms today. Orchestrating change on a number of fronts, balancing radical change with incremental improvement, is what distinguishes ambidextrous organizations from those that succumb to legacy assets that have degenerated to liabilities. O'Reilly and Tushman (2004) have found that successful ambidextrous firms separate their new exploratory units from their more traditional, exploitative ones. They create an environment that tolerates different processes, structures, and cultures at the same time. A business, these authors argue, does not necessarily have to escape its past in order to position itself for success in the future. Learning, and learning how to learn faster than the competition, goes hand in hand with ambidextrous change; increasingly this trait is distinguishing the successful firms from the "also-rans."

Key questions

- How well does the firm understand the key drivers of change in its business environment?
- How is this understanding being integrated into the firm's strategic thinking?
- Is there broad consensus regarding the strategic goals that must be achieved given the firm's specific competitive environment?
- Is there general agreement that the strategy of the firm is appropriate to today's and tomorrow's business environment?
- Has sufficient flexibility been built into the strategy to meet rapidly changing conditions?
- Does the firm's performance feedback system provide adequate warning when the need for change of direction arises?
- How capable is the firm of responding to emergent conditions?

Scoping the broader managerial context with respect to capabilities and innovation

How does one begin to make sense of the resulting conundrum? How does one even begin to approach the important task of "managing" capabilities and innovation strategically in such an environment? As paradigms change, so also must the thinking and mindset of those responsible for managing capabilities for competitive advantage change. The changing competitive landscape can be captured in various ways. One such way maps technology dynamics against market place dynamics (Figure 1.1).

We can segment the landscape very broadly into four quadrants. The lower left quadrant represents mature technologies in mature markets. The focus of business endeavors in this quadrant is on predictability, routine processes, and incremental change. Contributions to improvement are linear and additive. Processes and management systems are bureaucratic and rule-bound. Knowledge prevails in the codified form. Existing capabilities are exploited by incumbents while enabling them to build effective barriers to potential entrants.

The situation is quite different in the upper right quadrant, which is characterized by disruption and uncertainty. Technologies and processes are emergent, radical, and frame-breaking in nature. Change is unpredictable and its impact is highly non-linear. Entrants enjoy potential competitive

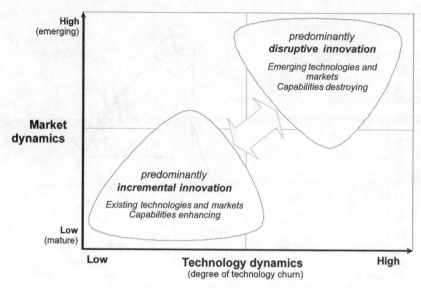

Figure 1.1 Innovation as a function of technology and market dynamics

advantage over incumbents as legacy capabilities prove to be liabilities in this environment. Firms competing in this environment must be adaptable and flexible. The nature of the emerging strategically relevant knowledge is largely tacit in nature.

In reality, firms more and more are experiencing combinations and composites of various shading of the extremes described in Figure 1.1 at any point in time. Competitive fronts are changing position continually; no single solution or approach adequately does justice to the demands of the shifting competitive environment. Firms must juggle multiple challenges in a competitive playing field that continually sets up new competitive targets.

Capabilities and market opportunity

Where does this leave the firm and its strategic capabilities? A simplified perspective of the competitive playing field can be drawn using two intersecting curves. The initially upper, downward-inclining curve represents an arbitrary market opportunity that presents itself to all potential competitors; the second, upwards-sweeping curve represents the competitive position of the individual competing firm (Figure 1.2). Both curves represent path-dependent trajectories of a sort; the market

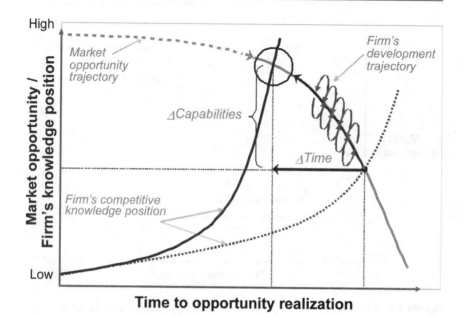

Figure 1.2 Market opportunity and the technology (knowledge) trajectory*

* The notion of intersecting curves representing market opportunity and the firms' knowledge position has been proposed earlier by William L. Miller and Langdon Morris (1999: xv).

opportunity trajectory shows itself as a decreasing time-dependent function in environments characterized by time-based competition.

The firm's unique competitive trajectory is path dependent, meaning that the firm's past determines its ability to build the requisite strategic capabilities to compete in emerging markets. The two trajectories intersect at a point representing the point at which the firm is in a position to respond successfully to the market opportunity. Each competing firm has its own unique competitive trajectory. Simply put, the strategic objective of a firm is to reposition its point of intersection further up along the market opportunity curve faster than its competitors. It does this by learning faster than the competition and channeling this learning into the development of its strategic capabilities, indicated in the diagram by the upward-moving spiral along the firm's development trajectory. The net vertical gain (Δ *capabilities*) achieved by the firm represents an enhanced knowledge position; the net horizontal gain (Δ *time*) represents the corresponding time-to-market advantage.

Strategic repositioning has several important management implications for the individual firm:

- **Value proposition.** Firms must review, and invariably, align their value proposition with the requirements of the new competitive position.
- **Business model.** Competitive repositioning typically calls for a newly defined business model that is in line with the new market conditions.
- **Capabilities.** Repositioning probably has the most important implications for the firm's capabilities. Capabilities, as will be shown in the next section, are inherently multi-dimensional, involving technological, organizational, cultural, and knowledge-relevant constituents, all of which must be taken into consideration in the repositioning.

Clearly, the framework depicted in Figure 1.2 presents a highly simplified view. In reality, firms are managing numerous such curves simultaneously. Often, repositioning occurs simultaneously in various markets and competitive areas. Depending on the dynamics of the competitive environment, competition for resources and managerial attention varies in these situations. Companies must succeed in exploiting and deploying their capabilities across a complex array of market opportunities in order to achieve strategic advantage.

Unanticipated legacy blessings

With its only 1.4 million inhabitants, Estonia has established itself in a leadership position in information and communication technologies that has already outpaced many of its new and much wealthier European neighbours. Estonia is reaping the rich benefits of a Soviet-era legacy that unwittingly laid the roots of a capabilities base in a way that could hardly have been anticipated at the time. The Soviet Union took great pains to squelch any ambitions for freedom and independence in the Baltic States by discouraging courses in philosophy and the social sciences at Estonian universities during the Soviet era. Philosophy, the Soviets reasoned, is a dangerous elixir among a people longing for the brief independence they had lost. Study programs in computer science, cybernetics, artificial intelligence, and information technology, on the other hand, were strongly encouraged. Estonians developed extraordinary capabilities in these fields. The Soviets responded by placing one of their most important centres of artificial intelligence research in Tallinn. Much of the software programming and development for the Soviet space program was carried out at this centre.

Following independence in 1991, this legacy helped propel Estonia to the remarkable post-Soviet success it is currently experiencing. The resourceful Estonians have used their knack of technology and open embracement of change to build one of the most advanced information and communication technology infrastructures in the world. Estonia's economy has benefited greatly. Although half of the country is covered in forests, Estonia's economy is humming below the trees. With economic growth rates projected at 6.0 percent for 2005, Estonia's economy is more in line with that of emerging Asia than with most of its European neighbours.

As a nation, Estonia represents the new global competitor on the block in many ways. It is has been very quick to respond to new market opportunities as they emerge. Swedish companies, for example, are known to often test new ideas first in Estonia. Estonians also foster a unique attitude toward innovation. Linnar Viik, a lecturer at Tallinn Technical University expresses it this way: "People like to say, don't touch things that work. But Estonians like to look behind the thing and wonder whether there's anything we can change about it. In Estonia you might say, if it works, you can break it."

Source: Levine (2004b).

Capabilities and technological innovation

The production of new knowledge is a key output in science and technology-based industries. The production of new knowledge has been compared to bubbles effervescing from knowledge that is deeply embedded within the firm. Some are more energetic than others. While some of these may simply fizzle out, dissipate and simply disappear, others may interact and coalesce with other bubbles to form major opportunities. Even the best scientists and researchers cannot predict the fate of any particular bubble.

New knowledge production is the source of innovation. Not surprisingly, innovation shares many of the characteristics of knowledge that make it difficult to "manage." Innovation as a capability features three major managerial problems (Drew and Turner 2004):

1 **Innovation is inherently fraught with risk and uncertainty.** Innovations are typically associated with late market launch and runaway

budgets. Many potential innovations that start out as technological successes end up as commercial failures.

2 **Innovation as a process is difficult to manage successfully.** Even the strongest advocates of process-driven innovation will admit that serendipity invariably plays a significant role in the innovation process. The randomness introduced by serendipity introduces nonlinearity and dynamics to the process.

3 **Leading at innovation does not guarantee appropriation of the rewards.** Xerox's research laboratories pioneered many outstanding advances in consumer electronics, including the personal computer, the computer mouse, and the Ethernet, but the profits were reaped largely by competitors such as IBM and Microsoft.

Managing innovation as a capability for strategic advantage requires multiple levels of managerial wherewithal. It requires the ability to recognize patterns of impending change and emergent opportunities in the firm's macro environment just as much as it demands rapid exploitation of new knowledge ever closer to the point at which market opportunities emerge.

Key questions

- What are the most profitable and exciting opportunities that the market offers today?
- Which of these is the firm currently ready to pursue?
- What are the capabilities, knowledge, and attitudes that are required?
- Which of these are available today?
- Which will need to be acquired?
- What current skills, capabilities, and knowledge could the firm apply immediately to get a head start in exploiting these opportunities?
- How are current capabilities being used to exploit today's emerging market opportunities?
- What new skills and capabilities does the firm have to acquire to better exploit emerging opportunities?
- What new skills and capabilities does the firm have to develop or acquire to create the new rules of the game by which others have to play in the most profitable emerging markets?

Concluding remarks

Recent economic, geopolitical and technological developments are changing the world irrevocably. Change is occurring primarily in the areas of science and technology, globalization of the economy, rate and mode of knowledge production, and the way organizations are evolving. This change has had an unprecedented and profound impact on the way firms are competing. New rules of the game are emerging that demand new approaches to the way firms manage their strategic capabilities and their innovation. As new market opportunities emerge, firms that learn to deploy their capabilities faster and in more innovative ways succeed in capturing the new opportunities ahead of the competition.

CHAPTER 2

Capabilities as strategic resources

Introduction

In the past decade and a half considerable research effort has been put into understanding the role of the firm's resources and competitive capabilities in determining and executing appropriate strategies. Prahalad and Hamel's (1990) seminal work on core competencies was highly influential in shifting the focus of management onto the firm's strategic resources, particularly its capabilities. The authors argued that competitive advantage does not reside in industry structure or the firm's participation in specific strategic groups, but rather in its possession and strategic deployment of unique and difficult to imitate bundles of skills, knowledge, and capabilities.

In this chapter, we:

- examine capabilities from the perspective of the resource-based view of the firm
- examine unique properties and traits of capabilities relating to their tacitness and path dependence
- explore capabilities and their knowledge dependency, including embedded functional organizational knowledge
- derive managerial implications relating to managing capabilities as strategic resources.

Capabilities and the resource-based view of the firm

Prahalad and Hamel's work immediately captured the interest of management practitioners and thinkers alike. It appeared that management was ready to embrace the notion that competitive strategy must go beyond industry structure, cash flow, and management control. The time was right for suggesting that that competitive strategy must also consider the organization's knowledge, technology, and skills, and the synergies between these.

Not that Prahalad and Hamel's core ideas were entirely new. A number of other authors, notably Wernerfelt (1984), Rumelt (1994) and Barney (1991) had introduced the notion of core competencies as an expression of the resource-based view of the firm in earlier papers. However, it can be said that Prahalad and Hamel's work (1994) irrevocably laid the groundwork for much of the thinking that has since coalesced into the school of strategic management known as the resource-based view of the firm.

This theory has a tradition in economics that reaches back to the earlier work of Penrose (1959) and Schumpeter (1934). It relates superior performance of the firm to its distinctive, difficult-to-duplicate resources. Thereby, the resource-based view of the firm stands in contrast to the structural forces approach to competitive advantage, which argues that advantage results from securing a defensible position in the market on the basis of cost or differentiation. In spite of its earlier traditions, most management scholars agree that the publications of Prahalad and Hamel, Wernerfelt (1984) and Barney (1991) and a few others in the early 1990s represent the conceptual foundations of the resource-based view of the firm for the field of strategy.

Barney's work, in particular, provides the basis for much of the subsequent thinking in business strategy; its economic argument enables us to develop the link between strategic resources and strategic capabilities. In Barney's view, essentially all organizations can build and maintain long-term strategic advantage as a result of creating and exploiting bundles of valued resources that other organizations cannot readily imitate. Barney develops three assumptions and four characteristics underlying this assertion. The assumptions are:

1 **Resource heterogeneity.** Resources are unevenly distributed amongst potential competitors; not all organizations have identical resource bundles.
2 **Resource immobility.** Strategic resources are inherently difficult to transfer.
3 **Appropriability.** It is assumed that organizations are in a position to extract some net value from their resource bundle, therefore the definition of value is context-dependent.

On the basis of these assumptions, Barney argues that the firm's strategic resource bundles, if they are to provide long-term strategic advantage, must exhibit the following attributes:

1 **Valuable:** that is, the resource bundle makes a measurable value contribution to the firm, though the contribution may not necessarily be quantitatively verifiable.
2 **Rare:** which is defined here in the sense of less than necessarily required for perfect competition.
3 **Non-substitutable:** alludes to the unique character of the resource bundle; no alternative resource bundle is capable of providing the same value contribution to customers or stakeholders.
4 **Durable:** thought to be the most complex construct of the four, this attribute of a strategic resource relates to its inimitability, and reflects a combination of path-dependence, the tacit nature of strategic resources, and their causal ambiguity.

On the basis of these assumptions and necessary attributes, we are provided with an 'acid test' to determine whether any given resource bundles in the firm are capable of indeed providing long-term strategic advantage. Barney's model is directly applicable to strategic capabilities, since these are one of the firm's most important resource bundles.

The resource-based view is not without its caveats. There are a few that are particularly relevant in the case of strategic capabilities. The same qualities that make strategically relevant capabilities difficult to imitate and transfer make them difficult to 'manage' within the firm. Moreover, the firm may not be able to analyze, and ultimately exploit its really valuable capabilities, since these are typically deeply embedded in the firm's tacit realm. This makes them difficult to identify in the first place. Finally, the firm's capabilities may actually reflect unintended consequences rather than deliberate strategic action on its part, throwing up the issue of social complexity and causal ambiguity. It has been argued that the resource-base view does not generate sufficiently clear prescriptions for managers. Priem and Butler (2001), however, note that 'how' questions relevant to the deliberate management of capabilities are increasingly being investigated empirically by management researchers.

Capabilities and organizational knowledge

Knowledge is increasingly being recognized to be one of the firm's most strategically important resources. Although an appreciation and understanding of *knowledge* per se has been with us since the dawn of civilization, *knowledge management* as such is a relatively new management topic that had its formal beginnings only about a decade and a half ago. Knowledge management, despite many open questions regarding its exact scope and definition, is challenging many managers today on how their firms are managing and exploiting their strategically relevant knowledge. This is, in part, fueled by an inherent recognition that knowledge is central to the success of business in an economy that is increasing by being driven by knowledge in its many forms. It is further fueled by a growing interest amongst investors in the measurement and valuation of intellectual capital, and the representation of this value in the balance sheet of the enterprise (for example see Roos et al 1997, Edvinsson and Malone 1997, Andriessen 2003).

Firms that possess superior intellectual resources can understand how to exploit and develop their traditional resources more effectively than their competitors, even if some of these traditional resources are not unique. Knowledge can therefore be considered to be the firm's most important strategic resource. Equally important is the firm's capability to acquire, integrate, store, retrieve, and share knowledge for building and sustaining competitive advantage. Knowledge, Zack (2001) points out, enhances the firm's fundamental ability to compete.

Much of the organization's strategically relevant knowledge exists in a tacit rather than explicit form (Birchall and Tovstiga 2004a). For the most part, this knowledge resides in the form of people-embedded knowledge. This leaves firms at risk if key personnel are attracted elsewhere. Competitive advantage is gained through the deliberate and purposeful management of the firm's stock of strategically relevant knowledge. For the most part, the firm's knowledge is embedded in its portfolio of competencies and capabilities.

Competence or capability?

The terms *competence* and *capability* are sometimes used interchangeably in the literature. We reserve the term *competence* for those knowledge-embedded resource bundles that span multiple businesses; that is, their competitive impact extends beyond a single business unit. Thompson and Strickland (2001) go on to differentiate between *core* and *distinct* competencies. The former are activities the company does well relative to other internal activities; the latter are activities the firm does well relative to its competitors. We prefer to use *core* to designate those competencies that differentiate a firm competitively across the entire company relative to its competitors.

Capabilities, in our terminology, are combinations and bundles of constituent knowledge, skills, and learning accumulated over time. Much of the knowledge embedded in capabilities is tacit in nature, making it difficult to identify and manage. Capabilities typically reside in teams and departments. Clusters of *core* capabilities constitute the building blocks of *core* competencies.

Capabilities and embedded functional knowledge

Capabilities are bundles of constituent skills and technologies—rather than single discrete skills or technologies—that create disproportionate value for the customer, differentiate its owner from competitors, and allow entrance to new markets (Hamel 1994). From a competitive perspective, the value aspect is critical. Capabilities are strategically relevant only if they make a significant contribution to the creation and delivery of better value for the firm's customers and other stakeholders.

Hamel identifies three key sets of functional capabilities that emerge from the firm's collective set of knowledge-based skills and technologies:

1 **Process-related capabilities:** competencies such as quality, cycle time management, just-in-time management. These allow the firm to do things more quickly, flexibly, and with a higher degree of reliability than competitors.
2 **Market-interface capabilities:** where the term "marketing" is used to embrace management of product/brand development, pricing, communication, sales and distribution, service—in short, these comprise the market interface knowledge-based capabilities that are non-technical in nature.
3 **Functionality-related capabilities:** skills and technologies which enable the firm to integrate into its services and products unique functionality; resulting, in turn, in distinctive customer benefits.

We refer to these capabilities of this type as *primary* capabilities; they are the most obvious and apparent of the firm's strategic capabilities. In a later section of this chapter we introduce the notion of *secondary* capabilities. These are largely organizational knowledge-based capabilities that are no less critical to the success of the firm, though they are highly tacit in nature.

Capabilities and multidimensionality

Leonard-Barton (1995) has argued that the firm's primary capabilities, in particular its technological capabilities, can be broken down into at least four interdependent dimensions (Figure 2.1). Two of these are knowledge competence repositories: (1) people-embodied knowledge and skills, and (2) physical technical systems; the remaining two are organizational knowledge control and channeling mechanisms: (3) managerial systems, and (4) organizational culture, values, and norms.

1 **People-embodied knowledge and skills.** This includes accumulated employee knowledge and skills. In addition to knowledge of techniques specific to the firm, this includes industry specific, scientific, and professional knowledge. People-embodied knowledge can be both deep and broad; for example, deep understanding in narrow areas coupled with understanding of the interfaces between the specific and the general to make it possible to relate the in-depth knowledge to its wider application and thus cultivate new or improved applications. The firm-specific knowledge is generally the least codified and therefore the most difficult to replicate and hence transfer.
2 **Physical technical systems.** This includes knowledge embedded in technical systems and processes such as manufacturing layouts and configurations, linked databases, and software. Physically embedded knowledge remains even after the originators have moved on. The rationale for the system may well be forgotten and become tacit in nature as a result. But it remains accessible to the organization as a result of it having been embedded into its systems.
3 **Managerial systems.** Managerial systems exist to create and control knowledge; these might include formalized procedures for decision making. They provide the infrastructure of the organizational environment required by the capability. But they also include the many implicit ways of managing organizations which seem to be part of the fabric and are learnt over time by working within the firm and passed on from one group to another.
4 **Culture, values, and norms.** The dominant values and norms can be seen as the glue that underpins the organization and determines how it

functions. No two organizations are alike. Often the dominant culture was set by the founders of the business, and in many organizations it is enduring. Even when organizations are envied for the particular characteristics of their culture it is impossible to copy and replicate. Some organizations clearly have a culture which fosters innovation—typified by encouraging experimentation, openness, "no-blame," and learning from experience. We all recognize that it is extremely difficult to transform an organization that has always been is a follower, a "me-too," into an industry leadership position.

A primary capability inherently exhibits elements of all four dimensions. This is not to say that all four dimensions are equally represented in a capability, but all four dimensions are necessarily present to some extent. This premise has important implications for the management of capabilities. A capability, for example, "cannot walk out of the door," that is, an individual person cannot constitute a capability. Capabilities may, however, reside in teams, or in other organizational units. An example of this might be a design capability that resides within a team of development engineers. Of the four requisite elements constituting the capability, the most apparent is the physical-technical dimension which, for example, might consist of a computer aided design (CAD) support system. People-embodied knowledge and skills, another dimension of the capability, encompasses the experience and expertise of the individual members of the design team in using the CAD system in a variety of applications. Managerial systems, the third element, provide the required organizational environment and working infrastructure for the capability to be

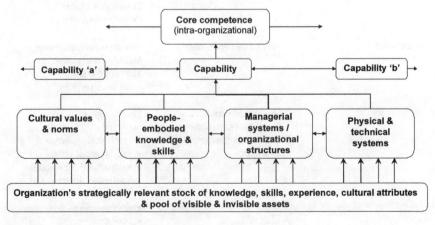

Figure 2.1 Dimensions of a capability

effective and efficient. This might include, for example, an appropriate incentives and reward system that provides motivation for excellent performance. Finally, the least obvious and most complex of the four dimensions, culture, values, and norms, addresses the social environment and process for learning, innovation, and change within the team.

Quélin (1997) proposes an organizational structure for capabilities by differentiating between levels at which these capabilities are found within the organization and their specific function (see Table 2.1).

Capabilities and embedded organizational knowledge

Quélin's framework categorizes combinative, integrative, and absorptive capabilities that cut vertically across all levels of the organization's capabilities. It also introduces organizational capabilities at the highest level of the organization. The firm's primary and organizational capabilities complement one another. Organizational capabilities draw on

Table 2.1 Capabilities and organizational structure

Level in organization	Capability cluster	Specific capability
Higher level	Organizational capabilities	Coordinating management processes Decision-making processes Designing incentive structures Performance management
Intermediary	Cross-functional capabilities	New product development Customer support Quality management
Functional	Functional capabilities	Research & development Manufacturing Marketing & sales After-sales services
Elementary	Specialized capabilities Single task capabilities Individual's specialized knowledge	Product line associated capabilities • technical expertise • commercial skills Infrastructural capabilities • networks (internal and external) • connectivity • computing • database, software

Table 2.2 Organizational capabilities

	Individual	Collective / organizational
Technical	Individual's functional, technical competence	Organization's core competencies
Social	Individual's leadership ability	Organization's capabilities

the organization's collective knowledge and the way in which aspects of it are brought together to achieve competitive advantage. Organizational capabilities are largely tacit and invisible to the eye of the observer. Ulrich and Smallwood (2004) categorize them as the organization's social and collective knowledge (Table 2.2)—representing the firm's collective skills, abilities, and expertise that evolve as a result of deliberate investment on the part of the firm in staffing, training, compensation, and overall investments in human resources.

Capabilities in the lower right quadrant, the firm's organizational capabilities, are deeply embedded in the organization's culture and unique identity—the organization's so-called "DNA." Organizational capabilities are not readily measurable; hence managers often neglect them in favor of more easily measurable tangible assets such as physical assets and financials. The firm's intangibles, its organizational capabilities, provide the firm with significantly more relevant forward-looking measures and indicators for potential future performance. Ulrich and Smallwood suggest 11 such capabilities-related measures:

1 Talent: successfully attracting competent and committed people.
2 Speed: carrying out important change expediently.
3 Shared mindset and coherent brand identity: maintaining positive and consistent images and experiences in the minds of both employees and customers.
4 Accountability: achieving high performance from employees.
5 Collaboration: working across firm boundaries efficiently with leverage.
6 Learning: generating and generalizing ideas with impact.
7 Leadership: embedding leaders throughout the organization.
8 Customer connectivity: building enduring relationships of trust with targeted customers.
9 Strategic unity: articulating and sharing a strategic point of view.
10 Innovation: exploiting new content and process.
11 Efficiency: managing costs.

Making good companies great

Collins's research (2001), over a five-year period, in which he examined the underlying variables that drive sustainable success in
companies that are already successful, provides further evidence of
the importance of the firm's organizational capabilities. Collins
found that even in companies such as Nucor, a pioneering leader in
the use of technology that revolutionized the steelmaking industry,
technology per se was subordinate to organizational capabilities that
build on the unique culture and the people of the company. Great
companies, Collins's findings suggest, first invest in building the
requisite culture and disciplined thought and action around (1) the
unique capabilities that propel them to be the best in their class; (2)
a deep understanding of their basis of competitive advantage, and (3)
the core values that these firms adhere to with deep passion.

Source: Collins (2001).

Secondary capabilities

The firm's *secondary* capabilities are organizational capabilities that that
enable and support the firm's primary functional capabilities. The firm's
capabilities are neither stable over time nor uniform at any point in time
(Bogner and Thomas 1994). In rapidly changing competitive environments capabilities have a limited shelf-life. Firms are therefore required
to continually renew their portfolio of capabilities. Successful players do
this by continually building and deploying new capabilities, for which
they need to source external knowledge (Teece and Pisano 1998). The
firm's secondary capabilities enable and support the difficult task of
sourcing and internalizing new, external knowledge into its existing portfolio of capabilities. In Chapter 4 we elaborate on the firm's secondary
capabilities.

Capabilities and learning

Organizational learning is a critical organizational capability. A capability's development path is essentially determined by the organization's
ability to learn. Learning is an ongoing process of experimentation,
feedback and evaluation, and renewed experimentation. Capabilities
represent an accumulation of learning over time. They reflect a firm's

deep understanding or unique ability in some specific area relevant to the firm's business that is advanced compared to other competitors in the industry. Either way, the notion of a capability encompasses the "ability to do" that has been acquired through learning over time. This ability to do enables the firm to actively apply knowledge to a task and thereby to generate "actionable knowledge." In this sense, capabilities are not traditional assets in the accounting meaning of the term. That is, capabilities are not inanimate things; rather they represent, in the words of Hamel (1994), a "messy accumulation of learning."

We also refer to this messy accumulation of learning as *experiential* knowledge—knowledge gained through experience. Experiential knowledge is predominantly tacit in nature. It is extremely difficult to capture and to codify. Of the firm's strategic resources, this is what distinguishes capabilities from the firm's other asset-based strategic resources. They differ from the firm's other assets in that they are deeply embedded in the firm's experience base, practices, and culture.

Teece, Pisano, and Shuen (1998) have argued that an important aspect of the dynamic nature of strategic capabilities is their relationship to development through learning. That is, the firm's strategic capabilities must adapt, become regenerated and renewed in response to changes in the firm's competitive environment. Capabilities that endow the firm with competitive superiority are continually subject to erosion by changes and shifts in the market. In the face of this reality, strategic management of capabilities assumes three key tasks. First, capabilities that differentiate the firm competitively must be protected. Barriers must be put in the way of competitors who seek to imitate them. Second, existing capabilities must be regenerated or renewed. This might be done by reconfiguring or rejuvenating old capabilities, thereby endowing existing capabilities with enhanced properties. Third, new capabilities must be built continually to replace those that ultimately cease to provide competitive advantage.

The mechanism for both renewal and building of new capabilities is organizational learning. Organizational learning is driven by the organization's knowledge processes—the acquisition, integration, assimilation, and exploitation of new knowledge.

Organizational learning itself is a strategic capability. Helleloid and Simonin (1994) argue that sustained competitive advantage is derived from core capabilities that are continually upgraded and developed in advance of competitors, and that sustainable competitive advantage demands that an organization possesses at least one core capability which enables the organization to adapt its capabilities in response to changing market and environment conditions. Hall (1997) discusses capabilities renewal and learning from the systemic perspective of the firm; he argues that innovation and change supporting the organization's learning process and capabilities renewal occur in a state bounded by instability and stability.

Capabilities and learning are inextricably linked to organizational change. In very rapidly changing environments, it may happen that too many aspects of the firm's learning environment are forced to change simultaneously. The firm's ability to make sense of cause–effect relationships may be confounded due to a lag in the firm's ability to form the requisite cognitive structures. The organization's rate of learning may diminish as a result. The development of capabilities through systematic organizational learning is therefore constrained by the firm's ability to absorb and react to change in its competitive environment.

Capabilities and tacitness

Capabilities differ from the firm's other assets in that they are embedded in the organization's processes, practices, and culture. The *people-embodied knowledge and skills* and *cultural values and norms* dimensions of capabilities constitute the tacit nature of knowledge embedded in the firm's strategic capabilities. Polanyi (1967) describes tacit and explicit knowledge as being personal, context-specific, and therefore difficult to formalize and to communicate. It is often ambiguous and experiential, and therefore highly complex. Knowledge embedded in capabilities exhibits its tacit character in varying degrees, much as Schein's (1992) levels of culture in the organization suggest varying depths of consciousness within the firm. Much of the strategically important knowledge embedded in capabilities is situated at the lowest levels of the firm's consciousness. This makes capabilities difficult to manage—to share, exchange, transfer, and imitate. Teece et al (1990) argue that capabilities are sticky. This characteristic of capabilities presents the firm with both opportunities and challenges: Other competitors, constrained by their own capabilities, cannot readily acquire a successful firm's core capabilities. The firm, on the other hand, may not even be fully aware of its own core capabilities.

The scheme presented in Figure 2.2 proposes a cascading model of tacitness ranging from knowledge that is yet codifiable (exhibiting a low degree of tacitness) through to knowledge that exhibits a high degree of causal ambiguity (exhibiting a high degree of tacitness). Clearly, there are limitations to the extent to which tacitness can be assessed; the scheme in

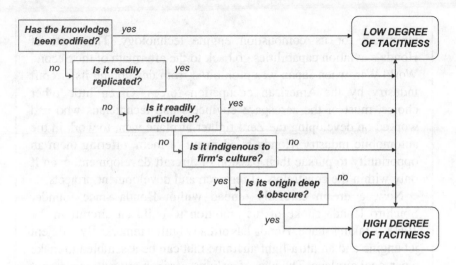

Figure 2.2 Capabilities-embedded knowledge and degree of tacitness

Figure 2.2 is simply to suggest a first approach to this intrinsically complex question (Birchall and Tovstiga 2004a).

Capabilities and path dependence

Capabilities are path dependent. They are not only inherited from the past, they are also constrained by the firm's past. That is, to understand a firm's capabilities today, we must examine the firm's historical development. Likewise, the capabilities that a firm will have at its disposal in the future will depend on where the firm stands today in terms of its current capabilities, its organizational practices, processes, and culture. The firm's past investment patterns and its repertoire of processes, routines, and practices define what it is capable of developing and/or absorbing in terms of new capabilities. Often, capabilities have their origin in the circumstances that existed at the time of those companies' foundation and early development.

Honda and microaviation

Honda Motor is not normally associated with aviation. Yet when Honda's president Takeo Fukui dreams about airplanes for the masses, he is not straying far from the roots of the company renowned for its combustion engine technology. The roots of Honda's aviation capabilities go back to the aftermath of the Second World War, when Japan was prohibited from developing its aircraft industry by the American occupation forces. Given little other choice, most of the aerospace engineers and technicians who had worked on developing the Zero fighter airplane went to work in the automobile industry. Honda hired many of them, offering them an opportunity to pursue their passion of aircraft development, even if only within the constraints of research and development projects.

Now, a dream carefully tended within Honda since founder Soichiro Honda spoke of his ambition to build an aircraft in the 1960s is taking shape. Honda has already built a remarkably efficient jet engine and an ultra-light airframe that can be assembled to make a personal airplane. The idea of a flying car in every garage may not yet be taken seriously by many. Honda, however, is not alone today in pursuing this dream. United Technologies' Pratt and Whitney and Williams International are in the process of developing tiny turbofan engines for such aircraft manufacturers as Adam Aircraft, Eclipse Aviation, and Cessna. These planes are being priced at US$2 million. Honda, having already attacked US automobile makers in the 1970s with inexpensive and efficient cars, is targeting a big piece of the microaviation market by focusing on affordability, light weight, fuel efficiency, reliability, and low cost of ownership.

Should Honda's microaviation dream ever come true, it will surely be the biggest revolution in travel since the commercial jet. And in no small way, Honda's stake in this new market would reflect its history of capabilities in aviation that go back to its founding.

Source: Fulford and Huang (2004).

Capabilities evolve along a development trajectory that traces the capabilities' path over time. Development trajectories consist of bundles of multiple strands that collectively and interactively determine the strategic relevance of the resulting capabilities. Component strands consist of internal factors including the organization's social processes, and external factors including external source technology. Table 2.3 provides some examples of core capabilities and their history.

A capability's development trajectory requires deliberate and focused management attention. It must not be left to chance. It must begin with a

Table 2.3 Core capabilities and path dependence

Firm	Core capability	History leading to capability
Honda	Drive train and small engine technology.	Post-war formation of gasoline engine manufacturing company; industry expertise brought in from aircraft engineering when US occupation forces prohibited Japan from further developing aircraft industry.
Royal Dutch / Shell Group	Coordinating a decentralized global network of more than 200 operating firms in over 145 countries.	Formed in 1907 by joining competing Royal Dutch Petroleum (founded to exploit colonial Indonesian oil reserves) and Shell Transport & Trading (founded to sell Russian oil in China and the Far East).
Canon	Integration of microelectronics, optics and electronic imaging.	Evolved from Precision Optical Industry Company (1937); evolution from pre- and post-war manufacturer of cameras to business machines (1960s) to image information processing (1970s) and diversification and global expansion post 1980s.
BP	"Elephant hunting," that is, discovering the large "company maker" oil fields in oil industry parlance.	Origins go back to 1909 to formation of Anglo Persian Oil Company to exploit Persian oil reserves; further stations included exploration and production of Forties field (North Sea) and Prudhoe Bay (Alaska).

clear articulation of the organization's strategy, and a realization that every strategic position is linked to some set of knowledge resources and capabilities. The strategic choices that the firm makes regarding which technologies, processes, product and/or service offering it intends to compete on determine the knowledge, skills, and capabilities it requires to compete effectively.

The progress of the trajectory reflects the firm's ability to transform itself to meet the demands of the changing competitive environment. The firm does this by sourcing, integrating, building, and embedding new internal or external knowledge into existing or new capabilities that enable the firm to compete more effectively in the new business environment. Innovation, learning, and the firm's ability to change contribute to the development of capabilities. Management's task is to create the right organizational conditions and environment for these processes to occur. This includes setting the right organizational context, which, for example, might consist of nurturing a culture of openness to new ideas, from both inside and outside the company (De Geus 1995). Covey (1994) suggests that managers may, paradoxically, have to give up a degree of direct control of their organization in order to "manage" it more effectively.

Concluding remarks

Capabilities are the scarce, intangible resources the firms deploys to distinguish itself in its strategy, and ultimately competitive performance, relative to its competitors. Capabilities display varying degrees of competitive impact. The firm's core capabilities make a disproportionate contribution to the firm's ability to create customer value, or to the efficiency with which that efficiency is delivered; they are difficult to imitate, and they provide a basis for entering new markets. Toward these objectives, the firm deploys capabilities of various types. We have differentiated mainly between the firm's *functional* capabilities and its *organizational* capabilities. Although less obvious than the firm's primarily functional capabilities, and therefore often neglected by the firm's managers, organizational capabilities are really one of the firm's key strategic assets.

CHAPTER 3

Capabilities and competitive advantage

Introduction

What is competitive advantage? How does a firm achieve competitive advantage, and how does competitive advantage manifest itself? How is competitive advantage sustained in highly competitive and fast-moving markets? What is the role of the firm's strategic capabilities in creating and sustaining competitive advantage? Over the years, management thinkers and practitioners alike have pondered these questions from various perspectives.

In this chapter, we:

- explore the notion of competitive advantage
- explore how capabilities contribute to the firm's position of competitive advantage
- examine capabilities and competitive advantage from the perspective of the impact of strategic capabilities and their potential to create value and profit earning potential.

Competitive advantage

Pietersen (2002) argues that business leaders today, regardless of industry or markets, must focus on developing a good understanding about: (1) the dynamic nature and character of the environment in which the firm must compete and win; (2) the few things the organization must do outstandingly well to win and go on winning in this environment; and (3) what the firm can and should do in order to mobilize and implement these measures faster and more effectively than the competition.

Grant (2002) suggests that a firm "possesses a competitive advantage over its rivals when it earns a persistently higher rate of profit." Competitive advantage, according to Grant, relates directly to the ability of the firm to outperform competitors on the basis of superior profitability. Other management thinkers have pointed out, however, that competitive advantage may not necessarily be revealed only in terms of higher profitability, as might be the case when the firm chooses to trade current profit for investment in market share or technology. Longevity and the sustainability of firms have in the past also been brought into association with competitiveness. Profitability and sustainability, though, do not necessarily correlate, although there does appear to be some evidence of late suggesting that in increasingly knowledge-dominated business environments there might indeed be congruence between the two (De Geus 1999).

Over the years, business strategists have sought to address these issues in various ways. Conventional management wisdom at one point in time related competitive advantage to cost leadership, then to differentiation advantage (Porter 1980, 1985). The inherent assumption was that market share was the key link to superior competitiveness. Strategy became a search for "fit" between the firm's strengths and weaknesses and its competitive environment.

Management thinking has moved on to the understanding that competitive advantage must go beyond simply seeking to achieve equilibrium in the market place, since striving for fit does not allow firms to react quickly enough in dynamically changing environments. Competitive environments are inherently unstable; disequilibrium is caused by change which may be externally or internally driven. External change might be driven by:

- changing customer demands and expectations
- technological change
- changing political and societal trends.

External change might well be driven by factors that lie outside the immediate industry of the competing firm.

Change that is internal to the industry may also drive the emergence of disequilibrium in a firm's competitive environment. This comes about as a result of some firms' ability to clearly differentiate themselves from their competitors on the basis of factors internal to the industry. These might include particular industry-specific skill sets or capabilities. Prahalad and Hamel, in their landmark book *Competing for the Future* (1994), emphasize the importance of firms proactively occupying the "competitive high ground" in their industry. They lay out a broad blueprint for appropriate pre-emptive strategic stances firms might act on in the face of impending changes in their competitive environment. In their view, the race to creating competitive advantage occurs in three distinct, overlapping stages:

1 **Competition for industry foresight and intellectual leadership.** This provides the basis for scoping current and potential new industry boundaries: that is, new competitive space created. The objective at this stage is to imagine new competitive space.
2 **Competition to foreshorten migration paths.** This focuses on accumulating the necessary capabilities or gaining complementary access to these through strategic partnering, exploiting market position, and achieving agreement around emerging standards. The objective of this second stage is to shape the emergence of the new competitive space.
3 **Competition for market position and share.** This involves building the requisite capabilities for maintaining and extending market position through delivery of value; depending on the dynamics and maturity of markets, this might be in the form of innovative product functionality, price, service offerings, or various combinations of these factors.

We argue that the firm's capabilities play a critical role in all of the three stages; that a well-managed portfolio of knowledge-based capabilities is a prerequisite for building a strong and sustainable competitive advantage. Key competitive knowledge—primarily tacit knowledge embedded in complex organizational routines and evolving from experience over time—tends to be unique and difficult to replicate, imitate, and transfer (Birchall and Tovstiga 2001, Zack 2001). These features of a capability carry a number of important implications for competitive differentiation. One of these has to do with the ease with which a capability can be replicated, transferred, or lost to a competitor. For example, a high degree of tacitness can be an effective barrier to diffusion of knowledge. From the external perspective, this represents a protective mechanism; for internal operations, this represents a challenge to be overcome; that is, firms must maintain mechanisms for consciously and deliberately managing their stock of tacit knowledge.

We explore how capabilities endow strategic advantage to the firm in the remaining sections of this chapter.

Key questions

- What are the unique characteristics of the competitive environment that determine how the firm must compete in order to win?
- What are those few things the organization must do outstandingly well in order to win in this environment?
- What does it take to mobilize the organization to implement these things faster and more effectively than the competition?

Capabilities and competitive advantage

Traditionally, two prominent perspectives have fueled the debate on competitive advantage. On the one hand, the structural forces approach states that competitive advantage is derived from securing a defensible position on the basis of cost or differentiation in selected segments of the total market. On the other hand, the resource-based view traces superior competitive performance to the distinctive resources of the firm. These resources, as we have seen in the previous chapter, consist of integrated combinations of assets and capabilities.

Day (1997) points out that positions of advantage address the *what* of competitive advantage, while superior resources, including the firm's assets and capabilities, addresses the *how* of competitive advantage. Neither of the two views provides the complete picture; taken together, however, the two views provide an indication of the firm's ability to compete in its markets.

The notion that competitive advantage is achieved through the exploitation of the firm's capabilities goes back as far as Penrose (1959). Only in the last decade, however, has management thinking moved towards recognizing the importance of capabilities renewal and regeneration in response to shifts in the business environment. A number of management thinkers in the late 1980s and early 1990s began showing how firms can develop their strategic capabilities to keep pace with rapidly changing environments (Hayes, Wheelwright and Clark 1998, Prahalad and Hamel 1990, Dierickx and Cool 1989, Chandler 1990).

Teece and Pisano (1998), in particular, have taken this notion further, developing a coherent framework that both integrates existing conceptual and empirical knowledge and is prescriptive in nature. Teece and Pisano argue that dynamic capabilities must be viewed against the strategic dimensions of the firm, which are its *managerial* and *organizational processes*, its present *position*, and the *paths* available to it. Dynamic capabilities are the subset of the firm's core or distinctive competencies that enable it to build its competitive position in changing market circumstances by allowing the firm to create new products and processes in responses to these. *Managerial* and *organizational processes*, in the terminology of Teece and Pisano, refer to the way things are done in the firm, its routines, practices, and learning. *Position* refers to the firm's current endowment of technology, intellectual property, and relational capital. *Paths* relate to strategic alternatives available to the firm. Paths refer to not only possible future options, but also the firm's history. Where the firm can go in the future is determined by the path it has taken in the past; the notion of *path dependence* recognizes that the firm's future options are determined by its history.

Capabilities must change as the competitive environment of the firm changes. Core capabilities have a limited shelf-life in the sense that those qualities and aspects of a capability that make it strategically relevant today gradually deteriorate with time. This might happen for a number of reasons. Capabilities may lose relevance as new markets demand different sets of skills. Key elements contributing to the strategic importance of a capability may cease to exist, while emerging market conditions render past capabilities obsolete. In fact, the firm's existing capabilities might stand in the way of it developing the required new ones. Leonard-Barton (1995) refers to aging, obsolete capabilities as *core rigidities*.

Kellogg's and the bagel

There was a time when the debate at Kellogg's headquarters in Battle Creek, Michigan centred on whether the market trend was towards hot or cold breakfast cereals. It appeared that little could challenge Kellogg's market position with its dominant cornflakes brand. Then along came the inconspicuous bagel. The bagel, a traditional food favoured by Jewish New Yorkers, required both boiling and baking. It has a short shelf life and its manufacture formerly required expensive equipment. However, in the 1960s, Daniel Thompson invented a small, inexpensive bagel-making machine that soon had mom-and-pop stores selling freshly baked bagels. Consumers quickly developed a taste for the inexpensive and tasty food. Bagels could also be consumed on the run, making them a particularly popular alternative to a traditional sit-down cereal breakfast with the growing suburban population that commuted to work in the big cities every morning. Bagels quickly became a serious challenge to Kellogg's breakfast cereal market. The legacy cereal manufacturer was caught off guard by the change in consumer taste; sales of cornflakes and other breakfast cereals dropped.

In 1996, Kellogg's responded by buying Lender's Bagels, a frozen bagel product sold through supermarket channels like cereal foods. Kellogg's miscalculated seriously by buying a market stake in frozen bagels just at a point when freshly made bagels were becoming the craze of the nation. In 1999, Kellogg's sold Lender's to Aurora for US$275 million, having paid US$455 million three years earlier. Kellogg's woes did not stop there. The traditional breakfast food market has experienced another significant shift with the emergence and explosive growth of national coffee-shop chains such as Starbucks. Busy city-dwellers and commuters more than ever are opting for a coffee and bagel on-the-go over traditional sit-down breakfast fare. Kellogg's, it appears, has had to learn the hard way that indirect competitors can change the tide of competitive advantage in virtually any industry. Moreover, Kellogg's saw its legacy assets quickly degenerate to core rigidities in markets that began dancing to a new tune.

Source: Pietersen (2002).

Capabilities and strategic impact

A firm's capabilities may vary in their strategic impact. Not all capabilities possess the same potential for strategic impact. The strategic impact of capabilities may range from core to supporting, depending on their potential for contributing to the competitive impact of the firm. *Core* capabilities are the most important. They provide the firm with sustainable competitive advantage, they are built up over time, are deeply embedded in the firm, and therefore difficult to transfer. Core capabilities are those on which the firm stakes its claim to competitive uniqueness; these set the firm apart from its competitors.

Somewhat lower on the scale of importance are the firm's *enabling* capabilities. These are important to the firm, but they do not distinguish the firm competitively from its competitors. They *enable* the firm's core capabilities. Often, they constitute a minimum basis of competitiveness in the firm's industry and markets; that is, they qualify the firm for competition but do not provide potential for competitive differentiation. Often, enabling capabilities are former core capabilities that have lost their strategic impact through changes in the competitive environment.

Supporting or *supplemental* capabilities exhibit the least degree of strategic impact. They are "nice to have," but not essential to the firm for competitive advantage, and they support the firm's core capabilities, but can readily be imitated by competitors. They fulfill only a marginally important role in the firm. Supporting capabilities could readily be outsourced without any serious compromise to the firm's competitive position (Leonard-Barton 1995).

Capabilities and profit-earning potential

Capabilities endow firms with competitive advantage. Competitive advantage enables the firm to achieve a higher degree of profitability relative to competing firms. How do capabilities contribute to the firm's profit-earning potential? In order to establish this link, we must examine some fundamental attributes of strategic capabilities. Grant (2002) has proposed a number of attributes which are clustered into three broad categories.

First, we have attributes relating to the *scarcity* and *relevance* of capabilities. These attributes determine the *degree of competitive advantage* established through capabilities. A capability must be scarce, that is, it must be difficult to acquire and/or it must not be widely available. Second, a capability must be relevant; it must be required and it must make a significant contribution to the firm's competitive potential.

Sustainability is a second broad clustering of attributes contributing to the profit earning potential of a capability. Attributes such as *durability, mobility*, and *replicability* determine the sustainability of a capability. *Durability* refers to the degree to which a capability is resilient to change and erosion of relevance. While change may make certain capabilities obsolete over time, other capabilities, such as reputation, may remain resilient even in the face of change. Examples of resilient reputation can be found in brand names such as Coca-Cola and Kellogg's that have stood the test of time. *Mobility* of a capability is another attribute related to its sustainability. The less mobile a capability is, the greater is its potential for sustainability. The tacit knowledge content of strategically relevant capabilities makes them difficult to transfer. Often this may reflect the high degree of causal ambiguity associated with largely tacit capabilities. Sustainability in this case exhibits a flip side; difficult to transfer capabilities are often difficult to mobilize *within* the firm as well. The real challenge for the firm lies in ensuring sufficient mobility of capabilities within the firm's own organizational boundaries while building appropriate barriers for mobility across the firm's boundaries. Strategically relevant capabilities are difficult to *replicate*. This attribute relates to the tacit nature of capabilities and the often encountered causal ambiguity associated with organizational knowledge that is deeply embedded within the culture and practices of the organization.

The third category, *appropriability* addresses the ownership and property rights issues associated with capabilities on a number of levels. To the extent that strategically relevant capabilities consist of largely people-embodied knowledge, the boundary between the knowledge owned by the employee and the collective knowledge of the firm is becoming increasingly difficult to delineate. Intellectual property rights—questions relating to who ultimately owns the knowledge produced in an organization—are becoming an increasingly important issue. The less clearly intellectual property rights can be defined in firms, the more important this issue is for the relative bargaining power of individual employees in the firm. The more the firm succeeds in building up a collectively shared stock of knowledge, skills, and capabilities (that is, the more deeply individual skills are embedded and integrated into the firm's processes and practices), the greater the potential of the firm to exploit its capabilities for competitive advantage.

Capabilities and value creation

Competitive advantage is directly related to the firm's ability to create value for customers and stakeholders. This might happen through delivering better value than the competition to the firm's customers, and/or achieving higher profitability for the firm and for its shareholders.

An effective competitive strategy seeks to deploy the firm's strategic capabilities in the pursuit of both objectives. The key to enacting this strategy lies in establishing the link between value definition, generation, and delivery and the firm's strategic capabilities shown in Figure 3.1. Value is defined and ultimately delivered in the market place. The firm's *value proposition* is an articulation of its strategic intent; it articulates *what* value the firm proposes to create and *how* it intends to deliver the value to the market. It expresses the firm's understanding of its *raison*

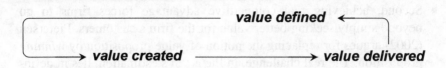

Figure 3.1 Value definition, creation, and delivery cycle

d'être, its "reason for being." It is also an articulation of the firm's differential value offering to its customers and stakeholders.

A valid *value proposition* provides a powerful basis for competitive differentiation. It may take on a variety of forms. Treacy and Wiersema (1995) suggest three possible value disciplines that form the basis of the corresponding value proposition to the firm's customers. The first value discipline focuses on *operational excellence*, providing the firm with the possibility to compete on an effective cost–price basis. Bulk processing industries such as hydrocarbon refineries or steelmaking companies typically adhere to this value discipline. The second value discipline focuses on *product leadership*. The value proposition in this case is based on the firm's ability to establish a leadership position in delivering innovative products that push current performance limits. Manufacturers of innovative consumer electronics products such as Sony, Philips, and Canon compete on this proposition.

The third value discipline is *customer intimacy*. Its adherents focus on cultivating relationships with specific customers, satisfying unique needs which often only the firm in question can fulfil by virtue of the close relationship it nurtures with the customer. Service industries—for example, banks, consultancies, airlines, and hotels—typically seek to excel at this value discipline.

Treacy and Wiersema (1995) argue that firms invariably focus on one of the value disciplines; that the firm's choice of value discipline in effect defines what a company does and therefore what it is. This does not imply, however, that it is free to neglect the other two. While it excels at its chosen value discipline, the firm must maintain at least industry parity in the other two. In our view, Treacy and Wiersema's framework provides a useful starting point for thinking about value in the context of capabilities. However, it does oversimplify reality:

- First, real business environments often do not allow for the clean segmentation suggested by the Treacy and Wiersema framework. Often firms must deliver a combination of value disciplines in order to compete effectively in the market place. This is particularly the case for companies competing in diversified markets.

- Second, achieving real competitive advantage forces firms to go beyond simply seeking better value for the firm's customers. Pietersen (2002) argues for replacing the notion of value proposition by *winning* proposition. The real challenge, in Pietersen's estimation, lies in defining and leveraging a winning proposition, which creates clearly differentiated value on all fronts; it creates greater value for the customer and superior profits for the firm and its stakeholders.

How does the firm create value? We propose a cascading model that traces the firm's ultimate delivery of value to the market back through its business processes to its repository of knowledge and capabilities. We begin by looking at the firm and its value-creating processes (Figure 3.2). A firm creates value on the basis of its business processes. Business processes generate net value, whereby the net value produced by a business process is the difference between the value entering and leaving that process.

Some business processes are more important than others by virtue of the fact that their net value creation potential is greater than others. In other words, the relative importance of any single business process is determined by its potential for contributing to the value implied by the firm's value proposition. Those capable of generating the greatest contribution are the firm's *core* business processes. These must be closely aligned with the firm's overall business strategy. Core business processes, in turn, are enabled by the firm's capabilities. The firm's *core capabilities* are particularly relevant to the firm's core business processes. The firm's capabilities ultimately draw on the firm's repository of knowledge. They are rooted in the firm's stock of strategically relevant knowledge, skills, and people-embodied experiential knowledge. Clusters of this knowledge, integrated with managerial systems, the firm's culture and physical technical systems combine to form capabilities.

Key questions

- How well does the firm understand its winning proposition?
- How valid is it today; how is it changing?
- To what extent is the winning proposition shared by both employees and customers?
- What are the firm's critical juncture points in its value delivery system?

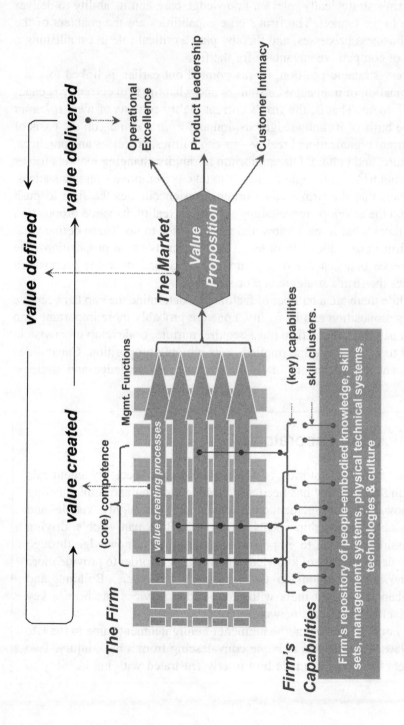

Figure 3.2 Schematic showing the link between a firm's capabilities and its delivery of value

The firm's core business processes therefore provide the link between the firm's strategically relevant knowledge base and its ability to deliver value to the market. The firm's core capabilities are the enablers of the core business processes, and thereby play a critical role in establishing a basis of competitive advantage for the firm.

Every strategic position, it was pointed out earlier, is linked to some combination of intellectual resources and what the firm currently is capable of doing. That is, the firm's current reality consists of *what it knows* on the basis of its knowledge position and *what it can do* on the basis of its current organizational reality—its capabilities, processes and practices, structure, and culture. Disequilibrium in rapidly changing markets forces firms not to seek strategic fit, rather to take pre-emptive strategic stances. It means that the firm's value proposition encourages the firm to push beyond the envelope representing its current reality. Its value proposition articulates what it must know and must be able to do. These define what the firm must achieve in order to deliver on its value proposition. The difference between the firm's current reality and its value proposition defines the firm's strategic *gap* or *stretch*.

While there are a number of factors that determine the gap between the firm's proposition and its reality, none are probably more important than the capabilities that a firm must acquire, nurture, or develop otherwise in order to create the value implied in its winning proposition. Capabilities represent a key element in closing the firm's knowledge and strategic gaps.

Buckman Laboratories

Buckman Laboratories is a Memphis-based speciality chemicals manufacturer that has been a pioneer in creating and implementing knowledge management solutions under the highly visible and visionary leadership of its CEO Bob Buckman. Bob's driving passion has been to empower employees with knowledge through the deliberate use of knowledge networking in order to provide more innovative solutions to the company's customers. Building and enhancing the business with value-added services has been a key driver behind Bob's networking efforts.

For Bob Buckman, the moment of enlightenment came in the late 1980s when he was at home convalescing from a back injury. Two weeks in bed had made him utterly frustrated with his inability to know what was going on in the firm. Bob began to map out a vision of a knowledge-driven company connected across all its 80 countries by an electronic network that would allow all its 1200 associates—as Buckman employees are known—access to the best knowledge practices, experience, and skills available to the company.

Bob made his vision come true on his return to the office. The heart of the knowledge management and transfer of best practices system called K'Netox[r] which was introduced in 1992. Each associate was provided with a laptop computer, which is important given the geographic dispersion of the associates around the globe. The system relies on the participation of all Buckman associates. Anyone can post a question on the network and expect to receive a response within 48 hours. The results have by far surpassed Bob's original expectations. Response time to customers has been reduced to hours rather than days or even weeks. New product-related revenues are reported to have increased by 10 percent and sales of new products are 50 percent higher.

Buckman Labs' pioneering approach to knowledge networking has been instrumental in establishing its competitive position in the value-added services area. Competing in this area has required Buckman Labs to build and maintain superior knowledge and capabilities in using its chemicals in various microbiocidal treatment applications to solve its customers' problems. Buckman Labs' strategic intent consisted in closing the gap between areas where it already had well-developed knowledge and expertise and those where its knowledge was more limited. Buckman Labs' knowledge networking capabilities where critical to closing the strategic and knowledge gaps very quickly. One Buckman associate has expressed the outcome in the following way: "When you ask one person a question, you have the power of 1200 employees behind you—including our CEO Bob Buckman."

Source: Buckman (2001).

Concluding remarks

Competitive advantage is the ability of the firm to outperform competitors on the basis of profitability. Competitive advantage is related to the strategic resources available to the firm, the degree to which the firm exploits and deploys these resources, and the extent to which it succeeds in creating the appropriate organizational enabling conditions for their deployment. Capabilities are one of the most strategically relevant resources available to the firm. They enable the firm to perform at the level that is required for success. Strategic capabilities consist mainly of tacit knowledge; the firm's bundles of skill sets, people-embodied knowledge, experience, and attitudes that are significantly more difficult to "manage" than the firm's physical resources. Capabilities endow competitive advantage by virtue of their uniqueness, inimitability, and their contribution toward generating better customer value.

CHAPTER 4

Managing capabilities for strategic advantage

Introduction

Rapid change in the global competitive environment is continually challenging firms to manage their portfolio of capabilities for maximum impact. Managers are being challenged to exploit their current capabilities while nurturing the development of new ones in anticipation of emerging and future markets. The firm's knowledge is its "key economic resource and the dominant—and perhaps even the only—source of competitive advantage" (Drucker 1999). The firm's knowledge manifests itself in its set of strategic capabilities. The strategic management of these demands deliberate and focused effort on the part of managers; it is a task that cannot be left to chance.

In this chapter, we:

- develop an overview of the task of the strategic management of capabilities
- derive guidelines for the specific tasks concerning
  - selecting capabilities
  - building capabilities
  - deploying capabilities
  - protecting capabilities.

Strategic management of capabilities

The field of strategic management of capabilities is an evolving management discipline. There is at this time no consensus on any model of "best practice" in this area. Companies are likely to approach the task in varying ways, differing in their ability to select, build, deploy, and protect their capabilities. The objective of this chapter is simply to provide an overview of the management tasks, and thereby provide some guidelines along which a firm's capability to manage its core capabilities may be assessed.

Chiesa and Barbeschi (1994) refer to capabilities management as "a guided process for resource management." The process implied here has a number of important dimensions that must be considered:

1 **Time**. Capabilities represent an accumulation of learning over time. Typical timescales for capability building are of the order of years, perhaps even decades. Strategically relevant capabilities cannot simply be purchased and deployed from one day to another.
2 **Deliberate strategy**. Strategic capabilities management demands a deliberate and focused strategy over time. The strategic management of capabilities can be viewed as a multi-strand trajectory that must be aligned with the firm's overall business strategy along all the various stages of its development. The notion of capabilities management in terms of a trajectory is consistent with path dependence and the dynamic nature of capabilities discussed in the previous chapter.
3 **Secondary capabilities**. The strategic management of the firm's capabilities requires the enabling support of secondary capabilities that ensure the effective exploitation and deployment of the firm's primary capabilities. Secondary capabilities are often neglected by managers because they are not as obvious as the firm's primary capabilities; they are typically soft skills-related and therefore difficult to "manage." They are entrepreneurial in nature, and range from supporting the strategic visioning of the firm's future competitive position, managing strategic partnerships and network relationships, through to the actual internalization of new, externally sourced knowledge into the firm's existing portfolio of capabilities.

According to Hamel (1994), there are four broad categories of tasks in the management of core capabilities: selecting, building, deploying, and protecting capabilities. The four dimensions are not orthogonal; rather, they are mutually dependent and exhibit overlap. Each of these has a number of subordinate tasks, as indicated in the following overview:

1 **Selecting capabilities:**
   – identifying the firm's stock of strategically relevant knowledge
   – assessing strategic impact of the firm's capabilities
   – ranking capabilities according to competitive impact

- identifying current gaps in the capabilities portfolio
- identifying capabilities that will be needed in the future
- identifying potential sources of external knowledge.

2 **Building capabilities:**
- acquiring capabilities
- creating new knowledge
- developing new capabilities through recombination of old and new capabilities
- accessing new capabilities through strategic partnering
- renewing existing capabilities through learning.

3 **Deploying capabilities:**
- leveraging capabilities
- transferring capabilities
- exploiting capabilities
- internalizing and integrating new knowledge into capabilities
- recombining and reconfiguring capabilities.

4 **Protecting capabilities:**
- pre-emptive deployment of capabilities
- divesting obsolete capabilities.

In the following sections, each task will be considered briefly, in turn.

Selecting capabilities

The old management adage "you can't manage something you don't know you have" holds true for capabilities. Put in a slightly different way, it might be said that a firm cannot actively manage its core capabilities if the firm's managers do not share a view of what those capabilities are. Hamel (1994) argues that the clarity of a firm's definition of its core capabilities is probably the most rudimentary test of the firm's ability to manage its core capabilities. Thus, the first task in managing core capabilities is to take stock of the firm's core capabilities. In many firms, this process is carried out in a haphazard and often political manner. Admittedly, the task is not simple. The firm's core capabilities are often entwined in the products and services in which they are embedded. It is very difficult to disentangle the capabilities, to differentiate the core from the non-core, and to cluster resulting capabilities in a meaningful and transparent manner. Often, the more competitively relevant a capability is, the less obvious it is; the tacit knowledge content of the firm's core capabilities defies exact approaches to its analysis.

Adrian Ward, leader of learning and change at Hughes S&C, observed, "[the] company suffers from 'islands of knowledge', deep pockets of expertise that have trouble developing synergies among themselves."

Lew Platt, CEO of Hewlett-Packard, is purported to have said, "If HP knew what HP knows, we would be three times as profitable."

Source: *Financial Times*, March 7, 1999.

Knowledge maps that capture, identify, and lay open the firm's knowledge in its various forms are a first step toward managing the firm's capabilities. While the assumption is often made that firms know what they know, in reality they mostly don't. Astonishingly, despite the wide consensus on the importance of knowledge, many firms still do not have at their disposal even the most rudimentary tools for assessing the breadth and depth of their capabilities-embedded knowledge. The strategic capabilities portfolio mapping approach developed by Birchall and Tovstiga (1999) is based on a systematic and stage-wise analysis of the firm's portfolio of capabilities. It has proven to be a suitable tool for analyzing the strategic positioning of the firm's portfolio of capabilities in terms of competitive impact (emerging, pacing, core or base) and competitive position (the firm's degree of control over its portfolio of capabilities and its ability to exploit its current portfolio).

Figure 4.1 shows a simplified outcome of a capabilities portfolio mapping exercise. Shown for the purpose of illustration are two existing, internal capabilities, C^1_{int} and C^2_{int}, and their positioning with respect to strategic impact and position. The banana-shaped envelope represents the approximate perimeter of a strategically balanced portfolio. Clearly, C^2_{int} represents an aging capability whereas C^1_{int} represents a capability that has already demonstrated its potential for competitive differentiation. The challenge in implementing a competitive strategy lies in identifying and developing those capabilities that constitute the critical building blocks of the firm's core competencies. Invariably, these will be the ones demonstrating *pacing* or *core* competitive impact and a *strong* competitive position. These, in turn, will exert the greatest impact on the important success factors of the firm's industry.

A suitable knowledge mapping methodology can be a powerful strategic management tool. A knowledge mapping approach such as the one described above accounts for the fact that knowledge is a dynamic entity.

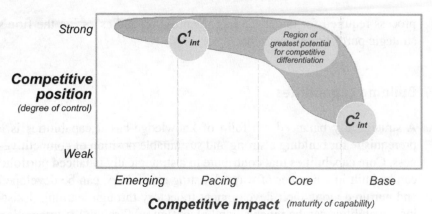

Figure 4.1 Capabilities portfolio mapping showing envelope of a strategically balanced portfolio and example of positioning of two capabilities in terms of competitive position and impact

A carefully done mapping analysis can provide valuable strategic insight on various levels. First, it provides a snapshot of where the firm stands today with respect to its current and desired strategic knowledge profile, thereby enabling the identification of internal knowledge gaps. Second, a comparative mapping of the firm's competitors and potential strategic partners enables an assessment of where the firm stands in relation to its competitors and potential partners. External knowledge gaps can be identified. Most importantly, however, a strategic mapping approach can be used to plot the historical path and future trajectory of the firm's competitive knowledge position.

On the basis of the resulting capabilities map, a firm can then proceed to determine what knowledge should be developed internally, what needs to be acquired externally, and how to go about accomplishing these tasks in the most effective manner. Capability portfolio maps can be used for identifying the portfolio's current strengths, its vulnerabilities, and strategic gaps. Moreover, they can be used to project the firm's current portfolio into the future by constructing scenarios showing how the firm might develop its current position of competitiveness to sustain a strategically balanced portfolio in the future. On the basis of these scenarios and the strategic gap analyses, the organization can prioritize actions, martial resources, and plan and drive the requisite organizational measures for closing the gaps.

In Appendix A, we have provided a capabilities mapping methodology that has been developed and applied by the authors with numerous companies. The purpose of the methodology is to help guide the thinking process required for understanding, identifying, and assessing the firm's strategic portfolio of capabilities.

Building capabilities

A strategically balanced portfolio of knowledge-based capabilities is a prerequisite for building a strong and sustainable position of competitiveness. Core capabilities that contribute to a strategically balanced portfolio can be built in a number of ways. Existing capabilities can be developed and nurtured along their development trajectory through learning. Existing capabilities can be renewed and reconfigured through the integration of new external knowledge that is acquired through strategic partnering. Alternatively, capabilities can be built from new knowledge that is created within the firm.

Creating new knowledge

Building capabilities from knowledge created within in the firm is one of the most important tasks of core capabilities management. Nonaka and Takeuchi's (1995) theory of organizational knowledge creation provides one of the most comprehensive conceptual frameworks for describing how new knowledge is created in the firm. Nonaka and Takeuchi describe how innovative organizations, when responding to a changing environment, in effect create new knowledge as a result of knowledge conversion between either of two modes of knowledge— the tacit and the explicit forms. Knowledge creation can take place in four ways:

1 **Socialization** (tacit knowledge to tacit knowledge).
2 **Externalization** (tacit knowledge to explicit knowledge).
3 **Internalization** (explicit knowledge to tacit knowledge).
4 **Combination** (explicit knowledge to explicit knowledge).

Knowledge creation occurs as a result of a spiral interaction between the two knowledge modes and at various organizational levels, although the authors argue that the key to knowledge creation really lies in the externalization process which involves the mobilization and conversion of tacit knowledge. When shared across the organization, the newly created knowledge, in turn, contributes to increased learning in the organization.

Nonaka and Takeuchi (1995) point out that it is the task of management to create the proper context for the knowledge processes to run their course effectively. They propose five conditions—management practices and processes—that ensure the appropriate environment within the firm for effective knowledge creation:

1 **Intent.** Knowledge creation is driven by the organization's strategic aspirations. A first step to that end involves creating a deeply and widely shared knowledge vision throughout the organization.
2 **Autonomy.** At the individual level, members of the organization are encouraged to act autonomously as far as circumstances permit. At a higher organizational level, autonomy translates to self-organizing, cross-functional teams.
3 **Fluctuation and creative chaos.** A high degree of interaction between the organization and its external environment ensures the breakdown of encumbering routines, habits, and thinking paradigms. This encourages reflection and dialogue within the organization, which in turn promotes the creation of new concepts.
4 **Redundancy.** Ensuring information flows that go clearly beyond the immediate operational requirements might at first appear to be a wasteful and inefficient practice. Nonaka and Takeuchi, however, argue that sharing redundant information promotes the sharing of tacit knowledge to the extent that it helps in the articulation of tacit content; this is particularly important in the early phases of development work.
5 **Requisite variety.** An organization's internal diversity and capabilities to cope with contingencies must match the variety and complexity of its competitive environment. Building capabilities for combining information differently, flexibly, and quickly enhances speed and innovation.

Finally, Nonaka and Takeuchi (1995) integrate the four modes of knowledge conversion and the five enabling practices into a five-phase model of organizational knowledge creation that consists of:

1 **Sharing of tacit knowledge.** Sharing on this level occurs mainly through the socialization mode of knowledge conversion.
2 **Creating concepts.** Concepts are created through the conversion of the shared tacit knowledge into explicit knowledge (externalization).
3 **Justifying concepts.** This phase introduces an internal verification mechanism to the organizational knowledge creation process.

4 **Building an archetype.** A form of rapid prototyping, this phase can involve the development of either "hard" products or "soft" new organizational knowledge; various forms of explicit knowledge are combined in this phase.

5 **Cross-leveling knowledge.** A final phase, cross-leveling ensures that knowledge is exchanged widely both within the organization and across the firm's boundaries.

Creating the right organizational context for building capabilities

One of the important strategic advantages the firm gains by building its own capabilities is that the firm alone determines the context within which knowledge is embedded into its new capabilities. Tacit knowledge—the factor that accounts for the greatest competitive impact of a capability—is highly context-specific. The mobilization, conversion, and sharing of tacit knowledge are critically dependent on the firm's internal context—the unique features of the firm's current reality, which are determined by its learning culture, knowledge base, and enabling practices. These factors constitute the firm's knowledge and learning infrastructure.

- **Enabling practices.** These provide the appropriate organizational conditions for enabling the rich exchange and sharing of knowledge at the individual and team levels of the firm (Nonaka and Takeuchi 1995).
- **Knowledge base.** The firm's knowledge base reflects the inherent knowledge practices, propensities, and learning patterns and orientations of the organization (Nevis, DiBella and Gould 1995).
- **Learning culture.** The organization's learning culture dimension describes the shared values and orientations of the organization and its attitude towards learning; it indicates where and how learning takes place in the organization by taking into consideration the organization's learning focus, attitude toward experimentation, and prevailing leadership style.

The firm's knowledge context can also be described as its "knowledge practice field," the internal environment in which the firm's enabling practices, learning culture, and knowledge base interact to generate new knowledge, as indicated in Figure 4.2 (Tovstiga 1999).

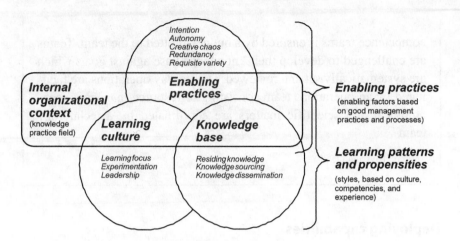

Figure 4.2. Dimensions of the organization's knowledge and learning
              environment

Capabilities development at SKF Engineering & Research Centre

The SKF Engineering and Research Centre, located near Utrecht, Netherlands, is the high-powered and innovative central research establishment of the Swedish SKF Group, the world's leading manufacturer of roller bearings and seals. Several years ago one particular group within this organization, the Bearing Theory & Testing (BTT) group, opted for a unique multi-competence structure based on competence teams.

Each competence team represents a unit of a larger "community of knowledge practice" composed of a number of competence teams. Each member of the organization is expected to join three competence teams, two to actively contribute to, and one to learn in. The competence teams are led by team leaders who assume the responsibility for their team's competence development and function as a resource in two other competence teams. There is no hierarchical structure within the teams; teams assume the responsibility for the scientific correctness of their results.

The competence team leader is chosen by the competence team members, and functions as chairperson of the competence team meetings. The operational and developmental autonomy of the competence teams is ensured by a budget allotted to the team. Teams are challenged to develop their knowledge base against goals which are systematically set and reviewed. Day-to-day operations are facilitated by an operations team consisting of resource managers; technological and scientific matters are coordinated by a technology team.

Source: Tovstiga (1999).

Deploying capabilities

Firms deploy their current portfolio of knowledge-based capabilities to gain strategic advantage in their competitive environments. Capabilities are dynamic entities, hence their deployment necessarily implies motion. Important factors are the rate of motion and the direction of motion of their deployment. The direction of motion is important from a competitive positioning perspective. With reference to Figure 4.1, the direction of motion should be toward a position of core competitive impact and strong competitive position. Management's task is to drive the development of the capability's trajectory in this direction. The rate of movement is equally important since speed matters in competitive environments. The strategic objective is invariably to learn faster than the competition, to arrive at a position of competitive advantage before the competition.

Firms deploy their capabilities in various ways. They *leverage* their existing capabilities by transferring these rapidly across multiple businesses and into new markets. Furthermore, successful firms exploit their existing position of competitive advantage by *internalizing* new knowledge to replenish their capabilities, and thereby counter rapid changes in the firm's business environment. This is important, since a firm's capabilities are neither stable over time nor uniform at any point in time (Bogner and Thomas 1994). Both mechanisms require timely responsiveness, rapid and flexible innovation, and the appropriate organizational skills and culture.

We shall focus on the internalization mechanism by showing how firms deploy their capabilities through integration of new knowledge and reconfiguration of existing capabilities to secure their position of competitive advantage.

Not that long ago, British Petroleum placed a full-page advertisement in a leading British daily paper announcing that it had learnt a new key technology for deep-sea oil exploration from its strategic partnership with Shell Oil Company in the Gulf of Mexico, and that it was using this new knowledge to initiate its own deep-sea exploration west of the Shetland Islands. BP exemplifies an emerging class of successful multinational firms that sees its ability to leverage its own capabilities-embedded knowledge with new knowledge brought into the organization from external sources as key to its competitive strategy. BP has shifted from conducting its own basic research to learning from strategic partners and quickly spreading that knowledge through the firm. To leverage maximum impact from this strategy, BP has had to nurture secondary capabilities that focus on making its new partnerships work.

Source: McDermott (1999).

Internalizing capabilities

Long-term sustained competitive advantage requires a continual upgrading and development of core capabilities in advance of competitors. Firms have recognized the need to look outside the firm for new sources of knowledge. They are seeking to leverage the superior innovation skills, knowledge bases, and processes of external partners. Acquiring and internalizing outside knowledge is rapidly becoming a critical factor for building a sustainable base of competitive advantage. This new challenge has given rise to the development and exploitation of an entirely new set of capabilities focused on *knowledge internalization*. This set supports the processes of knowledge scanning, evaluation, acquisition, adaptation, integration and internalization, and ultimately commercial exploitation of new, outside knowledge.

The strategic implications arising from strategic knowledge internalization are several-fold:

- The approach espousing the deployment of internal capabilities by enhancing them with new external knowledge is in accordance with Schumpeter's (1939) definition of innovation as a process of continually reconfiguring and internalizing fresh stocks of productive assets to enable future competitiveness. Rivalry to access new knowledge and to internalize the new knowledge in new and innovative ways is central to Schumpeter's process of creative destruction.

- The ability of a firm to source and use new knowledge is contingent on the firm's current portfolio of capabilities. Successful sourcing of strategically relevant new knowledge requires that the firm already has at least a shadow competence in the particular area.
- Sourcing external new knowledge invariably demands that the firm develops entirely new organizational capabilities devoted to the internalization and integration of knowledge from external sources with skills and knowledge currently existing within the firm. Knowledge sharing—both internally and across organizational boundaries—is essential for successful knowledge sourcing.
- The richest source of new knowledge and innovation is typically at the firm's interface to its external environment, for example, at the supplier–customer interface. Key issues here include: (1) not stifling the free flow of knowledge across the interface by insisting on "specified practices"; (2) focusing on the "what" rather than the "how" of outsourcing; and (3) building the necessary trust and experience across the interface by finding new methods of sharing benefits while protecting the proprietary rights of each party (Quinn 1999).

A knowledge internalization strategy can be viewed in terms of a trajectory that determines how new knowledge is sourced and internalized into the existing portfolio of capabilities, as shown in Figure 4.3.

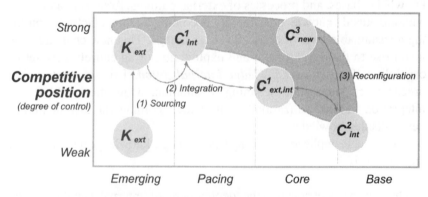

Figure 4.3 Knowledge internalization trajectory shown for deployment of capabilities

Figure 4.3 shows the path a trajectory might take in the case of a firm that has decided to deploy external knowledge (K_{ext}) to enhance an existing capability (C^1_{int}) that is yet evolving, and regenerate another existing capability (C^2_{int}) that is essentially obsolete. How does the firm go about doing this?

1 First, the firm sources new knowledge (K_{ext}) in its external environment. Successful sourcing begins with the effective management of strategic partnerships and external network relationships. These are typically the source of the new knowledge. Furthermore, sourcing demands secondary capabilities that enable the firm to continually scan, monitor, and evaluate relevant new knowledge in its environment. The sourcing of new knowledge should target new development platforms rather than specific products or projects. Note that the receiving firm is necessarily in a weak position with respect to K_{ext} since strategic control of the new knowledge clearly lies outside the firm.

2 The firm brings the new knowledge, K_{ext}, into position alongside an existing internal capability (C^1_{int}) in the first stage of the internalization process. Internalization involves the appropriate *integration*, that is, *adaptation* and *absorption* of the new knowledge, leading to the creation of an enhanced capability, $C^1_{ext,int}$. Relying on external knowledge comes at a price, however. The firm's competitive position with respect to the new knowledge-enhanced capability $C^1_{ext,int}$ is compromised by the fact that it has relied on deploying external knowledge for the enhanced capability. The strategic imperative for the firm is now to take appropriate measures to boost the enhanced capability $C^1_{ext,int}$ from a position of neutral competitiveness to a strong competitive position.

3 One option for doing this is to create an entirely new capability, C^3_{new}, through *recombination* and *reconfiguration* of the enhanced capability, $C^1_{ext,int}$, with existing capability, C^2_{int}. Reconfiguration of capability C^2_{int} with the knowledge-enhanced capability $C^1_{ext,int}$ leads to the new capability C^3_{new}, a new capability that endows the firm with unique competitive advantage.

Strategies for sourcing external knowledge

Various strategies exist for sourcing new external knowledge. Dussauge, Hart and Ramanantsoa (1992) have identified four possible mechanisms:

1 **Joint ventures and alliances.** The firm joins forces with other firms to

develop new knowledge. Alliances may take on two forms: *knowledge transfer alliances* tend to be more competitive and less cooperative than *knowledge sharing alliances* in which partners agree to develop new knowledge in common.

2 **External R&D contracts.** The firm subcontracts with an external knowledge provider such as a research laboratory, research centre, or university for the development of particular knowledge.

3 **Licenses.** Firms are allotted access to knowledge developed by firms operating in different industries or geographical areas. Firms are typically restricted by specifications regulating the deployment of knowledge brought in under licensing agreements. Fees are often directly linked to the profits achieved by deploying the licensed knowledge.

4 **Outright acquisition of a firm possessing the desired knowledge.** This assumes that a firm possessing the required knowledge exists and is available for acquisition.

Capabilities specifically focused on sourcing new knowledge

We introduced the notion of the firm's secondary capabilities in an earlier chapter. They are organizational capabilities that support and enable the firm's primary capabilities. When a firm acquires new knowledge, the intent is on enhancing the deployment of its primary capabilities. The firm's secondary capabilities help make this happen. For new knowledge sourcing purposes, we broadly categorize the firm's secondary capabilities into two groups.

The first group of secondary capabilities are *functionality-related* capabilities, structural mechanisms and management processes that provide the required infrastructure within the organization for sourcing and internalizing new knowledge. In particular, we find in this first group:

- **functionality-related capabilities** (information technologies) dedicated to processing, storing, categorizing, indexing, and linking knowledge units such as the Internet, groupware and e-mail
- **cross-functional team mechanisms** such as new product management capabilities, customer support capabilities, and quality management capabilities
- **management processes** such as coordination processes, decision processes, performance management, and incentive structures.

In the second group we find largely *soft* organizational capabilities that enable the organization to exploit its knowledge. Klein and Hiscocks (1994) suggest four categories of organizational capabilities that govern the way in which a firm acquires and deploys capabilities:

- **Learning** has an individual as well as an organizational dimension. In both cases, it involves the process by which repetition, experimentation, and review enable key tasks to be performed better and more quickly (Teece and Pisano 1998). Learning involves identifying and articulating common themes and platforms, and organizing them both intellectually and organizationally for enhanced use. Learning is a key factor in the absorption and adaptation of new knowledge into the organization.
- **Innovating** is required for combining and reconfiguring old and new knowledge in creative new ways. It also involves making links across and between boundaries of knowledge clusters. Innovation is a key factor in the integration and internalization of new knowledge into the firm's existing stock of knowledge.
- **Strategic visioning** is the implicit capability of the firm to envision the evolution of new knowledge developments. It involves developing a shared, common understanding of the patterns of market and technology evolution, and categorizing skills and knowledge clusters in terms of these emerging market opportunities in the firm itself, and influencing strategic development of capabilities in partner firms.
- **Embedding** knowledge involves minimizing knowledge loss and dissipation through staff turnover, disrupted and dispersed teams, and through skill sets and knowledge that are simply forgotten. Embedding is an internalization mechanism that focuses on the integration of new knowledge streams into the organization's existing stock of strategically relevant knowledge. Knowledge sharing—sharing of experiential knowledge through processes such as mentoring and team work—is a key mechanism of embedding.

Protecting capabilities

In fast-moving competitive environments, core capabilities are particularly vulnerable to erosion, dissipation, and degradation. This may happen in many ways. Capabilities may erode because of a lack of funding, particularly when intense business pressure and short-term business targets divert critical funds to investments that promise more obvious and shorter-term returns. Capabilities may become fragmented when firms diversify their business activities. They may be lost entirely when an underperforming business is divested or they may inadvertently migrate to alliance partners (Pralahad and Hamel 1994).

Traditional intellectual property protection strategies are largely irrelevant when it comes to protecting capabilities. We have argued that it is the tacit knowledge embedded in capabilities that makes them strategically important to the firm. Patents do not capture the tacit content of capabilities that makes them strategically important. Traditional measures for protecting tangible assets are largely unsuitable for protecting capabilities.

Capabilities can be protected in a number of ways. Pre-empting new competitive space by moving into an under-defended territory, a so-called "loose brick" strategy, is one approach to protecting capabilities. Honda's success in North America with its small motorcycles and Komatsu's entry into the Eastern European market with its heavy equipment are examples of cases in which the new entrants made their market debut while the incumbents' attention was directed elsewhere (Pralahad and Hamel 1994).

Protecting capabilities can also be achieved by changing the rules of competitive engagement in established markets. Dell Computer is an apt example. Dell, one of the fastest growing computer companies in the United States, could not in any way match IBM's direct sales force or Compaq's dealer network. Dell chose to change the rules of the game by developing and deploying new capabilities for marketing and distributing its computers. In its early days, Dell sold its computers by mail; today this business has evolved into a sophisticated and highly profitable online business. Industry incumbents have been left with legacy stakeholders that have kept them from deploying the web-based market channel capabilities that Dell has so effectively exploited. Protecting capabilities requires ongoing vigilance on the part of the firm's management. There are at present no quick and reliable measures for determining whether the firm is staying ahead of the competition with its core capabilities.

Key questions

- How does your firm go about "knowing what it does"?
- How does your firm go about identifying "what it does not know"?
- How does it go about generating and deploying new knowledge?
- What are the greatest challenges encountered in bringing new knowledge into the firm?

Concluding remarks

Capabilities deliver strategic advantage when they enable the company to deliver better value on the basis of the combined competencies and skills of its people. This process must not be left to chance. To the extent that capabilities can be "managed" at all, the task is a formidable one. What probably challenges managers most is the fact that capabilities are largely intangible. Intangibles are not visible, they are difficult to grasp and "sticky," and even more difficult to account for. The management of capabilities must therefore also be approached accordingly. While it is very difficult for managers to "manage" the capabilities per se, they can and must manage the organizational parameters that enable the firm's capabilities to unfold their full competitive potential. That is, the important task of managers is to create the right organizational context—processes, structure, practices, and culture—to enable the effective selection, building, deployment, and protection of its capabilities.

CHAPTER 5

Strategic capabilities and innovation

Introduction

Innovation is undoubtedly one of the most crucial strategic levers available to the firm. As firms are moving out of the difficult economic period brought on by the collapse of the dot.com bubble, innovation, it appears, is being "rediscovered." Many firms are now poised to venture beyond measures that are focused purely on retrenchment and cost reduction to embrace innovation as the engine for driving their new business growth. Innovation, however, is intimately linked with the firm's capabilities and ability to mobilize new knowledge through learning. The grouping of innovation, capabilities, and organizational learning is growing more important as business environments change more rapidly and the production of new knowledge accelerates as never before.

In this chapter, we:

- explore innovation and capabilities in the greater context of organizational knowledge, learning, and change
- introduce and develop the notions of institutional, revolutional, and evolutional innovation and discuss their managerial implications in the context of achieving successful innovation across a range of strategic options
- examine the role of organizational capabilities in enabling evolutional innovation.

Capabilities and innovation

Innovation is important to the firm, but it is not a stand-alone factor in the firm's arsenal of competitive weapons. It is inextricably linked to a number of other important organizational processes, such as knowledge, learning, and change. In order to understand the true competitive impli-cations of innovation, we must understand innovation in the greater context of these factors. We develop the argument in this chapter that the interaction between innovation and other related processes such as orga-nizational change, learning, and knowledge creation can be shown in terms of a cyclical relationship, as suggested in Figure 5.1 (Tovstiga 1999). Furthermore, we argue that it is the *collective* outcome of the effec-tive management of these factors that ultimately enables firms to build and exploit strategically relevant capabilities to its advantage.

From an experiential learning systems perspective, innovation has been linked to organizational learning both in concept and in empirical research. The learning systems approach views organizational change and innovation as experiential learning processes. Experiential learning on the basis of Nonaka and Takeuchi's (1995) concept of organizational knowledge creation introduced in Chapter 4 supports this view. Their notion of organizational knowledge creation draws on the premise that when organizations innovate, they actually create new knowledge through the mobilization and conversion of knowledge existing in vari-ous forms. In doing so, they not only re-create (that is change) their environment, the newly created knowledge is embedded in the organi-zation in the form of new capabilities. Viewing capabilities from the

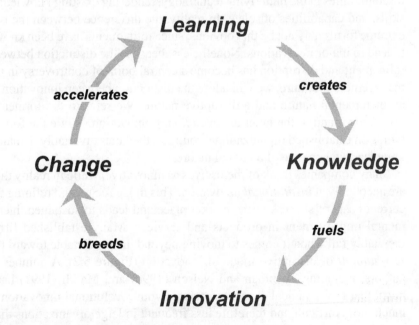

Figure 5.1 The organization's capabilities-building cycle

learning perspective is particularly appropriate because it takes into account the influence of the firm's history in shaping new capabilities through renewal and change. Capabilities development from this perspective expresses itself in the well-known *learning curve*.

Innovation has been defined as the process of bringing new, problem-solving ideas into use in the organization (Kanter 1983). Implicit to this definition is the notion that an innovation has a commercial impact of some sort: That is, innovation produces economic value of some sort to the organization's stakeholders. This may express itself in new business generated from the resulting new products. Innovation may also lead to more efficient operations, leading to cost savings. The commercial impact of innovation also expresses itself in a range of secondary benefits to the adopting organization. Secondary benefits may include, for example, the development of enhanced capabilities through innovation; it may also be the learning spill-over and transformation introduced to the organization through the innovation.

Innovation may take on a variety of forms. Innovation may range from *incremental refinement* to *frame-breaking* or *disruptive* change. The former focuses on improving the performance of existing technologies or capabilities by building on the organization's existing portfolio of knowledge, capabilities, and skills. The latter, disruptive form of innovation, involves discontinuities in the underlying technology, rendering existing knowledge, skills, and capabilities obsolete. In reality, the difference between the two extreme forms may not be that obvious, since refinements have been known to lead to major innovations. Nonetheless, because the distinction between refinement and disruption has become a central point of controversy in the management literature, we will adopt the distinction between innovation of an incremental nature and a disruptive nature. We refer to the former as *institutional* and to the latter as *revolutional* innovation. While the former builds on established organizational routines, the latter invariably demands organizational change of a radical nature.

Many companies think of themselves as innovative, while in reality they are adept only at *institutional* innovation. This mode focuses on refining the current basis of success in the market place and leads to sustained, incremental improvement in products and services. Many established firms inevitably fail when it comes to moving beyond the predictable toward the *revolutional* or disruptive mode of innovation (Figure 5.2). A number of authors, including Tushman and Nelson (1990) and March (1991) have noted that rapid, radical change associated with revolutional innovation is much more difficult and therefore less frequent in large organizations than change of the incremental, routine type. Organizational size, formalized structures and routines, and complexity are obstacles to innovation, and contribute to the competitive inertia often observed in established firms. Why this is so has been the subject of much debate over the years. Some management scholars have gone so far as to argue that there is no way out of the existing innovation conundrum, thereby suggesting that balancing institutional with revolutionary innovation within a single organization is simply not possible.

Christensen, Johnson, and Rigby (2002) suggest that few managers venture beyond the predictable and known, since when a core business is in the growth phase, venturing into unknown territory appears unnecessary. Alternatively, when a mature business is under pressure to perform in economically difficult times, investments to create new-growth businesses that tend to go beyond institutional innovation cannot ensure sufficient bottom-line profitability to satisfy investor pressure for rapid turnaround. In our view, it is not a question of "either–or"; sustainable growth can be ensured only by nurturing a strategic balance across a range of innovation options that includes both institutional and revolutionary innovation. Only an innovation strategy of such dimensions can deliver

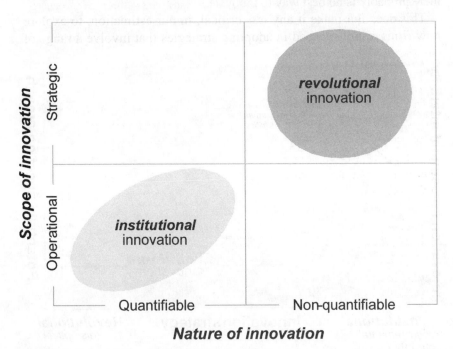

Figure 5.2 Institutional and revolutionary innovation as a function of the nature and scope of innovation

the synergies that enable firms to achieve the full competitive benefit of innovation. Few companies today succeed in achieving this objective, although many aspire to do so.

Various strategies for combining the institutional and the revolutional have been suggested and tried. The *corporate venturing* model has emerged as a model for nurturing exploratory business ventures in an environment that is not threatened by corporate interests. ABB, for example, set up a new-venture business but ended up abandoning the idea relatively quickly. The spin-off model is another strategy that has been tried by a number of large firms. Revolutionary new technologies are taken outside the parent organization entirely and put into an appropriate environment for development growth in the early stages of the technology. Successful spin-offs are sometimes reintroduced to the parent organization via a "spin-in" mechanism.

Generally, though, there has been no consensus on any one strategy suitable for managing innovation across the range of innovation strategies. Angle and Van de Ven (1989) suggest that just as management has come to realize that there is no single best way to "manage," we are learning that there probably is no best way to innovate.

This does not make it any less critical, in our estimation, to explore how firms might succeed in adopting strategies that involve a range of

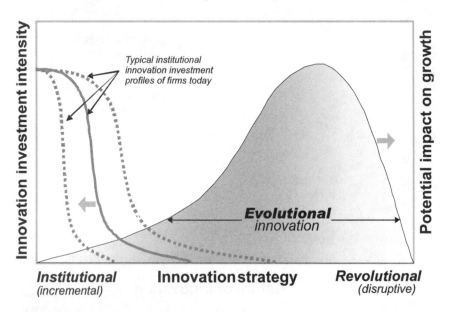

Figure 5.3 Innovation investment intensity and potential impact on growth as an outcome of innovation strategy

innovation options. The recent Henley–Arthur D. Little global innovation practices study (Birchall et al 2005) suggests that most firms do not engage in innovation beyond the institutional mode. Institutional innovation allows firms to achieve incremental improvements in existing products and processes to keep pace with the competition, but it does not provide the basis for achieving real business growth. Yet many of the same firms view innovation as a means for achieving business growth. Business growth through innovation is achieved when firms adopt strategies that deliberately extend beyond the institutional mode (Figure 5.3); that is, when firms select and execute evolutional innovation strategies.

We review three broad categories of innovation in the context of the framework proposed in Figures 5.2 and 5.3, and then explore and derive management implications for an appropriate overall innovation strategy. We adopt the categorization schemes proposed by Mezias and Boyle (2002). Two of the innovation themes relate to the two modes introduced earlier in this section, institutional and revolutional innovation. The third theme involves evolutional innovation, an innovation strategy that seeks to combine trade-offs inherent in each of the two extremes while maintaining a distinct chaotic nature of its own.

Key questions

- What is the firm's strategy behind its innovation investment profile?
- What portion of the overall investment in innovation targets innovation beyond institutional innovation?
- What is the anticipated impact of the firm's investment in innovation on business growth?
- What is its actually realized return on innovation?

Institutional innovation

Innovation has traditionally been viewed as the outcome of an organized, purposeful, and deliberate process. This view is in line with our definition of institutional innovation. It occurs by design and results from the organization's routines and procedures. It is closely linked to day-to-day operations, even if these are research-related. Institutional innovation introduces incremental change through a manipulation of bureaucratic rules that would normally tend to hinder its occurrence. That is, institutional innovation occurs in spite of organizational inertia that is biased towards continuity and preservation.

Inherent to the institutional mode is a tendency to maintain the status quo. Institutionalized environments feature a number of characteristics that have important implications for innovation of this type.

Institutional innovation:

- introduces incremental change, with a focus on preservation of the status quo
- features predictable, tried-and-proven processes
- produces largely additive, linear contributions in support of existing systems
- is rule-bound, based on bureaucratic systems, and risk-averse
- is capabilities-enhancing, thereby providing a strong basis for continuity
- is "quantifiable" within definable limits.

Many of the innovation approaches and models encountered in the innovation management literature have their origins in the institutional innovation mode. The purpose of these innovation models has been to show innovation as a mostly manageable process consisting of distinct and interlinked routine activities that are quantifiable at least within given boundaries. The Arthur D. Little innovation "rocket model" (Figure 5.4) is an example of an institutional innovation model.

This innovation model views innovation as a process that consists of a number of sub-activities ranging from business strategy visioning through to post-launch activities. The entire process is linked by continuous feedback loops, representing learning and the development of new knowledge. Two specific external sources of inputs representing customers and network partners contribute to the overall process at a variety of intersection points. The basic assumption of the framework is that innovation is a manageable process. Intervention is possible at the level of each of the individual activities. It also assumes that inputs and outputs of each of the individual activities may be measured on at least two levels, those of individual development projects and of the aggregate or portfolio of projects.

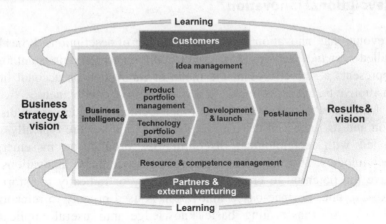

Figure 5.4 Arthur D. Little's innovation framework
Source: Arthur D. Little. Used with permission.

Other institutional innovation models include:

- The European Commission–Eurostat "Oslo Manual", which seeks to provide a unifying view on the innovation process and its economic impact for a range of industries. Currently in its second version, the Oslo Manual proposes a conceptual framework for innovation that brings together concepts, definitions, and methodology. It provides guidelines by which comparable innovation indicators can be developed in OECD countries, and presents these in an appropriate analytical and policy-related context.
- The EIRMA (European Industrial Research Management Association) innovation framework, which is described in the recent Working Group Report entitled "Assessing R&D Effectiveness" (EIRMA 2002). The approach adopted by EIRMA considers three phases within the innovation process: R&D inputs, the R&D processes themselves, and the effect of the R&D output. The model defines appropriate performance indicators for each of these. It also takes into consideration the interaction, communication, and transitions between these phases, and looks beyond parameters that sit strictly within the R&D function to link innovation effectiveness to other business functions. Despite the diversity and possible industries and company strategies, the framework succeeds in providing a relatively straightforward and consistent approach to assessing R&D and innovation effectiveness in the overall business context on the basis of a limited set of indicators.

Revolutional innovation

Revolutional innovation goes by any number of descriptions: It has been called *radical, frame-breaking,* and *discontinuous* by various authors. It represents a step-change in the mode of innovation on account of the disruptive nature of its impact in the competitive environment.

Much has been written in recent management literature about disruption and its impact in the market place. Disruptions are typically associated with technological discontinuities brought on by emerging technologies. They have been defined as science-based innovations that have the potential to create a new industry or radically transform an existing one. Science-based innovation is used broadly to refer to the process of transforming basic knowledge into useful application, whereby disruptive innovation triggers (1) expansion of the knowledge base, (2) change in existing markets, and (3) the creation of new markets (Day and Schoemaker 2000a).

More often than not, disruption has been viewed as a threat to industry incumbents that must be met with defensive counter measures. Indeed, as Bower and Christensen (1995), Christensen (1997), and Christensen and Overdorf (2000) in their seminal works on disruptive technologies, plus a number of other authors since, have shown that disruption has caused many established industry leaders to fail, and will likely continue to do so. Other researchers have argued, however, that disruptive innovation is inherently more about new opportunities than it is about destruction. For example, Gilbert (2003) argues that in every industry changed by disruption, the net affect has been total market growth, and moreover, that disruption can be a powerful driver of growth through new market discovery for incumbents as well as for upstarts.

Revolutional innovation is the outcome of disruption; it can be the result of a deliberate strategy or it can be an outcome of a serendipitous change of events. In the conceptual framework portrayed in Figure 5.2, it is positioned in the upper right quadrant, diagonally opposite to institutional innovation. As the figure implies, revolutional innovation defies traditional quantitative approaches to its measurement. Likewise it has a significantly longer time horizon; the scope of its focus is strategic. Revolutional innovation may also be viewed as involving a deliberate move from the invariably prevailing institutional innovation paradigm of an organization (Mezias and Glynn 1993).

The deliberate move beyond the status quo represented by revolutional innovation addresses two potential constraints imposed by institutional innovation in organizations. First, revolutional innovation strategies recognize that discontinuous change of the breakthrough type is generally not achievable within the bounds of the status quo, which seeks to preserve continuity within the organization; and second, resistance to change brought on by institutional innovation tends to ultimately block the successful implementation of that innovation within the organization.

Institutional innovation is inherently embedded in organizations focused on structure, mechanisms, and efficiency. A number of authors have argued that the dominant culture in organizations stifles true innovation (Kanter 1983). Evolutional innovation strategies, on the other hand, condone the deliberate breaking of habitual and routine ways of doing things (Senge 1990). The evolutional innovation environment is more amenable to organizational learning; it is continually evolving, organic, and typically unstructured. Revolutional strategies encourage skunkworks and ad hoc teams that operate outside the established organizational structure; they involve the questioning of prevailing assumptions and norms, playful exploration, and the relaxation of managerial impulses aimed at controlling and coordinating.

Typically, the individual innovation champion plays an important role in revolutional innovation; in fact, as Sahal (1981) points out, the determining factor in the adoption of new technologies may sometimes depend more on the individual innovator's ability to persist and procure the required resources than the quality of the original innovative idea. This fact introduces a significant degree of vulnerability to the revolutional approach, Tushman and Nadler (1986) argue, since individuals generally do not contribute to the organizational learning and innovation processes that are inherently group and inter-group phenomena. As a result, the efforts of individual contributors seldom result in the breakthrough approaches required for complex and disruptive innovation.

Revolutional innovation:

- introduces radical, frame-breaking and disruptive change
- features unpredictable, high-risk and largely emergent processes
- produces non-linear outcomes
- is experimental, exploratory in nature
- is capabilities-destroying
- largely defies quantification.

Another vulnerability associated with revolutional innovation strategies is its tax on organizational efficiency. Challenging assumptions, violating standing rules, and defying the current paradigm may be necessary for initiating radical change in organizations; they come at a potential price, however. Often, innovations originating outside the mainstream organization such in skunkwork teams are difficult to implement in the organization at large. Integrating innovation across diverse units of the organization may also be problematic, particularly when the innovating units adopt structural and cultural attributes that are viewed to be contrary to those of the parent organization.

Probably one of the most important managerial implications associated with revolutional innovation is its competence and capabilities-destroying character. Revolutional innovation introduces entirely new sets of capabilities to the strategic portfolio of a competing firm. Capabilities that in the past determined the basis of competitiveness quickly fade to obsolescence in the face of revolutional innovation. This makes incumbent firms particularly vulnerable, especially those that look back on a legacy of successful competitiveness in their markets. By the same token, young start-up firms often have an advantage; they often not only are at the front end of the revolutional innovation itself, they also tend to be more flexible and adaptable than their established competitors.

The tyranny of success

Numerous studies have pointed to the fact that incumbents were not all unaware of the new technologies that eventually disrupted their own competitive position as leaders in their markets. The *tyranny of success*—in which past success spells the death sentence for legacy leaders in rapidly changing markets—has left many anecdotes. The Swiss watch industry provides a classic example of a case in which incumbents not only invested in the development of revolutional technologies, but were also the creators and technical pioneers of them. Swiss watch companies invested in and invented quartz and digital watches, but stopped short of commercializing these radical new technologies. Japanese companies moved in to pick up where the Swiss companies left off. The rest is history. The Swiss watch industry did, however, regain competitive ground through the efforts of Hayek and his lifestyle creating Swatch creation in the early 1980s, thereby demonstrating the potential sustaining power of rekindled legacy.

We might be led to think on the basis of these arguments that innovation presents an intractable dilemma, given the limitations of both extreme forms, institutional and revolutional innovation. With the former seeking to preserve and the latter seeking to disrupt, both might be viewed as making competitive contributions in only a relatively narrow range of innovation strategies. Indeed, a recent joint Henley–Arthur D. Little global survey (Birchall et al 2005) of innovation practices substantiates this postulation. The majority of large established firms are firmly focused on institutional innovation, while young entrepreneurial start-up firms tend to engage in revolutional innovation.

Does this mean that established firms are limited only to the former, and that entrepreneurial firms cannot benefit from the supporting attributes of institutional innovation strategies? We suggest that this need not be the case. In the following section we develop the case of a hybrid innovation strategy that seeks to combine the competitive attributes of both institutional and revolutional innovation. The hybrid mode of innovation we refer to as *evolutional* or *sustainable* innovation. While we do not claim to be the first to propose this intermediate mode of innovation, we do develop the notion and bring it into the context of strategic capabilities and their management.

While the literature on revolutional innovation and its management is still emergent, there have been some attempts at bringing together the pertinent elements of revolutional innovation into the form of a model. Christensen and Raynor's (2003) resources, processes, and values (RPV) framework is one such model that seeks to define what an organization can and cannot accomplish in terms of the three factors, which in turn define its capabilities. Christensen and Raynor use this framework to assess an organization's capabilities and disabilities in the context of revolutional innovation.

Doering and Parayre (2000) suggest using a dynamic, iterative approach in the case of emerging technologies based on a systematic technology assessment process that includes scoping, searching, evaluating potential new technologies, and committing requisite organizational resources and capabilities. The authors argue that this approach is particularly crucial in the early stages of emerging technological disruption, when competitive advantage favours those firms that are most capable in choosing among the large number of technology options, not necessarily those that create them.

> ## Key questions
>
> - To what extent does the firm really understand its current basis of competitiveness?
> - To what extent is the firm exploiting its current competitive position?
> - What are its capabilities for becoming a potential disruptor in its industry?
> - How are the potential disruptors being identified and tracked?
> - What measures does the firm have in place for protecting its base of competitive advantage?

Evolutional or sustainable innovation

Organizations everywhere today face the dual and paradoxical challenge of operating efficiently today while at the same time innovating effectively for the future. Efficiency and effectiveness are often at odds with one another; the latter has a much longer time horizon and with it the inherent uncertainty associated with change in the competitive playing field, while the former seeks to preserve the status quo and to perfect the known. The tension lies in reconciling the future-oriented exploratory mindset with the operations-focused exploitation of today's competitive position.

The challenge today lies in managing both concerns simultaneously. To succeed in this endeavour, firms must understand and learn to manage the dynamics of innovation across a range of strategic innovation options, ranging from a purely protective stance to a potentially disruptive innovation strategy.

A recent study (Paap and Katz 2004) has shown that leading firms consistently fail at this strategic task. That is, they fail to maintain their leadership position when faced with disruption in their market place. It appears that the very factors determining a firm's success can also play a significant role in its demise in fast-changing markets. Factors such as the firm's unique capabilities, its supporting culture, its leadership and management focus, which contributed to the firm's competitive leadership position in the past, rapidly become liabilities and disablers when market dynamics change.

Evolutional or *sustainable* innovation is a dual innovation strategy that not only focuses on the financial success and penetration of the firm's current product and service offering, it also helps firms focus on building their long-term capabilities to commercialize emerging market opportunities.

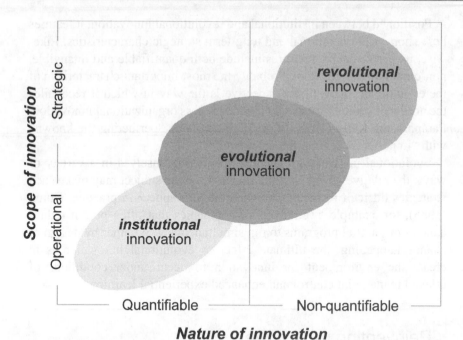

Figure 5.5 Evolutional innovation in relation to institutional and revolutional
innovation

Evolutional innovation strategies are less intentional than either institutional or revolutional strategies. They are emergent and probabilistic in nature. They are designed to help the organization move beyond its current capabilities by making the currently perceived boundaries and constraints unclear. Furthermore, evolutional innovation strategies straddle the regions defined by institutional and revolutional innovation, as suggested in Figure 5.5.

Evolutional innovation:

- is less intentional than either institutional or revolutional innovation
- is emergent, probabilistic, and inherently chaotic in nature
- involves using and experimenting with slack resources
- involves making routines, performance measurement, and controls less precise
- seeks to reconcile "perfecting the known" with "imperfectly seizing the unknown."

Positioned between institutional and revolutional innovation, it features both short-term operational and long-term strategic characteristics. Likewise, its performance measures include both quantifiable and intangible, non-quantitative indicators. Probably the most important characteristic of the evolutional innovation perspective is the way in which it reconciles the notion of serendipity and deliberate process organizational innovation. Paraphrasing Kelly (1998), it seeks to reconcile "perfecting the known" with "imperfectly seizing the unknown."

Evolutional innovation strategies manifest themselves in a variety of ways; the relative newness of the literature on the subject may make such strategies difficult to recognize when they do appear in practice. Quinn (1985), for example, reminds us of companies that often permit redundancies or parallel programs to run simultaneously. Whether by design or chance happening, the ultimate effect of evolutional innovation is to create the environment for innovation to occur under conditions of relaxed managerial control and enhanced experiential learning.

Reinventing wind power

The original idea is over 4000 years old and has its origins in ancient China. The innovation combines the age-old technology of kite-flying, new materials technology, and advanced automation technology. It promises to revolutionize the freight and passenger shipping industry.

The SkySails system consists of a towing kite filled with compressed air, an autopilot, and wind-optimised route management. Earlier attempts to realize this innovation had failed for lack of appropriate rope technology. New polymeric material technology has eliminated that obstacle. The 48 mm towropes made from the high-performance polyethylene fibre Dyneema—discovered and produced by DSM and purported to be 15 times stronger than steel—can withstand tractive forces of up to 150 tonnes. Using the SkySails system, fuel consumption can be reduced by up to 50 percent. Additional savings are made on lubricating oil, leading to significant reductions in the ship's operating costs. Moreover, savings are achieved on charges normally levied on atmospheric emissions.

The innovation exploits wind energy as a strong and reliable propulsion power by intelligently combining hardware and software technology with an eye to the requirements of modern shipping.

According to its innovators, almost every merchant and passenger vessel can be equipped or retrofitted with the SkySails system.

The potential advantages of this radical innovation are numerous. Depending on the type of ship, propulsion power, cruising speed, shipping routes, and oil prices, a ship uses up to €10 million worth of fuel per annum. Up to half of the ship's operating expenses are spent on fuel. These would be drastically cut by the application of the innovation. Alternatively, the system enables an increase in the average speed of the ship, enabling ship owners to transport more cargo and earn higher profits. The SkySails system is also said to improve the seaway performance and manoeuvring capability of the ship, thanks to the smoothing of the ride through the upward pull of the kite sail. This ensures higher security of the ship, enhanced well-being of the passengers on cruise ships, and better performance capability of the crew. Minimized slamming and torsion forces furthermore extend the life of the ship and minimize the negative effects of propelling-engine damage, for example by a turbo-super-charger. SkySails claims an amortization of the €300,000 to 2.5 million retrofitting investment within approximately two years.

The SkySails system is an appropriate example of an evolutionary innovation that does not entirely replace existing technology (it does not replace the traditional diesel ship engine), but rather brings old and new technology and capabilities together to create a unique and exciting business opportunity.

Sources: Hintermeier (2004) and http://skysails.info/.

Nonaka and Takeuchi's (1995) enabling conditions, including intention, autonomy, fluctuation and creative chaos, redundancy and requisite variety, provide the appropriate organizational setting for successful evolutional innovation. Implementing and embedding evolutional innovation in organizations is nonetheless a very difficult management task. It involves building and nurturing internally contradictory structures, processes, capabilities, and organizational cultures. Creating these apparently inconsistent structures is typically viewed by management as a threat to the firm's current business imperatives and basis of success.

Firms are typically at a loss over how to begin building an evolutional innovation capability. Often, the first impulse is to focus on resource allocation. Raising investments in innovation—resulting in increased budgets for research and development—is often perceived to be the way to move away from institutional innovation. Firms tend to neglect a number of other important dimensions, such as the mindset and aspirations of the organization, business proposition and model, organizational structure and processes, and organizational culture. These vary considerably across the range of innovation options for any particular dimension. Figure 5.6, for example, shows the profile of a firm that has apparent aspirations to extend its current portfolio of predominantly institutional innovation to potentially disruptive innovation. A scoreboard-like snapshot of where the firm currently stands with respect to its efforts and focus readily reveals that it is as yet firmly entrenched in the institutional innovation mode (Tovstiga and Birchall 2004).

Key questions

- What measures does the firm have in place for defending its current competitive position?
- What are appropriate measures for enhancing and strengthening the firm's current competitive position; for overcoming its vulnerabilities; for achieving a strategically balanced portfolio of innovation strategies?
- What are the appropriate pre-emptive growth strategies for the firm in seeking to push forward an exploitation-driven innovation?

Capabilities and evolutional innovation

Evolutional innovation is at least in part driven by serendipity, a phenomenon that defies precise definition. Hence, evolutional innovation is as much a phenomenon as it is a deliberately managed process. This brings evolutional innovation in line with the phenomenological view of innovation, an interpretation of innovation that subscribes to the view that while we may observe certain outcomes of the innovation phenomenon, we really do not understand all the mechanisms that drive innovation because of their complex nature. Hence innovation, according to this interpretation, may at best be described in qualitative terms and measures only. Van de Ven et al (1999) describe innovation as neither sequential nor orderly, but rather as a nonlinear dynamic system consisting of a cycle of divergent and convergent activities that may be repeated over time and at different organizational levels, provided that enabling and constraining

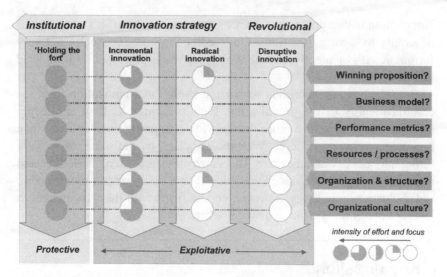

Figure 5.6 Innovation strategy option range and associated business dimensions, showing the profile of a typical institutional innovation-oriented firm

conditions prevail. Innovation in the view of this group of researchers is most aptly described as a journey that is responsive to a system of dynamic constraints and resources. Van de Ven et al (1999) specify some of the soft factors of the innovation phenomenon that do not readily lend themselves to measurement. These include:

- development of the organizational culture for innovation
- learning amongst innovation team members
- leadership behaviour of top managers or other important innovation decision makers.

The ability to innovate in the evolutional mode demands *organizational* capabilities that are for the most part intangible (Ulrich and Smallwood 2004). These capabilities are largely invisible; they are the outcome of investments in human resources, training, and strategic staffing over many years. They represent the manner in which people in the organization are integrated into the firm's structure and processes; how this complex mixture of skills, knowledge, and culture is brought together to create value.

Tom Kelley (2002), who is associated with Ideo, a US design consultancy specializing in product development and innovation, observes in describing how these soft factors collectively contribute to innovation,

"innovation is part golf swing, part secret recipe.... [But] it's not a matter of simply following directions. Our 'secret formula' is actually not very formulaic. It's a blend of methodologies, work practices, culture, and infrastructure."

Organizational capabilities supporting evolutional innovation form the cultural identity of the organization. Highly intangible, they are deeply embedded and therefore more difficult for competitors to duplicate than product strategy, or technology assets. They are, by the same token, very difficult to identify and measure. This is why they are often overlooked and neglected by managers, since their value cannot easily be communicated to stakeholders. Capabilities, however, endow firms with the wherewithal to leverage opportunity from dynamic markets.

> ## Key questions
>
> - Does the firm have the right resources and capabilities, the appropriate supporting processes and culture for executing an effective evolutional innovation strategy?
> - What would it take to transform the firm to more effectively execute evolutional innovation?

Concluding remarks

Innovation must be more than simply a shot in the dark. As trivial as it may seem, the prevailing fundamental premise of innovation is that innovation and the creation of new business are intrinsically unpredictable, and therefore prone to high failure rates. The tendency of innovation practice has consequently been to constrain innovation investment within "manageable" bounds, since investment in any other form of innovation is still viewed by those running the firm as a threat to the firm's current priorities, practices, and success. The result has been a largely institutionalized innovation paradigm that does not provide the business growth potential firms are seeking today.

We argue in this chapter that innovation need not be as random and failure-fraught as it has been made out to be in the past. We propose that firms stand the best chance of maximizing their bottom-line business impact through innovation through executing an innovation strategy that covers a range of options, ranging from protective innovation through to experimentation with disruptive forms of innovation. This requires a deliberate departure from conventional management thinking that seeks to control and to perfect; it requires organizations to simultaneously build internally contradictory and inconsistent structures, processes, capabilities, and cultures. Above all, organizations that learn to balance an attitude of efficiency and reliability with one that encourages experimentation and exploration also learn to minimize the negative randomness effects of innovation, thereby making successful innovation more than just a lucky bet.

CHAPTER 6

Evolutional innovation: deriving opportunity from disruption

Introduction

Evolutional innovation, we argued in the last chapter, provides the firm with the most viable basis for exploiting its capabilities toward capturing competitive advantage through innovation. Evolutional innovation seeks to derive opportunity from disruption by enabling the firm to bring into strategic balance the right mix of institutional and revolutional innovation strategies. It ensures the proper organizational context for building the requisite capabilities that enable the firm to capture market opportunity ahead of its competition. For this, firms are increasingly depending on secondary organizational capabilities such as innovation partnering and strategic networking, which enable them to fully exploit their primary capabilities.

In this chapter, we:

- explore the notion of disruption and put it into the context of evolutional innovation
- develop the concept of matching market opportunity with the firm's competitive position and capabilities
- develop the notion of evolutionary trajectories and their application to disruptive innovation
- examine organizational and managerial implications of deriving opportunity from disruptive innovation
- explore how changing competition is redefining the focus of capabilities management.

In many ways the focus of strategic management of innovation is shifting towards building and deploying the right set of secondary organizational capabilities. Under these conditions, disruption can be a tremendous opportunity for those firms that learn to play by the new rules.

Evolutional innovation: deriving opportunity from disruption

Disruption, Gilbert (2003) points out, is often thought of as a sudden occurrence that emerges out of nowhere to upset the established market. Not so, he argues, and goes on to describe three distinct phases of disruption. In a first phase, innovation creates a new, non-competitive market space outside the existing market. In a second phase, the new market encroaches on the existing market; growth of the established market slows as a result. The third phase sees acceleration in the growth and maturation of the disruptive innovation and a significant reduction in the size of the existing market. Managers of incumbent companies typically fail to recognize disruptions as opportunities because the potential new markets lie outside their existing resource base. Incumbents may perceive markets developing, but legacy thinking prevents their management from recognizing the developing market as the threat it really poses to them.

Encyclopaedia Britannica (EB) and its forced plunge into digital publishing provides a striking example of an incumbent that has been forced to abandon its legacy industry: In the early days of Microsoft's *Encarta*, the idea of a digital version of an encyclopedia was not taken seriously by EB's senior managers. In dismissing *Encarta* as a frivolous toy, they failed entirely to recognize the threat of the new digital disruptor. The emergence of mass digitalization had introduced a new twist to the value proposition of the market traditionally served by EB. "Assuaging parental guilt," long the implicit driver of EB's success in its traditional printed encyclopedia market, was now being achieved by the personal computer. Hence the personal computer emerged as the new, real competitor to Britannica's printed version of an encyclopedia. *Encarta* was merely the mock-up competitor. For EB's management, this realization came almost too late. Disruption has forced the 235-year old firm, still the most venerable and most authoritative encyclopedia in the English-speaking world, to relaunch itself as a dot.com in a digital world. Past successes and strong corporate cultures are irrelevant in the face of disruption; in fact, they tend to blind business leaders to developments in the market place that do not fit into their collective mental framework (Evans and Wurster 2000, Shapiro and Varian 1999).

Opportunity borne on the wings of flight

A different perspective on the nature of disruption and its diffusion is provided by Carr (2004). He argues that when a disruptive new technology arrives on the scene, the greatest business opportunities often lie not in the disruption per se but in trying to work around it. Carr cites the example of the telegraph system. When it was introduced in the early nineteenth century, the line network was far from seamless. There were infrastructural gaps and users often had to find ingenious ways to overcome them. One of the most prominent gaps lay in the heart of Europe, where the Belgian line ended in Brussels and the German line extended only as far as Aachen, situated near the Belgian border. Transcontinental telegraph messages had to be manually transcribed and transported across the approximately 120 kilometres separating the two cities by land.

A small company recognized a niche business opportunity in this gap. In 1849 it invested in a flock of 45 carrier pigeons that would deliver news and stock prices between Brussels and Aachen. Transmission times were reduced to two hours, beating the railroad by six hours. Within a few years the entrepreneurial company developed to become one of the leading telegraph agencies, specializing in the rapid communication of time-sensitive financial information.

The entrepreneur was Paul Julius Reuters, the founder of Reuters, today the world's largest international multimedia news agency. Most recently, Reuters launched Reuters Messaging, a reliable, high-security, high-speed instant messaging service developed specifically for the global financial services industry. Developed by Reuters and Microsoft and more than 30 financial institutions, the service allows financial professionals to communicate instantly with their colleagues and customers.

Source: Carr (2004).

Radical or disruptive innovations represent new market opportunities, even though they initially deliver performance that is inferior to established products, and therefore do not appeal to an established customer base. This makes them unattractive to successful players, who are dependent on growth based on economies of scale. At the disruptive phase of an innovation, customers do not yet know what they want. Investors are equally reluctant to sink capital into ventures for which markets are only emerging. Disruptive technologies do, however, possess features that appeal to a new and different group of customers. These may include new technical functionality, convenience, or price. The early users of the disruptive technology are a much smaller and less profitable group than the customers for an established product. A new market emerges around these early users, and early entrants to the playing field drive the disruptive innovation along a trajectory featuring high market opportunity (Figure 6.1). As the disruptive innovation evolves and matures to acceptable performance and superior pricing, it encroaches on the market of the established technology. With time and maturation, the initially "disruptive" innovation becomes ever less so, attracting more and more entrants to the market. This results in a drop in the curve.

Potential players, whether incumbents or new entrants, initially find themselves positioned in the left segment of the lower curve, as depicted in Figure 6.1. Disruptive innovations typically make claim to a new value proposition, a new business model, and new sets of capabilities or embedded knowledge (typically embedded in the new technology, although new knowledge often also extends to new ways of approaching the business opportunity). It can be argued that for most firms, the major challenge lies in building and nurturing the right capabilities basis. Developing and deploying new strategically relevant knowledge in the form of

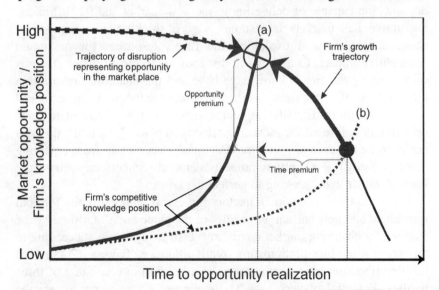

Figure 6.1 Market opportunity and the firm's knowledge position in disruptive markets

capabilities, we have seen in earlier chapters, is a daunting task that requires deliberate effort over time. In order to compete effectively, the firm needs to do this faster than the competition.

The challenge for firms wishing to compete on the basis of the new disruptive innovation translates to moving upward along the curve representing the market opportunity, that is, from point "b" to point "a" in Figure 6.1. This segment of the curve represents the firm's path of growth. As the firm builds capabilities, it builds competitive strength and repositions itself for competition in the emerging market. At point "a" the firm has succeeded in achieving the requisite knowledge position on the basis of its strategic capabilities, and has built the enabling organizational environment (structure, processes, culture) around these. The challenge for the individual firm, whether incumbent or entrant, is to arrive at point "a" along the market opportunity trajectory before its competitors.

Gilbert (2003) argues that there are several critical factors to successful navigation along the market opportunity trajectory. The first is recognizing that established players have more time than they often think to meet the requirements for early entry, provided they learn to play by the new rules established by the new market. Disruptions can take significant time—sometimes even years—before they seriously encroach on the existing market. A key challenge for the firm is to learn to look beyond its current customers. A second critical factor is succeeding in building an organization capable of delivering to the new market and its customers. Disruptive, new markets demand new ways of thinking about competing; about developing and exploiting the firm's resources for maximum competitive impact. Competing in disruptive markets ultimately focuses on managing the firm's knowledge base and the enabling organization around it, enabling the firm to seize opportunity in the market place ahead of its competitors. Equally important, firms must be prepared to seize opportunity before all the facts are perfectly in place. Invariably, this will not even be the case at point "a." Capturing opportunity from emerging markets, Kelly (1998) aptly reminds us, demands "imperfectly seizing the known" rather than "seeking to perfect the known."

The disruptive innovation trajectory represents an opportunity for both incumbent and new entrant. New rules of the game are established by the continually changing market environment. In many ways, succeeding in this arena resembles participating in a hurdle race. Tripsas (2000: 184) has described the trajectory in terms of a hurdle run consisting of three hurdles. Potential players, whether incumbent or new entrant, are the contestants in the race. The first hurdle is the decision whether to enter the race at all; whether to invest in acquiring, building, or developing the new technology. The second hurdle is the organizational challenge of applying that investment toward building and nurturing the required resource base, that is, the required set of capabilities. When the firm has successfully built the required set of capabilities to compete, the third hurdle facing the firm is the actual commercialization of that technology.

Key questions

- What mechanisms does the firm have in place for building a good understanding of what the next opportunity is going to be?
- How does the firm develop an understanding of how that market is going to work?
- On what basis are decisions made in the firm whether or not to participate in the emerging market opportunity?

Many firms already fail to clear the first hurdle. Disruptive innovations are risky. Emerging markets, if at all present, are small and the new technology characteristically does not appeal to the existing customer base. The result is that many potential entrants get "cold feet" at the first hurdle.

Off by a country mile

Emerging markets are notoriously unpredictable. In the mid-1980s, when mobile telephony was just emerging, AT&T consulted McKinsey & Co. for an estimate on the potential size of the cellular telephone market. The worldwide potential was estimated to be 900,000 units. Today we have 1.52 billion global mobile users, with China leading the pack. We also know that about 900,000 new users are added to the growing list of mobile-telephone subscribers *every three days*. In emerging markets, initial expectations are almost always wrong. Error magnitudes in estimates of market potential are typically of the order of multiples rather than percentages.

Sources: Govindarajan and Trimble (2004);
         http://www.cellular.co.za/stats/stats-main.htm.

Those firms that do succeed in making it over the first hurdle face the challenge of building new technological and organizational capabilities. Established firms often quickly get bogged down by legacy assets that express themselves in strong organizational routines and procedures that have ensured success in the past. These may be largely irrelevant for capturing opportunity in the new market, however. Worse, existing capabilities often turn out to be liabilities, or in the words of Leonard-Barton (1995), *core rigidities*, in developing products based on radically new technologies. This explains why initial new products made by incumbents are often inferior to those developed by new entrants.

The technical inferiority of incumbents often trails along and translates into inferior market position as companies approach the final, technology commercialization stage. Technological superiority does not necessarily guarantee success at the commercialization stage, since the outcome of technology commercialization is generally not decided in the laboratory alone. In order to succeed at commercialization, companies typically need to develop a broader perspective on competing in the newly emerging market. Market dynamics play an important role in determining the final outcome of the last hurdle. As numerous examples have shown, it is not even always the better technology that achieves success in the market. Network externalities, for example, played an important part in establishing Microsoft's dominant position over Apple. Many would argue that Apple still has the better technology, but that it has lost out to Microsoft's shrewder tactics in the market place.

Ultimately, whether or not a firm succeeds at clearing all three hurdles comes down to how successful it is at building the new sets of knowledge demanded by the disruptive innovation. Capabilities define what the firm can and cannot do, at all stages of the race. The strategic capabilities portfolio framework developed by Birchall and Tovstiga (2001) which was presented in Chapter 3 provides a practical tool for tracking the evolution of disruptive innovation in terms of capabilities. Figure 6.2 shows a mapping of competitive impact (maturity of the technology or capability) against competitive position (the firm's degree of control over that technology or capability). The banana-shaped area, as argued in Chapter 3, represents the bounds of a strategically balanced portfolio of technologies or capabilities.

When using the framework it is important to differentiate, however, between first, the disruption itself, typically a technological breakthrough (which itself may evolve into a capability) leading to a disruptive product and market opportunity, and second, the firm's portfolio of capabilities which supports and enables the firm to capture the opportunity created by

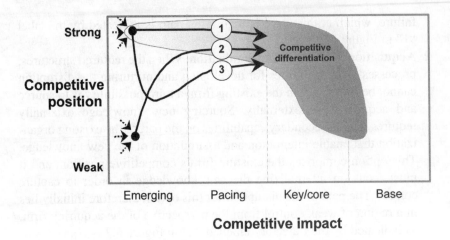

Competitive impact

Figure 6.2 A conceptual framework showing possible paths for evolving disruptive innovation

the disruption. The two are distinct, though interdependent—perhaps one can think of them as two sides of a coin. Returning to the analogy of the hurdle race, we can think of the disruptive innovation as the entity that needs to clear all the hurdles on its way to commercialization. Helping it to achieve that objective are the organization's capabilities. These, however, must also evolve along with the disruptive innovation.

Christensen and Overdorf (2000) use the term *capability migration* to describe this evolutionary development of capabilities. Capabilities migration reflects the fact that companies compete differently at different stages along a disruptive innovation's evolutionary trajectory, and that the competing firm requires different capabilities at different stages along the disruption's trajectory.

Evolutionary paths of disruptive technologies

Christensen and Overdorf (2000) suggest three possible trajectories along which the disruptive innovation can evolve:

1 **In-house development.** The disruption is developed within the corporate boundaries of the firm. The assumption is that the appropriate and new organizational space, structure, processes, and capabilities are created for nurturing the new technological disruption to commercialization. The advantage for the firm is that it maintains a high degree of control over the disruption. On the cost side, the firm carries the risk of

failure, which at this stage is high. This path is indicated by the label "1" in Figure 6.2.

2 **Acquisition of a different organization.** When the required structures, processes and capabilities for developing and nurturing the disruption cannot be found within the existing firm, a third possibility is to source and acquire these externally. Sourcing new knowledge externally requires special secondary capabilities on the part of the existing organization that enable integration and assimilation of the new knowledge. This option comprises the existing firm's competitive position, and it must focus on internalizing the new knowledge in order to capture control. The path of the disruption for this option therefore initially lies in a region of weak control from the perspective of the acquiring firm, as indicated by the trajectory labelled "2" in Figure 6.2.

3 **Spin-out to an independent organization.** The disruption is taken out of the existing organization; a new organization is created and the required structures, processes, capabilities, and culture are developed in this new environment. Often, this is the only survival route for disruptions originating in large established companies. Once mature and proven, the initially disruptive technology may be taken back into the established firm via a so-called *spin-in*. Motorola has done pioneering work in this area. The path marked "3" shows this route. The dip in the curve suggests that, from the perspective of the existing firm, there is a compromise on competitive position when the disruption is handed over to the newly created firm. The parent firm regains control through spin-in, as indicated by the rising trajectory in Figure 6.2.

Managerial focus on capabilities in the emerging region of the portfolio (those appearing in the "emerging" column of Figure 6.2) must be on creating the conditions within the organization that favor and encourage pre-emptive and discovery-driven innovation. Managerial action in the "key/core" region must be exploitative in nature; the focus is on deliberate exploitation of the differentiation attained on the basis of the current competitive base. At the same time, effort must be expended to protect the competitive edge achieved. As capabilities mature from emerging, progressing toward pacing and ultimately key/core, firms may be reliant on external help in order to provide the development trajectory with the requisite momentum. External help may take on a variety of forms; the most common ones include *strategic partnering* and *innovation consortia*. Finally, as pointed out in earlier chapters, strategic capabilities are dynamic entities—that is, they have limited "shelf-lives." Market environments change, resulting in shifting competitive requirements that demand changes in the firm's capabilities. Capabilities also have a tendency to erode over time. Those that were at one point in time unique to the firm, endowing the firm with a key/core position of differentiation, inevitably move on to become obsolete as more and more competitors gain access to the once unique knowledge. Hence, key/core capabilities must be protected while those tending toward obsolescence must be regenerated or reconfigured.

Key questions

- What mechanisms and tools does the firm have in place for determining the dynamics and the nature of competition in the industry?
- How are emerging markets being identified and analyzed?
- Are they more competence-enhancing or more competence destroying?
- How great is the threat of new entrants; what are the firm's potential blind spots?
- Do opportunities exist for pre-emptive disruption?
- What are the firm's strategic intent, key technologies, strategic capabilities (market interface, organizational), key competitive knowledge?
- What is the firm's position on the competitive knowledge trajectory, and how is it being monitored?
- What are the firm's vulnerabilities in view of potential disruption in the firm's markets?

Implications and challenges for management

Companies facing disruption in their traditional industries and markets face a dilemma. Traditionally, companies have been designed and run to perform well and to optimize their performance. Capturing opportunity from disruption demands that companies evolve quickly, often radically, rather than focus on operating optimally. Disruptions represent discontinuities that require successful players to "jump to the next curve," representing the next wave of market opportunity.

Firms react in very different ways. Many are traumatized by the discontinuity. Typically, these are the industry incumbents that are saddled with legacy assets, and that have a propensity for "sticking with the familiar." Past successes, a lack of appropriate in-house capability to appraise the emerging technology, and a proprietary mindset get in the way of these firms (Day and Schoemaker 2000a). They characteristically foster an organizational "culture of optimization" that seeks to maintain quality, keep costs down, keep the product moving, and generally "manage" crises in day-to-day operations.

Other firms prepare to "make the leap." These firms have a very different mindset from the former group. They nurture organizational cultures that are eager to pursue new quests. They also ask very different questions, such as: What is going to be the next big thing? How are we going to be part of it? How is that market going to work? How are we going to lock in the new market; that is, how are we going to capture the market in such a way as to make it inaccessible to other competitors (Arthur 1999)?

Jumping the curve successfully challenges firms to deploy a variety of innovation strategies over the course of a market opportunity. Initially, firms deploy revolutional innovation to bring a radical new product to market. The value of this new market offering lies in its functionality— that it is, the radical new product or service features some radically different functionality that attracts a specific group of lead users. The secondary organizational capabilities required for managing this stage of the innovation support the discovery and mobilization of new knowledge in order to secure the functionality of the new offering, which is situated at the lower left origin of the innovation trajectory portrayed in Figure 6.3. This might involve managing internal skunkworks, or a strategic partnership with, and external partner for, the co-development of the new market offering; alternatively, it might involve the effective leveraging of a network that includes lead users of the new technology.

As the market offering matures, that is, as it progresses along the innovation trajectory, different sets of organizational capabilities are required. As the firm moves into the maturing stage of the innovation trajectory, it relies more and more on institutionalized capabilities for establishing adequate routines, processes, and structures required for building appropriate protective barriers around the market offering as more and more competitors seek to enter that market. The secondary capabilities might support establishing the proper economies of scale, securing cost advantage over new entrants, and implementing an effective intellectual property strategy.

When the original innovation nears the point where market stagnation threatens to set in, the firm must again revert to a revolutionary innovation strategy, by jumping to the curve representing the next innovation and market opportunity. Evolutional innovation spans the entire spectrum

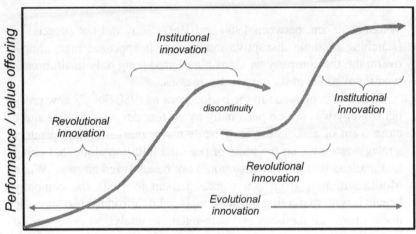

Figure 6.3 Innovation cycles and management implications for their strategic management

of innovation strategies that firms execute over multiple innovation cycles.

What differentiates those firms that succeed in making the leap to the next curve from those that do not? Mindset most certainly does, as the preceding discussion suggests. But even firms that bring the right mindset to the game are at risk. Tripsas (2000) suggests that too often even these firms are so focused on the difficult task of developing the radically new technological capability that they neglect to see the broader picture. They assume, for example, that once the technological innovation has been developed they can rely on existing strategies to bring it to market. They fail to realize that disruptive innovation invariably demands new business models and new resource requirements. Often firms also neglect to develop new complementary resources and capabilities—and they fail to realize that they are up against a new set of competitors.

Losing a legacy

Sony used to have an innovation track record that positioned it amongst the world's most successful industry disruptors. It introduced no less than 12 fundamentally disruptive technologies between 1950 and 1980, which created hot new markets, and upstaged industry leaders with products ranging from radios to the

Walkman. Then, between 1980 and 1997, Sony did not succeed in launching a single disruptive innovation. It appeared that, almost overnight, the company was capable of producing only institutional-type innovations in its product businesses.

What had happened? In the period prior to 1980 Sony's new product strategy was driven personally by co-founder Akio Morita and a close team of associates. They made major marketing and product strategy decisions on the basis of personal intuition alone, believing that markets that did not exist could not be analyzed anyway. When Morita withdrew from active management in 1980, the company began hiring marketing professionals who introduced systematic market research methods and data-intensive analytical processes to Sony. While these new approaches worked well to enhance Sony's business in existing markets, they also spelt the end of Sony's legacy as an industry disruptor.

Source: Christensen, Johnson, and Rigby (2002).

Foster and Kaplan (2001) argue that many companies need to be *redesigned* if they are to meet the challenges of disruption. Companies need to learn to compete differently. In order to accommodate disruption, firms must move away from rigid organizational designs which were conceived for repetitive transactions, routinized operations, and optimization. In order to accommodate disruptive innovation, firms need to become *flexible*. Flexibility, argues Bahrami (1996), inherently enables firms to continually respond to unanticipated changes in the market; to adjust to the unexpected consequences of predictable change; and to precipitate intentional change when called for by unexpected events in the competitive environment.

Flexibility is a multi-dimensional trait that demands agility and versatility. It is also associated with change, innovation, and novelty, and is coupled with robustness, resilience, and capabilities that evolve over time. One of the key building blocks of the flexible organization, according to Bahrami, is a capability-based view of the organization, which first recognizes the core capability of the technology-based firm ultimately to be the knowledge of its people, and second, views the firm more in terms of a montage of individual capabilities, informal networks, and relationships than in terms of predetermined roles, positions, and formal hierarchical relationships.

Disruption need not be a source of dilemma for managers and their firms. Indeed, disruption always has been, and will continue to be, a tremendous opportunity for those firms that learn to play by the new rules. Capturing opportunity from disruption poses a challenge to managers to rethink the competitive position and strategic stance of their firms. Just as important, however, disruption challenges the mindset of managers. Kelly (1998) aptly reminds us that capturing opportunity from disruption has to do with designing the organization and its capabilities for "imperfectly seizing the unknown" rather than "perfecting the known."

Key questions

- What is the most appropriate strategic posture for your firm in its current competitive situation?
- How will the requisite organizational transformation be initiated and driven?
- What are the appropriate organizational levers available to the firm for changing its culture and, ultimately, its current paradigm?
- To what extent has the organization internalized the new rules of the game?

Learning to derive opportunity from disruption

Day and Schoemaker (2000b) suggest that managers operating in markets prone to disruption must learn to become comfortable with high levels of paradox and ambiguity. They point out some of the key paradoxes:

1 **Learning to commit strongly while keeping options open.** Commitments to investment in emerging technologies must be balanced with flexibility. Hedging on alternative directions, particularly in the face of aggressive and focused competition, is costly and dilutes commitment. In practice, it has been shown that it is desirable in the early stages of the development of a revolutionary innovation to keep options open by only committing to investments in stages, and by following multiple technology paths, and possibly delaying some projects. It is important to keep in mind as well that few technologies or product ideas are

inherently disruptive when they emerge; they must be deliberately shaped.

2 **Learning to balance the perils and the promise of pioneering.** Day and Schoemaker (2000a) point out that while winners are often pioneers, most pioneers fail. Pioneering, they point out, is inherently risky. Moving forward in short and calculated stages can help to minimize the risk. This might include using techniques such as exploratory marketing to test the viability of a revolutionary idea. Partnering to share risk is another approach used by pioneers to increase the odds of success in unknown territory.

3 **Learning to exploit existing capabilities while experimenting with new organizational structures.** Past successes often create traps for large organizations when they venture into new competitive territory. The business dimensions discussed in the previous chapter—the business propositions and models, performance metrics, resources and process, the organization culture—that are at the root of the firm's current success are often no longer suitable when a new basis of competition emerges. Firms recently have turned to setting up separate organizations, for example, spin-offs—with appropriate cultural attributes, organizational structures, and performance measures—to deal with the emerging technology business. This strategy comes with a risk, however; the more separate the organization becomes, the more difficult it becomes to establish and exploit synergies with the parent organization. Both spin-off and parent organization stand to lose when this is allowed to happen.

4 **Learning to compete and to collaborate, simultaneously.** Competing in emerging markets can be brutal when firms stake their entire future on the success of their investments. Failure is typically not an option in these situations. Yet, more and more, firms are realizing that they are not able "go it alone." With new knowledge emerging at accelerated rates in networks strung across the globe, they are realizing the benefits of "co-option"—a judicious mix of cooperation and competition in increasingly complex webs of relationships emerging around emerging technologies. Often, companies are collaborating in one area while competing in another. The recently launched semiconductor manufacturing facility near Grenoble, France shared by arch-competitors Philips, STMicroelectronics, and Motorola on a time-share basis is a case in point (see boxed insert).

When one plus two yield more than three

STMicroelectronics, the Franco-Italian chipmaker, is one of the world's largest semiconductor companies with some 50,000 people and a sales volume of US$9 billion. It is a survivor in an industry that leaves less and less room for strategic error. STMicro's recent move has been to join up with its arch-competitors, Philips and Motorola, to jointly run a shared research and production facility on the outskirts of Crolles, an idyllic French village nestled in an Alpine valley near Grenoble. The triple alliance is aiming for world leadership in nanometric technology applied to systems on a chip (SoC). The combined resources and capabilities of the three firms will focus on the development of next-generation CMOS technology.

The new joint R&D centre and laboratory opened its doors in early 2003. The shared facilities at Crolles are used to design and develop the new semiconductor technology. Researchers from all three companies work together to develop the basic nanometric processes and fabrication technologies that are used for cutting, etching, and installing the basic circuits on the 300 mm wavers. Then, each company in turn runs its plates through the finishing stages that customize the final product.

A fourth alliance partner, Taiwan's TSMC, the world's largest contract manufacturer of semiconductors, is involved at the earliest stages by providing outsourcing services to all three Crolles partners. The strategic alliance will not provide STMicro with access to any of its partners' customers, but it gives all three partners unprecedented opportunity to lead in the co-development of key capabilities in a fast-moving market. Observes Pasquale Pistorio, CEO of STMicro, "We can beat anyone but Intel." Given that the three companies have a pooled research budget of US$15 billion for developing the state-of-the art in semiconductor capabilities, the strategic alliance is indeed a competitive force to be reckoned with.

Source: Orr (2003).

Exploiting new opportunities for competitive advantage

More and more, paradoxes and ambiguities of the type outlined above are determining the nature of competition in our changing business environment.

Successful innovators today are challenging traditional paradigms with new approaches that are increasingly focusing on these soft, enabling organizational skill sets and capabilities to enable evolutional innovation in their competitive markets.

This is changing the scope and emphasis of the strategic management of capabilities in important ways. In intensely competitive markets, the life-cycle of capabilities is becoming ever shorter. Firms are being forced to replenish their stock of strategic capabilities ever more frequently. Traditional approaches to in-sourcing are neither any longer affordable, nor do they allow firms to react quickly enough to changes in the environment. Innovation leaders are therefore focusing on new approaches to revamping their capabilities. Firms are either, one, accelerating the development of capabilities currently in the in the pipeline, such as capability C_1 in Figure 6.4, thereby nudging them toward a strong and core competitive position (represented by $C_{primary}$ in Figure 6.4); or two, repositioning existing capabilities that are in danger of degenerating into obsolescence (such as capabilities represented by C_2 and C_3 in Figure 6.4).

For this, they are relying chiefly on the influx of new knowledge and skills from outside the firm. The knowledge flow mechanism, in turn, is primarily dependent on the firm's secondary organizational skill sets and capabilities. Therefore, in many ways, competitive position in the market place is being determined by the firm's success at these capabilities—its understanding of the markets and its market orientation, its abilities to nurture and exploit strategic partnerships, and its ability to manage networks for gaining access to critical knowledge. The strategic management of capabilities, we argue, is

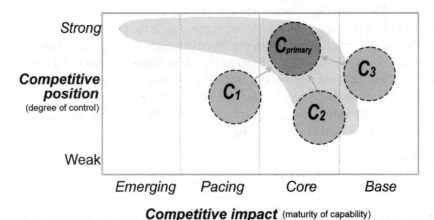

Figure 6.4 Positioning the firm's primary capabilities alongside its soft, enabling organizational capabilities

shifting away from a singular focus on the firm's primary capabilities to a more comprehensive management perspective that has an emphasis on soft, enabling organizational capabilities.

Concluding remarks

Disruption is more about new market opportunity than it is about the threat of stealth attacks on incumbents. It will continue to be a major source of new business growth in the economy—for those firms, whether incumbent or new entrant, who learn to play by the new rules. Disruption and its inherent potential for growth favour those firms that build and nurture organizations that learn to imperfectly seize the unknown rather than seek to perfect the known. Firms are achieving this by focusing deliberate attention on soft, organizational capabilities that are redefining the way firms are approaching innovation. We devote the following chapters to exploring some of these evolutionary mechanisms.

PART II

CHAPTER 7

Market orientation and innovation success

Introduction

The ultimate test of the effectiveness of innovation is its success in the market place in giving the firm greater profits than the investment costs. So it seems logical that an understanding of what the market wants is a good starting point for the innovation process. This was recognized by Cooper who, writing as early as 1993, stated, "one should seek the customer input and feedback at every step of the way throughout the entire development phase as the product takes shape." Rothwell et al (1974) had earlier put forward a similar viewpoint when they said, "User needs must be precisely determined and met and it is important that these needs are monitored throughout the course of the innovation since they rarely remain completely static."

In this chapter we set out to address a number of issues in relation to the role of the market in innovation processes:

- What is the evidence that a market orientation leads to improved innovation performance?
- What is the relationship between the nature of the innovation effort, customer involvement, and success in innovation?
- What types of customers should be involved in the innovation process and at what cost?
- How can firms go beyond current customers to work on more radical innovations?
- How can the firm establish the direction of its future efforts in seeking to meet customer needs that have not yet been identified?
- What capabilities set is needed by the firm to succeed in engaging the market place in its innovation efforts?

Market orientation

Companies that really understand the market place and respond in timely fashion to changing customer needs have been described as *market oriented*. Market orientation has its roots in marketing theory as the operationalization of the marketing concept, and is concerned with learning about the market by developing an understanding of the market and using it for marketing decisions and actions. It becomes the basis of organizational behaviours with regard to the firm's business stakeholders (customers, competitors, and internal functions), all of which have an impact on organizational performance. Han, Kim, and Srivastava (1998) suggest that basically it is a corporate culture characterized by the organization's disposition to continuously deliver superior value to its customers. So the market-oriented firm has an organization-wide commitment to continuous information gathering and coordination of customer needs, competitor's capabilities and the provisions of other significant market agents and authorities. This results in an integrated effort on the part of the employees and across departments in organizations.

Han et al (1998) go on to identify three core components of market orientation: *customer orientation, competitor orientation*, and *inter-functional coordination*. They suggest that customer orientation is insufficient on its own. An effective strategy requires more than simply customer-centred methods. Competitor orientation essentially focuses on the following questions:

- Who are the competitors?
- What technologies do they offer?
- Do they represent an attractive alternative from the perspective of the target customers?

Competitor-oriented firms seek to establish their own strengths and weaknesses across the enterprise, in terms of not only products and their marketing, but also processes and organization. They regularly review their capabilities relative to others in terms of people-embodied knowledge and skills, physical and technical systems, managerial systems, organizational structures, and cultural values and norms.

So just how important is market orientation to innovation? Montoya-Weiss and Calatone (1994), from their research, conclude that a large number of studies state that, among others, factors related to market orientation determine new product performance. That is, these factors are either a part of market orientation (such as proficiency of predevelopment activities, proficiency of marketing activities, and protocol) or a consequence of having a market orientation (such as product advantage). They identify two dimensions. The first, based on ideas put forward by behaviourists, is that market orientation is the generation and dissemination of market intelligence as well as a responsiveness to this market intelligence (that is, the cross-functional activities directed at creating and satisfying customers through continuous needs assessment). The second is based on notions of organizational cognition, where market orientation is seen as a culture or set of shared beliefs that puts the customer's interests first and then has in place the required knowledge systems and structures to achieve this. Montoya-Weiss and Calatone suggest that competitive advantage through market orientation can really only be based on the basic cultural differences, as outward behaviours are easily copied. They see organizational learning as a capability that integrates both perspectives.

Based on their later research, Kok, Hillebrand, and Biemans (2003) conclude, "hardly any study reports on the conceptualization and operationalization of market orientation in the managerial context of a specific critical process like product development." They see this as necessary in order to assist managers in identifying appropriate actions to improve performance, and also to know how to improve market orientation within their organizations.

Jaworski and Kohli (1993) assert that market-oriented behaviour yields superior innovation and greater new product success. Incorporation of customer needs and competitor positioning into the new product development (NPD) process can lead to well-defined goals that result in speed to market. Clarity of project goals is also seen by Kessler and Chakravarthy (1996) as having a positive impact on innovation speed. The ambiguity in project goals can be reduced by the use of real-time product definition, driven by frequent repeated interactions with customers. From their research into a sample of 453 companies in four diverse industries (automotive, electronics, publishing, and manufacturing), Jaworski and Kohli (1993) conclude that, in turbulent environments, through boundary-spanning activities such as the active involvement of NPD staff in corporate strategy planning and the involvement of corporate planners in NPD activities, positive results will be achieved. Management also needs to recognize that risky investments and risky decisions have to be taken in such conditions.

Knowledge management systems, according to Kok, Hillebrand, and Biemans (2003), offer both formal and informal ways of controlling and creating knowledge and skills that enable market learning. Systems are aimed at both creating market information processing knowledge and skills (*knowledge-creating systems*) and controlling the use of market information processing knowledge and skills (*knowledge-controlling systems*). Knowledge-creating systems enable the processing of information, resulting in new knowledge and skills that may lead to modification of technical and/or managerial knowledge systems. Kok et al suggest that Total Quality Management (TQM) and other techniques may be useful here, but there are many approaches. Knowledge-controlling systems facilitate the systematic use of knowledge and skills and the operation of technical systems. Here, the organizational structures may help or hinder. The NPD process offers one way of controlling the use of market information if procedures are consciously built in. Another way is the product development strategy, and techniques such as technology roadmaps can help. The knowledge management approach needs to enable the interpretation of information and its reformulation so as to be useful for decision making in relation to innovation strategy and operations.

Costs versus benefits of customer involvement in the innovation process

An interesting issue facing firms is "Who takes the initiative?" Birchall and Armstrong (2004), from a study of 240 companies based in seven European countries, reported that closeness to customers and demanding customers have a positive impact on self-reported innovation performance. But a good question that merits an answer is, should the firm be aiming to acquire particularly demanding customers in order to be pushed to innovate? In such cases the customer has probably already identified a need for such product or service enhancement, and so the prospective market for the product or service seems more secure. Or should the firm seek to understand customer behaviour surrounding the use of its products and services, then go off into itself to identify improvements which, when completed, are presented to the enthusiastic customer?

How can the firm do as suggested in Chapter 6 and "go beyond the current customers"? Should the firm wait to be solicited by its customers, or should it actively seek to engage customers? Much seems to depend upon the type of market conditions. For example, the market for industrial goods differs from that for consumer goods. In the industrial sector customers typically have a higher level of expertise regarding the product. But in the business-to-business context the customer may place a price on involvement in the development of the firm's products and services. It might weigh up the cost benefits of perhaps a closer engagement with one supplier versus requiring competitiveness between suppliers. According to resource dependence theory, one of the fundamental strategies to reduce dependence is coordination with the resource owner—information on customer needs and user experiences is a resource (Gruner and Hamburg, 2000), and a closer relationship can lock in the other party.

Understanding the customer's point of view is part of market orientation, and this applies as much to understanding motivations for, and expectations from, engagement in the front-end innovation process as to other elements of the innovation process. Customer-related information can only really be obtained from customers. It should be borne in mind that customers do have discretion over giving this information. The cost of information to the firm may well be the readiness to exchange information that might be of commercial use to the customer.

But some information is readily available without seeking the customer's agreement for its use. One rich source is unsolicited information in the form of complaints, and suggestions that flow from this interaction. Sadly, the potential is often lost because this process is often seen by organizations as a means of quality control rather than product development, and hence the information gets used only partially. In some cultural contexts, of course, this approach is not successful because of a predisposition against complaining. One must understand the motivations for complaining, but really it is the identification of those few ideas that can really make a difference to the value of the product or service in the eyes of the customer that is being mined from the general data available. It is not possible to predict the likely source of the obscure comment or complaint that can trigger, in the right context, that radically different solution.

Complaints can also be useful in providing comparisons with competing products, but often users have limited experience with alternatives, and in any case the firm should not really be seeking innovations which end up as "me-too" products. Also, little is known about the origin of complaints, and so they may represent a segment of the market that the firm does not seek to serve. E-mail is making it much easier for customers to send in complaints, and also much cheaper for the provider to receive and record complaints. But the processing costs can be high, and unless those sifting through have the skills and motivation to reframe complaints as ideas and recognize the potential, there is little likelihood of this proving productive.

Novel design can disrupt well-established markets

Not all disruption comes about from developments in technology, management processes, or channels to market. Where products and services are mature, firms may need to seek novel solutions to the problems of developing their market place. A strong market orientation can help in product development so as to attract new customers and retain them. The aesthetic design of products, focusing on product appeal, can help in this.

This short case study is about a development in a well-established and mature market—toothbrushes. It is based on the work of Barré & Associés, a French design agency. Its work is strongly influenced by the founder's expressed philosophy—the *Oblique vision*® (Barré, 2001):

> when you can no longer see the horizon, change direction ... our markets are mature or in decline and everyone has arrived at a level of excellence and works with good designers ... we set out to identify innovative moves that the competition has not exploited.

The agency worked for Elida Fabergé to develop the Signal Croissance toothbrush aimed at the children's toothbrush market. Starting with a launch in 1991 the company has further developed the concept, and by doing so has been successful in increasing its European market share from 8 per cent to 42 per cent, and also retaining a leadership in spite of a strong response from the competition.

To develop new insights the agency used an approach based on working from all the negative feelings about the product and then looking for new solutions. It then looks for the most promising improvements, described as 'the axis of seduction." In the case of the toothbrush it set about making the brushing of teeth fun. It borrowed ideas from Disney and attempted to 'transform an inanimate object into a playmate." The concept was progressed further by involving groups of children in creativity meetings, and then by using drawings produced by these children to stimulate new ideas. Testing mock-ups with user groups led to a shortlist of preferred designs.

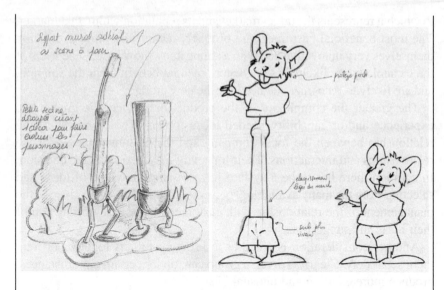

Sources: based on Gotzsch (2003). Images by Barré & Associés, used with permission.

One key question is how to reward the originator of ideas. This issue taxes those running internal suggestion schemes, but the issues are possibly greater for those seeking to engage customers and suppliers. Where a monetary value can be assigned to the idea, for example through patent recognition, it is possible to operate a personal or team reward scheme which is transparent. But in many cases this is just not possible, as when the idea gets incorporated into a complex product and it has no clear impact on the price charged nor the cost of manufacture.

Where customers have been invited to participate, they may well have higher expectations of reward. Clearly where the customer has proprietary knowledge the firm must itself expect to pay a reward, perhaps in the form of early access to new products, exclusive use for a period, additional services to support the new product, or product/service discounts. Where the source of ideas is individuals, they may well be satisfied by an acknowledgement or some form of recognition, which by its prominence enhances the self-worth of the individual.

For the firm seeking to work with customers, choices have to be made about which customers are likely to present the greatest benefits. The answer might be one, or a large number. It might well not be the largest customer by volume, although a major customer might have an expectation of involvement. The customer's financial attractiveness relates to the degree to which it represents the target market and its reputation within that market. The most beneficial customers are probably technically attractive, being themselves very innovative and with a strong know-how base. Lead users of the technology are likely to see greater potential benefit from the solution, and are likely to recognize the need for the new product.

The greater the complexity of the product or service, the greater the experience and/or capability needed of customers. The closeness of the relationship between the focal company and the customer, the wider the relationships and interactions. Their longevity may also sway the decision. In addition there has to be a system for assessing the value of ideas and selecting from the many available. Then consideration has to be given to the management of the relationship with customers in the case of rejection of their ideas and suggestions.

Another consideration is whether to bring customers together or treat them separately. Clearly a diverse group can, under certain circumstances, produce more exciting and unusual ideas.

Is the firm engaging individuals or companies, and in what way? Clearly the higher the degree of involvement (duration, frequency of meetings and exchanges, number of people), the greater the cost. Brockhoff (2003) categorizes the form of advice as by weak control, by doing, or by strong control. All relationships have opportunity costs, and perhaps even unwanted outcomes: for example, the customer might be guilty of actually slowing down development, for many reasons. Customers will not behave as predicted or expected on all occasions, and customer involvement does not guarantee success.

Key questions

- Does the firm have a clear notion of how far it needs to be market-oriented?
- How is the degree of market orientation measured by the firm?
- How well developed is the culture of market orientation in the firm?
- How effective is the firm at collecting, analyzing, and sharing customer information?
- How is market orientation converted into innovative new products and services?

Stages of the development process and customer involvement

Is customer involvement of greater value at particular points in the innovation process, with perhaps different customers, and contacts at different levels within their organizations, at each stage in the process? For customers, idea generation is probably at low cost. Clearly lead users are useful when prototyping or evaluating alternative concepts in prototype form. Also, where the product has to be integrated by the customer into a larger product, early involvement is appropriate as it is likely to allow simultaneous engineering. Product pre-announcements to particular customers are sometimes used to test reactions before market launch. When they start to use the product, customers can help recognize market potential in areas not previously envisaged. After-launch experience can result in early modifications and give the customer tangible benefits as well as providing a reference site.

On the other side, the question arises how customers select suppliers to work with. Again, do they choose one or many, those with the best track record of innovation, those with whom they have long-standing relationships? One key consideration for customers is to determine the capabilities and track record of suppliers in taking forward ideas for new products and services (Brockhoff 2003). Again the review framework proposed earlier, of people-embodied knowledge and skills, physical and technical systems, managerial systems, organizational structures, and cultural values and norms, is useful in this context.

Another factor impacting on the nature of involvement is the risk of disclosure. A key issue for both parties is the protection of intellectual property. The supplier may well feel the need to protect supplier-specific information from transfer to customers to avoid the possibility of it being transferred, either inadvertently or deliberately, to competing suppliers. The more radical the innovation and its significance to the supplier's business, the greater the need for non-disclosure contracts or high trust levels, which are normally the result of long-term relationships. Systems for the processing of information flow need careful management. Also concerns may be expressed about the possibility of customer opportunism, possibly going as far as taking over leadership in development or combining experiences with different suppliers.

Gruner and Hamburg (2000) studied over 300 companies in the German machine industry through questionnaire survey to establish the impact on innovation success of interaction with the customer at the various stages of new product development. They focused on mid-range innovations (not revolutional but also not institutional). Six stages in the NPD process were identified—initial screening, preliminary market assessment, preliminary technical assessment, product development, in-house product testing, and market launch. They studied the intensity of interaction in relation to the degree to which it went beyond the standards of market research; the duration of joint work; the frequency of meetings; the number of personnel involved from customer organizations; the perceived intensity of customer interaction; and the number of involved companies. While the study has limitations, it did produce some interesting results which question some assumptions about customer involvement more generally. Their results are shown in Table 7.1.

From this it can be seen that in practice the intensity of interaction reported varies across phases of NPD. The impact of interaction also varies. Certainly it would appear that interaction in the early and late phases has a pay-off. Project definition and engineering are believed to benefit least because it is expected that the firm has superior competencies in this area on which they can rely. Firms also feel that customers can add more value at the more concrete concept review rather that to the ideas phase. At the prototype phase customers can still have an impact on the final product, and can use their experiences to provide a detailed critique based on practical insights. Customers really can have little impact once the product is at the launch phase.

Table 7.1 Interaction with customers during stages in new product development and success

Phase	Impact	Reported interaction intensity (1= none, 7 = maximum interaction)
Idea generation	Positive impact	2.42
Product concept development	Positive impact and stronger than idea generation	2.58
Project definition	No significant impact	2.76
Engineering	No significant impact	2.42
Prototype testing	Positive impact and larger than elsewhere	3.38
Market launch	Positive impact and weakest of all	4.14

Environmental turbulence—is a different approach needed?

Calato, Garcia, and Dröge (2003) point out that turbulent environments have features such as high levels of inter-period change which create uncertainty and unpredictability, sharp discontinuities in demand and growth rate, temporary competitive advantages which are continually created or eroded, and low barriers to entry and exit which continuously change the competitive structure of the industry. So a turbulent environment increases the risk and uncertainty in the NPD strategic planning process:

> In turbulent environments NP managers must cope with uncertainty regarding their customers' needs, uncertainty as to which are the best long-term technology and market paths to follow and uncertainty as to levels of resources to commit to various endeavours.

Mohr and Shooshtari (2003) go on to suggest that high-technology products are characterized by a high degree of market and technological uncertainty, competitive volatility, high R&D expenditures, rapid obsolescence, and also benefits for the customer which arise due to the presence of external networks. That is, the value any customer gets is exponentially related to the number of other adopters, as in instant messaging applications:

> Many high-tech firms tend to be engineering oriented (or product driven) and exhibit a culture in which engineering knowledge is valued more that marketing acumen. This creates a double-jeopardy environment where the need for marketing skills is greater than other industry contexts, yet is less likely to be found or valued.

While a market orientation creates a culture seemingly well suited to developing superior value for customers through institutional innovations, continuous improvements to products and processes, it does not appear to fit the needs of a turbulent environment. For example, does the organization have the luxury of the time for extensive data collection and analysis—a scientific approach? Those reviewing market orientation and innovation from a marketing perspective are seen to place their emphasis on a market orientation, but in contrast much management research is focused on entrepreneurship and an entrepreneurial orientation. Since market-oriented firms focus on responding to well-articulated customer needs, they tend to work within the current capability domain of the firm, and as a result they are likely to miss opportunities for developing radically different new products beyond the capability of existing customers to articulate.

An entrepreneurial orientation is seen as offering a proactive and aggressive focus on innovations that meet emerging and unarticulated customer needs so as to pre-empt the competition (Atuahene-Gima and Ko 2001). This is aiming to lead the customer rather than be led by the customer. Successful firms in this environment are characterized by a high degree of innovativeness, risk taking, and proactiveness. The learning and selection mechanisms engender exploration and risk-seeking behaviours in the product innovation process. New resource combinations are speedily brought together from both within and outside the firm's boundaries. Prior assumptions about how best to operate are constantly being questioned. But firms adopting this orientation may well be technology-driven, and engage in endeavours with a high risk of market failure. They can be blinded by the success of their technological developments. Hence, Atuahene-Gima and Ko (2001) assert that "firms need to strike a self-reinforcing balance between market and entrepreneurship orientations to engender effective product development and performance." They see this interaction between the market and the entrepreneurial orientation as a significant means of organizational adaptation. An organizational orientation provides the means for social learning and selection, linking strategic intent to operational activities. Desired behaviors are reinforced through a mix of control systems and reward structures.

From their research into over 180 Australian companies, Atuahene-Gima and Ko (2001) report that market/entrepreneurship-oriented firms have a higher new product performance and are more effective in the product innovation process overall than other firms. There was no evidence reported to suggest that these firms were being faced with a more hostile environment or more intense competition. Entrepreneurship-oriented firms appeared to place more emphasis on human resource practices than the market/entrepreneurship-oriented, but the latter provided greater managerial support for specific innovation projects.

An engineering organization developing an understanding of customer needs

Cummins, the engine manufacturer, embarked on a number of extensive data-gathering activities as part of their product development process:

- Advising councils were set up including key customers and distributors to discuss product needs and design ideas.
- Project design and marketing personnel interviewed individual users of engines produced by Cummins and various competitors.
- Project managers and design engineers interviewed truck fleet managers as well as truckers at truck stops.
- Engineers rode with truck owner-operators for long periods.
- First-hand knowledge identified features not previously seen as important, and served to clarify design goals and reduce conflicts over design features.

Different customers in different parts of the world and in different businesses were found to have different needs, so how can they be reconciled?

Source: Swink, Sandvig, and Mabert (1996).

Key questions

- Does the firm have a clear, well-documented innovation process?
- Does the firm have policies and procedures for customer involvement at the various stages of the innovation process for the different forms of innovation?
- Does the firm have systems and processes for assessing and progressing ideas gleaned from the market place?
- Is there any recent evidence, including anecdotal evidence, that intellectual property policies are failing to provide adequate protection?

Integrating future market opportunities, technological advances, firm capabilities, and strategic intent

The key aim of innovation in products or processes is to better meet a customer need so as to generate profitable long-term business. But the innovation has to fit into the firm's future strategic positioning and provide for ongoing business development. To achieve this there has to be an integration of opportunities through technology development, customers' changing lifestyles and needs, and the organization's capability to deliver.

In an earlier book (Birchall and Tovstiga 2002), the authors developed the notion of *Future Proofing*. Future proofing sets out to minimize the risks of investing in organizational capabilities which soon become obsolete, and are then prohibitively expensive to reconfigure and reshape or dispose of, even if this is feasible without putting the total business at risk. The overall aim is to find a way forward for the organization which ensures that future market obsolescence is minimized. This is done by developing technologies and designing them into products and services, such that resources developed and deployed are flexible and open-ended enough to allow for growth, by combining a concern for the changing needs of stakeholders with affordability. The focus is on getting a balance between specificity of resources and their flexibility—there is a trade-off to be struck between the lower costs of specificity and the higher costs of flexibility and adaptability.

In that book we demonstrated how the application of a range of techniques can enable informed strategic formulation, and more effective

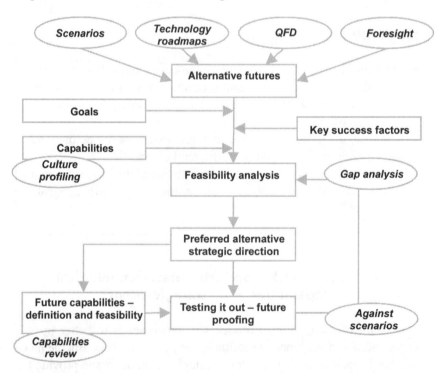

Figure 7.1 The future proofing process

development and deployment of organizational resources, so as to meet a range of possible futures—in short, future proofing. In seeking to establish those areas "at risk" to rapid change, strategies can then be developed to minimize the chance of expensive redundancy while better meeting customer needs.

The overall aim of an exercise in future proofing is to achieve a blueprint for action that has been widely tested for validity and is widely accepted as an appropriate way forward. In arriving at the blueprint, the models and assumptions underpinning the conceptualization should have been made explicit, and thoroughly tested across a range of experts from a diversity of disciplines and background experiences.

A range of tools can be used in the process of future proofing, but essential to the process is the development of a picture of customer needs and wants into the future. The basic process is illustrated in Figure 7.1.

The starting point is the identification of alternative scenarios for the specific unit of analysis of interest, be it a product, service, or industry. In preparation for the scenario exercise, background information should be collected about the business environment and the changes taking place, particularly on the technology front.

Foresight as background to future proofing

Foresight studies carried out at industry or national level can be very useful as an input to a *scenario exercise* undertaken by the firm. Foresight programs bring together experts from a wide range of backgrounds to build common perceptions of long-term trends, in order to identify areas of strategic research and the emerging generic technologies likely to yield the greatest economic and social welfare. While early government-sponsored Foresights were mainly concerned primarily with technological developments, a recognition of the interactions between technological developments and social and cultural circumstances has led to a broadening of Foresight to areas such as the Ageing Population, Crime Prevention, and Sustainability, as well as the broadening of technology-related fields to include societal impact (see the UK website at www. foresight. gov.uk).

So Foresight is a process by which a fuller understanding of the forces shaping the long-term future is put together. Experts are brought together to develop a vision which is strongly underpinned by a rationale—what are the key factors driving us in the direction of this vision? Since Foresight does not claim to predict a certain future situation, but recognizes that a range of possibilities exists, it attempts to shape or create paths for development.

Van der Meulen and Lohnberg (2001) put it like this:

> Foresight may be described both as a production of information, in order to reduce uncertainties about technological development, and as an interaction process between actors to co-ordinate their research, development and innovation activities. But the resulting information and co-ordination are not like any other. The specific nature of foresight lies in its focus on expectations and its inherent uncertainty because of the unpredictability of the future. The paradox then is that if foresight is successful, organizations reduce uncertainty and improve their ability to develop technology strategies by relying on necessarily uncertain intelligence, rather than on, for example, the certainty of past performance or present markets.

Rather than relying on the outputs from any single national program, businesses can access a range of initiatives to survey the differing national expectations. This includes studies by the governments of Japan, the UK, and Germany. The US approach focuses on critical technologies crucial to improving competitiveness and other societal needs. The US studies have been targeted and not long-running (for example, the "clean car"). France and the Netherlands have also favoured an approach based on critical technologies. Smaller countries, such as Austria and Sweden, and regions, such as Bordeaux in France, have more recently instigated Foresight exercises.

Expectations clearly influence technology strategy. Technological communities share technological visions, and the expectations generated lead to the shaping of strategies. In formulating strategies, organizations seek to reduce risk by seeking opinion from experts and stakeholders, and building the best informed foresight they can achieve. But these expectations then shape future actions. One often-quoted example is Moore's Law of the doubling of storage capacity on a chip in 18–24 months. It had no scientific basis but in the 1980s this became a target for competing chip manufacturers. It shaped the industry as it underpinned the innovation dynamic. Late delivery had high costs; as chips became increasingly more expensive to develop, the risks involved increased considerably. Moore's Law became a self-fulfilling "expectancy" (Van der Meulen and Lohnberg 2001).

In order to gain the benefits from Foresight, it is necessary to integrate foresight, assessment, and policy evaluation into the business's strategic intelligence system. This strategic intelligence system (whether it is at the level of the business unit or the business overall) has a major focus on learning, and relates closely to the notions of the learning organization. The outcome being sought from the exercise by the organization is "anticipatory intelligence." Such intelligence is based not only on the "what" but also the "why" and "'how."

National, industry and company-specific *technology roadmaps* also serve to inform this stage in the overall process of future proofing. These government-sponsored maps are much more specific than Foresight exercises about the likely development of relevant technologies in key business sectors for the national economy, and are used to set national and industry targets for R&D development, so these are pre-competitive. Industry roadmaps are also pre-competitive, and again can be used to focus long-term R&D and also lead to cooperation by competitors within the industry, so as to accelerate development and reduce overall costs. Company-specific roadmaps are clearly not normally intended to be shared publicly, although it is likely that suppliers and customers will be involved in parts of the analysis. Also some of the expertise used in formulating the roadmap will come from universities, research establishments, and consultancies, so it is unlikely that the information will be proprietary, but it is the way in which the business configures the technologies and then develops control and mastery over those areas essential to its future that will give it competitive edge.

Scenarios in planning

Scenario literally means the written version of a play or story. Scenarios are "focused descriptions of fundamentally different futures presented in coherent script-like or narrative fashion" (Schoemaker 1995). Scenarios are plausible and challenging stories, not forecasts. They do not extrapolate from the past to predict what will happen in the future, but instead offer several very different stories of how the future might look. They are used by organizations in preparing themselves for discontinuities and sudden change. They can be used to create a common culture or language through which the future can be imagined and discussed. They also challenge the "mental models" commonly held by members of organizations. Their use can underpin organizational learning. They are "tools for foresight-discussions and documents whose purpose is not a prediction or a plan, but a change in the mindset of the people who use them" (De Geus 1999).

There are at least three schools of scenario planning. The first is the *intuitive school*, derived from Shell's experience It is largely qualitative, assuming that business decisions result from a process of finding and understanding complex interrelationships between internal and external factors (including economic, political, technological, social, and environmental factors). The *quantitative school* uses operational research techniques such as econometric forecasting and time series. The third, a *hybrid school*, uses both intuitive and quantitative approaches. Multiple scenarios are put together so that more than one future is considered. Having two is often seen as insufficient because they will be bipolar and leave little choice. Having three is seen as leading to a middle road being chosen. But more than four often leads to too much overlap.

Schoemaker (1995) stresses that final scenarios should meet three criteria:

- They should be different from one another and reflect different futures rather than be variations.
- They should be relevant and connect to mental maps and concerns of the users.
- They should be internally consistent and make sense in the context of the drivers being examined.

To assist businesses to look at the global implications, scenario building needs to do the following:

1 Take a holistic view in constructing scenarios to include a global perspective and multi-variable analysis.
2 Call on appropriate experts and thought leaders, wherever they are located, to assist in the process; and also to respect their inputs.
3 Use highly diverse teams to work on the scenarios and future proofing to reflect global perspectives and experiences.
4 Ensure that language or cultural differences do not inhibit contributions by experts.
5 Accelerate learning across the organization and across organizational boundaries to embrace a global view into organizational learning. It should develop a seeking culture, and one where insights about the impact of globalization get passed on and discussed within the organization.
6 Systematically record and analyze comments on the global aspects of the scenarios.
7 Test out the scenarios at regular intervals, with as broad a group as possible.
8 Adopt a mentality in which flexibility in planning is given high value.

9 Seek out and share with global organizations best practice processes for scenario building.

"Scenarios increase the organisation's capability to more skilfully observe its environment, leading to more robust long-term organisational learning." They are is seen as shifting strategic thinking from reactive to proactive and from internal to external.

Source: Kees van der Heijden (1996).

Scenario building normally involves a series of facilitated workshops. Elements typically included in this process are:

1 Reconsideration of vision and objectives.
2 Clarification of business ideas that will lead to success.
3 Identification of strategic priorities.
4 Identification of "gaps" between where the organization is now and where it would like to be in the future.
5 Identification of relevant actions to move the organization forward.

The point in time at which scenario planning is introduced to the organization may also be important in its eventual acceptance. Schoemaker (1995) suggests that scenarios are most beneficial when the organization:

- has experienced, or is about to experience, significant change
- faces great uncertainty that is straining managers' efforts to predict or adjust
- has difficulty thinking strategically or has a low quality of strategic thinking
- has a difficult time perceiving or generating new opportunities
- requires a common language and framework to advance change
- includes constituents with strong differences of opinion, including many viewpoints with merit.

If organizations are to benefit from scenario exercises they need to consider how both the process and the outputs will be used. Story telling is an important aspect in the application of scenarios in influencing organizational thinking. The construction of good-quality and memorable stories is part of the art of the scenario builder. The stories have to be plausible to gain credibility within the organization at large. But those constructing the stories need to recognize how their own bias will impact the story line(s) they develop. That is not to suggest a particular style of story, but considerable thought needs to be given to consideration of how the story will be presented and how it might impact. Above all the stories need to disturb the listener. If they fail in this they will soon be forgotten, and will not have the desired effect of galvanizing thinking, decision making and action. Great care also needs to be taken in selecting those to present the stories. Unless they themselves have credibility—"having been there, done it and got the T-shirt (or battle scars) to prove it"—the stories are unlikely to be well received.

Steve Denning of the World Bank has this to say on story telling in organizations:

Good organisational stories have five key characteristics:
Endurance (the stories go on through decades).
Salience (they have punch and emotional power).
Sense-making (they explain something).
Comfort (the story rings true to something people have experienced).
Authenticity (people trust the story-teller and believe the story).
Stories can be used in organisations to stimulate change, to convince people of what you want them to believe, to gain commitment and loyalty and to transfer knowledge. Some people are natural story-tellers, but it is a technique everyone can learn.

Source: quoted from a talk given to the Knowledge Management Forum at Henley in June, 2001.

There is undoubtedly the potential to extend the use of scenario building within organizations as a useful mechanism to increase organizational learning, and also to engage the organization in developing foresight and supporting the processes of innovation by giving it a common language and focus. The importance of the latter is stressed by Hamel and Prahalad (1994) as having the goal to "build the best possible assumption base about the future and thereby develop the prescience needed to proactively shape industry evolution." Mintzberg (1988) acknowledges with a health warning that, when looking at the external environment, "some of the softer techniques, such as scenario building, may be of use ... not to predict, but simply to interpret and clarify for managers what seems to be going on out there."

Clearly one important determinant of success at this stage in the process of future proofing is to build robust scenarios. This depends upon a number of factors relating to inputs, process, and outputs.

Trend analysis

Trend analysis is an important tool for future proofing. This and competitive intelligence are strategic exercises that seek to support and extend the firm's planning horizon into the future. The horizon can be two, five, or more years, depending on the business involved. The questions typically asked are:

- What trends will mature or emerge at that time?
- What will be the driving forces of the market?
- What will be the key success factors of the market?
- What new technologies might emerge that might prove to be disruptive and discontinuous?
- Who will the competitors be?
- What will the firm need in terms of capabilities and competencies to build a position of competitive advantage in the future?

In order to provide answers to these questions, managers must understand a highly complex set of interacting factors. They must understand the industry's history, time frames, structure, and stakeholders. The firm must also be clear about its own scope of competition. The firm must be capable of analyzing the external forces that shape its day-to-day operations and its strategic thrust. These may be grouped into five categories: economic, political, societal, technological, and industrial. For each, key trends are established and analyzed according to impact. The impact can be positive, neutral (indeterminate), or negative. The impact analysis provides a good opportunity for cross-checking key success factors determined in the analysis described in the previous section. Table 7.2 suggests a framework for examining trends and deriving the strategic impact for the firm.

The origins of trends analysis can be traced to the 1950s, when long-range planning was developed for anticipating growth and managing

Table 7.2 The possible strategic impacts of major trends

Timeframe and scope	Trends and uncertainties	Impact on firm?
1. What is the firm's **time frame**? • Pace of technological development? • Competitor's timeframe? • Investment intensity? • Political timeframe?	1. **economic** • Shift toward network-knowledge economy? • Impact of globalization? 2. **political** • Selective trade barriers / agreements?	Positive? Neutral?
2. What is the firm's **scope**? • Domestic versus global?	• Legislation? deregulation? • North–south / east–west migration?	Negative?
3. Who are the **stakeholders**? • Clients / shareholders / employees? • Investors / society at large?	3. **societal** • Increase in environmental sensitivity? 4. **technological** • Potential technological discontinuities? 5. **industrial** • Shifts; emergence of new industries?	

complexity (Aaker 1992). The assumption was that past trends would continue into the future. Today, keeping up to date on ever more rapidly changing competitive environment trends demands sophisticated business intelligence gathering, that may include formal as well as informal capabilities.

Formal capabilities include virtual and hard-wired networks around the world to monitor various developments such as patent applications, scientific and technical developments, processes for searching, filtering, and sorting information contained in volumes of published information and other codified information sources such as the Internet, and a formal system for touching networking with other innovative companies around the world. Formal capabilities may also include formalized techniques such as trend extrapolation, curve matching, Delphi, and relevance trees, scenarios, and cross impact analysis (Goodman and Lawless 1994).

Increasingly, the firm is being seen as a boundaryless entity that is tied into networks of firms and communities of commerce; the old "stand-alone" version of the firm is rapidly disappearing. New game rules and codes of conduct are emerging. The networked firm of the future must learn to position and balance the interests of the network with its own strategic interests and goals (Tovstiga and Fantner 2000).

Informal capabilities draw on informal, largely tacit flows of knowledge between organizations. People are at the heart of these networks; technology merely supports the exchange of information.

There are many approaches to business intelligence gathering. A critical factor is that methods should be chosen that consistently bring a diverse array of data that can be tested against the existing business models. Some of this data will fit the models; other data will inevitably not fit. This, however, is desirable since it will force an ongoing re-evaluation and rethink of the current business models, leading to a redoubling of efforts directed at building and nurturing a valid value proposition.

Formal business intelligence involves a variety of analyses that focus on what is happening in the firm's external environment. This external analysis includes the following categories (Aaker 1992):

- customer analysis: segments, motivations, latent needs
- competitive analysis: identity, strategic groups, performance, objectives, strategies, culture, cost structure, strengths, weaknesses, new business models
- market analysis: size, projected growth, profitability, entry barriers, cost structure, distribution system, trends, key success factors, measures of success
- environmental analysis: technological, governmental, economic, cultural, demographic, scenarios, information needs.

Technology roadmaps

At a firm level, the overarching aim of roadmapping is to achieve improved time-to-market and thereby a strengthened competitive position. In order to improve the product creation process, a long-term view of technology and market developments improves planning. The technique is being used to achieve better integration between the overall business strategy and its technology strategy. An agreed overall plan can also support people at all levels in achieving milestones, and can lead to greater commitment to their role in the overall process. It is to be hoped that roadmaps will stimulate creativity and innovation, directed with purpose.

> Roadmapping stimulates organizational learning through the encouragement of openness and ways of doing things better. It also supports

people at all levels in achieving milestones and becoming committed to their role in the overall process.

Pieter Groenveld (1997) who worked with Philips
Electronics in Eindhoven, the Netherlands

It is clear from articles written about roadmapping that many tools exist to support the process, with many organizations developing their own to suit their own particular requirements. Other well-understood tools are used in support of the process, such as quality function deployment (QFD), maturity grids, and the innovation matrix. But most start the process by defining markets and applications, so that products are specified in terms of customer requirements. It is then possible to identify technical functionality for the product, and those technologies needed to provide the functionality sought.

Roadmaps may be developed for a product, a range of products, components, or production processes. They may well cross organizational and company boundaries, reflecting the technical complexity of most products. The timescale will vary: The higher the level, probably the greater the timespan. The longer the timescale is, the greater is the need for visionary thinking, and the more the process will benefit from diversity in the background of participants directly involved in the development process. The various roadmaps developed across the organization need to be reconciled in order that there is overall coordination of a shared view. Roadmapping is normally an ongoing process.

In developing an industry roadmap, challenges can well be classified into two classes: first, the relatively near-term that need to be met by "technology solutions" currently under development, and second, those with no "known solutions" (of reasonable confidence). These are classified as "red," and signify that progress might end if breakthroughs are not achieved or a "work-around" developed.

Also included will be current best estimates of the timing of introduction. This may be broken down into research, development, prototyping, and manufacturing. They may be confined to "year of introduction," which is the estimate of the point at which the technology will be "at the leading-edge of ramp to volume manufacturing."

As noted above, QFD is an useful adjunct to the process. It focuses on functional requirements of customers, and facilitates translating these into technical features of the product. Here timescales and process technologies are not considered in detail. This can serve as a simpler starting point than a full roadmap. The next stage—the technology roadmap—can build on this output by adopting either a technology-push or a market-pull perspective. This shows either what technology is required to meet product functionality, or how technology will make possible different product functionality.

Philips has used a tool—the Blue Box Model—in which the uncertainty of product feasibility and commitment to resource allocation is shown. See Figure 7.2 (from Groenveld 1997). This is the basis of the innovation matrix (Figure 7.3), which shows technical uncertainty and hence risks, against the requirement of availability. This matrix identifies particular short-term needs with unproven technology problems. It also shows areas where technology, while available, is not needed for a considerable time—in other words, premature R&D spend—and areas where the business has access to proven technology essential for the mid-term—a desirable situation.

Technology roadmapping may then include:

1 Mapping the innovation matrix onto the product matrix; identifying gaps and establishing actions.
2 Reviewing the portfolio of technologies and assessing the overall balance of risks.

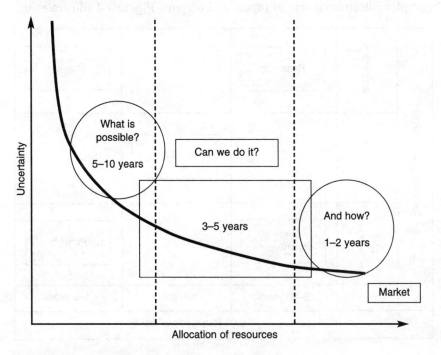

Figure 7.2 The blue box model from Groenveld

3 Reviewing the product portfolio to assess possible gaps within the future portfolio if technologies are not available within the timeframe.

Quality function deployment (QFD) is a useful tool as a preliminary to product or services roadmapping, because it emphasizes the position of the customer, and customer needs and preferences, and identifies the functional requirements of products. It also takes into consideration the firm's competitive position.

Quality function deployment

QFD was developed by the Japanese and first applied in the shipyards at Kobe in 1972. It has since been used in many organizations in the auto, IT, and consumer product industries. Essentially it aims to convert customer demands into quality characteristics to be the basis of a quality plan for the finished product or service. Weighting of the characteristics and customer desires in importance establishes the overall priorities to be worked towards. The charts also serve to map out what are generally complex interrelated sets of inputs and outputs. Figure 7.4 illustrates the

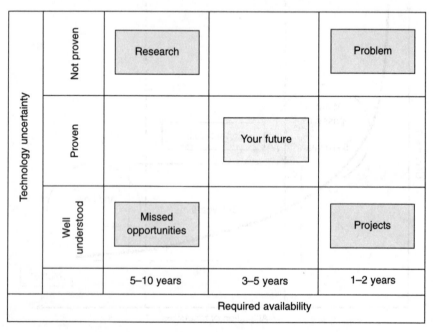

Figure 7.3 The innovation matrix from Groenveld

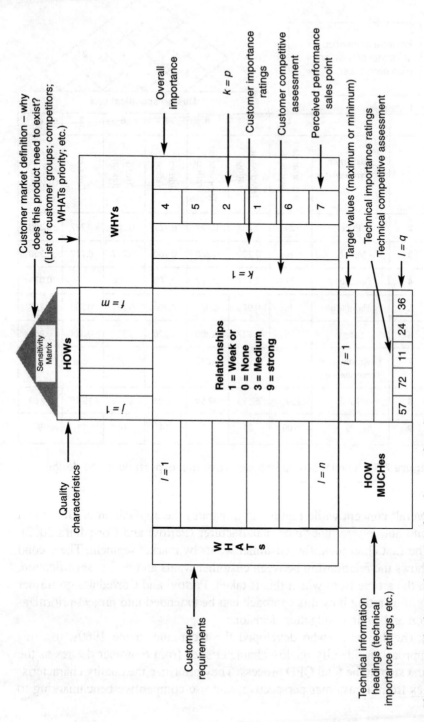

Figure 7.4 The basic elements of the house of quality

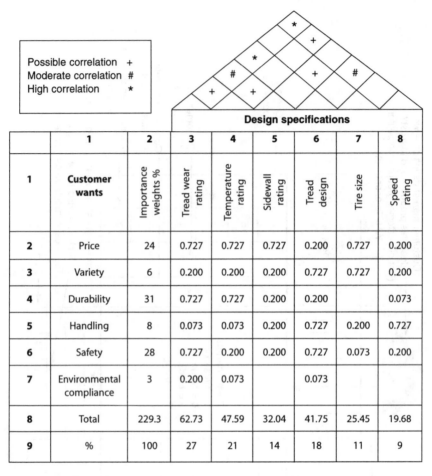

Figure 7.5 The relationship between customer expectations and design specification

overall concept while Figure 7.5 illustrates the application of QFD to an automotive tyre inner tube manufacturer (Partovi and Corredoira 2002). The first chart identifies customer wants by market segment. The second shows the relationship between customer wants and design specification. In the article from which this is taken, Partovi and Corredoira go further by illustrating how this approach can be extended into project prioritization and capital budgeting decisions.

The Japanese, who developed the technique in the 1960s, use this approach to identify quality characteristics from customer desires as the first step in the total QFD process. They prioritize the quality characteristics from a customer perspective, and use competitive benchmarking to inform the setting of target values. In a second phase, the relationship between the quality characteristics and the various design elements is examined and the component parts of the design are prioritized in terms of desired quality characteristic performance levels. In phase three, the important components are examined in relation to manufacturing processes, with the aim of identifying manufacturing operations that control the component target value, then process target specifications and values are set. Prioritized manufacturing processes and specifications are then used in the final phase to develop work package specifications, control and reaction plans, and training requirements. Such a comprehensive approach is seemingly widely adopted in Japan, but not in the United States, where stage one is popular with companies such as General Motors and Chrysler (Cristiano, Liker, and White 2000). Not only are such techniques used in manufacturing, they are also found in software development, service and process improvement. They are particularly useful where *concurrent engineering* is being deployed to cut down time from concept to market.

The technique performs well where good customer data is available— the "voice of the customer." In the United States, focus groups and one-to-one interviews are used extensively, whereas in Japan there is more reliance on customer complaints and warranty data. But unless "exciting" customer needs are identified, the product development is unlikely to "'break the mould." Certainly US companies in the survey by Cristiano, Liker, and White (2000) reported a higher level of breakthrough than Japanese companies. The Japanese saw the process as a useful contributor to organizational learning, particularly through the use of the results in training young engineers.

While there is clear merit in combining phase one of the QFD approach, commonly known as the 'House of Quality,' in a technology roadmapping exercise in order to speculate on customer preferences, needs or demands, prioritize, and then relate these to functionality and to benchmarks with competitors, the approach can also be applied in research portfolio analysis.

QFD has been applied in the US National Aeronautics and Space Administration (Kauffman, Ricks, and Shockcor 1999) to do just that. The QFD model is used to measure the direct impact of research work packages on the metrics developed for assessing progress towards strategic objectives (SOs). The researchers also looked at how Work Packages(WPs) interrelate to impact on the SOs. They illustrate the approach in relation to one of ten goals for NASA—"General aviation: Invigorate industry to deliver 10,000 (20,000) aircraft annually (20) years" (Table 7.3). Table 7.4 shows the SOs

Table 7.3 Three pillars and ten goals of NASA Research

Three pillars	Ten research goals
Global civil aviation: Provide the technical advances to maintain the nation's position in civil aviation	1 *Safety*: Reduce aircraft accident rate by a factor of 5(10) within 10(20) years 2 *Environmental*: Reduce emissions of future aircraft by a factor of 3(5) within 10(20) years 3 *Environmental*: Reduce noise levels of future aircraft by a factor of 2(4) from today's levels within 10(20) years 4 *Affordability*: While maintaining safety, triple the aviation system throughput in all weather conditions within 10 years 5 *Affordability*: Reduce the cost of air travel by 25%(50%) within 10(20) years
Revolutionary technology leaps: Explore technology to revolutionize air travel and create new markets for US industry	6 *High speed travel*: Reduce travel time to the Far East and Europe by 50% within 20 years at today's subsonic ticket prices 7 *General aviation*: Invigorate industry to deliver 10,000(20,000) aircraft annually within 10(20) years 8 *Advanced design tools*: Provide design tools to halve the development cycle time for aircraft
Access to space: Develop affordable and reliable access to space	9 *Payload cost*: Reduce the payload cost to low earth orbit from $10,000 per pound to $1000 per pound within 10 years 10 *Payload cost*: Reduce the payload cost to low earth orbit from $1000 per pound to $100 per pound by 2020

Table 7.4 Strategic objectives in relation to high-level goals

Strategic objective	Weight	Metric description and measures	Base line	Goal
Safety	30%	Fatal accidents per 100k flight hours	1.75	0.5
Affordability	20%	Cost per passenger mile	1.63	0.65
Reliability	15%	Trips per 100 cancelled due to malfunction	3.0	0.25
Weather	10%	Weather cancellations and redirections per 100 trips	10	0.5
Passenger comfort	15%	Combined cabin vibration and noise factors	92	50
Environment	10%	Emissions per operating hour	500	25

and their weighting to meet higher-level goals as well as the associated metrics. Five research work packages are evaluated for their impact against the SOs (Table 7.5). The interaction between WPs is shown in Table 7.6.

This approach has a number of benefits. In addition to challenging assumptions and raising the level of general awareness of the interactions

Table 7.5 Work packages and their impact on straegic objectives

Strategic objective	Weight	Research work packages				
		Flight systems	Propulsion systems	Integrated design and manufacture	Icing protection	Training systems
Safety	30%	9	9	1	1	9
Affordability	20%	3	3	9	9	9
Reliability	15%	9	9	1	1	1
Weather	10%	9	9	1	1	3
Passenger comfort	15%	1	3	3	3	1
Environment	10%	9	3	1	1	9

Table 7.6 The interaction between work packages

	Flight systems	Propulsion systems	Integrated design and manufacture	Icing protection	Training systems
Flight systems	1.0	0.23	0.23	0.077	0.69
Propulsion systems	0.23	1.0	0.23	0.077	0
Integrated design and manufacture	0.23	0.23	1.0	0.69	0.077
Icing protection	0.077	0.23	0.69	1.0	0.23
Training systems	0.69	0	0.077	0.23	1.0

and their importance, it highlights the probability of success and the potential impact on the overall program of failure. It also allows for adjustment over time of the SOs, possibly de-emphasizing SOs as they approach the achievement of the target metrics, and then redeployment of resources to areas where progress is inadequate.

QFD has a place in future proofing at several points in the process. First, it can support technology roadmapping, which is done as a preliminary to the scenario building. Such an analysis can guide the scenarios, because it can give a picture of the technologies likely to impact on customer needs, and how they might do so. But the approach is really more useful for shorter time horizons than those being applied to scenario building. However at later stages in the overall process of future proofing these charts can help in determining the mid-term development of technology, by again supporting the roadmapping process. The approach taken by the Japanese in extending the QFD to include manufacturing processes and develop much more detail, can also be used to test the feasibility of planned moves by the firm.

Pulling together the results of the analysis into a blueprint for action is a major challenge for the organization. It requires clear overall aims to be articulated. Then the alternative futures have to be assessed against the overall aims. This then enables the use of the methodology described in Appendix A to assess capabilities. This leads on to decisions about those areas over which the firm feels the greatest need for control. The key issue now is "How best can the firm gain the necessary control?"

By such a process the firm can map out alternative routes to its future based on the best possible estimates of what the market will be looking for and expecting in the timeframe set for the analysis. It will also enable the identification of "white spaces" based on gaps identified between the current uses of existing technologies and the potential uses of emerging technologies, some of which will not be apparent yet to the market.

Key questions

- How effectively are future customer needs identified and translated into an innovation strategy?
- How effective is organizational learning in support of innovation from customer interactions?
- Does the firm utilize methods such as foresight, scenarios, and technology roadmaps to support strategy development?
- Does the firm have a regular review along the lines of future proofing?
- How effective has the firm been at developing a long-term view of its needs for technology development?

Concluding remarks

In this chapter we have focused attention on issues in relation to customer involvement in the innovation process. We have identified issues that need consideration when developing a strategy for customer involvement. We have recognized that no one strategy fits all. Institutional, evolutional, and revolutional innovations all need somewhat different approaches. In addition, serving a business market will offer different challenges and opportunities from those of a consumer market. Fast-moving markets also place different demands than do the more stable. So the firm needs to consider its own particular circumstances and develop policies for customer engagement appropriate to its own needs and aspirations.

By carrying out a long-term review of the market, the firm seeks to address calls for analysis which integrate market opportunities, technological advances, firm capabilities, and strategic intent. To do this, time needs to be spent examining strategy formulation based on the best possible information and views. Techniques can help in this process and lead to "future proofing" by identifying the options available to the firm and ensuring that alternative routes are mapped out.

The capabilities needed for managing the market place relationships throughout the innovation process differ between the three main forms of innovation. The differences are summarized in Table 7.7. Here we have identified the differences emerging from this chapter which appear to have strong support from either empirical research or practice.

Table 7.7 The key capabilities needed for successful customer engagement in the innovation process

	Institutional	Evolutional	Revolutional
People-embodied knowledge and skills.	Skills in customer interaction. Market information processing. Analytical skills. Knowledge sharing. Sensitivity to intellectual property issues.	Sensing market changes. Questioning approach. Working outside the comfort zone. Knowledge of a range of scientific and technological disciplines and their potential market place applications.	Boundary spanning. Working in environment of constant change.
Management systems/organizational structures.	Clarity of long-term goals. Evaluation of ideas/fuzzy end decision-making.	Emphasis on "learning" and anticipation. Use of tools for future proofing. Mid- to long-term thinking.	Outward looking. Futures envisioning and strategic foresight. Entrepreneurial leadership. Highly visible. Risk taking. Proactive thinking. Networking.
Physical and technical systems.	Systems for customer data collection and verification. Means for triangulating customer information from various sources. Means for carrying out and sharing competitor analysis. Integration of systems to support knowledge creation and sharing.	Flexibility in systems to enable the building of quick responses to market changes. Strategic intelligence system.	
Cultural values and norms.	Valuing superior offerings to customers. Customers' interests come first. Intellectual property valued and protected.		A balanced view of the value of an entrepreneurial orientation vs. a market orientation with dominance to suit the stage of development. Technical uniqueness valued. Confidence in superior capabilities.

CHAPTER 8

Accelerating progress through partnering and alliancing

Introduction

In this chapter we examine the nature of alliances in their various forms. There is no doubt that alliances have become important to all sizeable organizations. But they are also important to smaller and medium-sized companies (SMEs), as these firms offer the large organization access to entrepreneurship and exciting new technological developments, and the SME can in turn gain through access to the expertise which resides in the large firm. In the knowledge economy, one of the key reasons for alliancing is to access capabilities not available or readily accessible within the organization itself. This can compensate for the lack of capability within the organization; it can lead to greater leverage of existing capabilities, a greater degree of control over key technologies, and a spreading of risk in development. But learning is a key motivator for firms.

In this chapter we set out to help the reader answer a number of key questions in relation to alliances:

- Why do firms need to form alliances at all?
- What form do alliances take, and under what circumstances are they appropriate?
- What are the principal challenges in forming, maintaining, and terminating alliances, and how can they best be tackled?
- How can the firm leverage benefit from alliances?
- How can the firm avoid the downsides of alliancing?
- How should the firm organize its alliance activities?
- How do international alliances differ from purely domestic alliance?

Unless the new knowledge gained through alliancing can be turned quickly to commercial advantage, the efforts will not be really beneficial. This is one of the big challenges facing the twenty-first century firm.

Partnerships and alliances

It would be difficult to find a firm that has an R&D capability which does not operate in partnership with other organizations in order to meet its innovation needs. The extent to which R&D partnerships exist is unknown, but figures available suggest a vast increase in their numbers even over the last ten years. This applies to firms of all sizes, although more so the larger the company. It has been estimated that firms such as Philips, Siemens, and Olivetti have managed hundreds of alliances simultaneously. But not only are the numbers of partnerships increasing, so is the proportion of R&D budgets spent on such ventures. This is despite what appear disappointing results from partnerships, with many failing to meet the original expectations. However, these results may well be no lower than the success rates achieved by internal R&D. But the failures are more visible than those within a single organization and they can be high in terms of opportunity costs—the rejected potential partners may not want to enter into later deals, the management time of extrication is high, and failure impacts on the firm's reputation with potential alliance partners.

Sony's partnership with suppliers

Today's business environment is constantly changing. To succeed in this shifting environment, Sony needs to build strong links with suppliers. It is important that Sony and its suppliers share policies, strategies, and technology. By working together, Sony and its suppliers can achieve higher goals and generate greater value for the future than would be possible alone.

Collaboration between Sony and its suppliers should ultimately be aimed at earning customer approval. This goal must form the common base of Sony procurement activities and its suppliers' sales activities. Sony calls suppliers capable of maintaining this kind of collaborative relationship "partners."

One of Sony's key goals is to give its worldwide customers satisfaction through its products. Sony must therefore constantly strive to develop products that are ever more innovative and captivating. The creation of these kinds of product relies to a great extent on the parts and materials used in them to realize its functions and performance.

Sony believes that cooperation as true partners is critical to supplying products that achieve high levels of customer satisfaction. Sony and its suppliers work together in a wide range of areas—by combining technological skills that complement each other, building powerful supply chains, preserving and enhancing the quality of parts, strictly complying with relevant laws and regulations, and contributing to society as a whole.

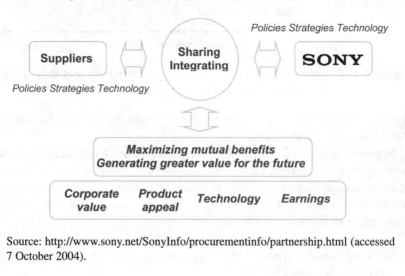

Source: http://www.sony.net/SonyInfo/procurementinfo/partnership.html (accessed 7 October 2004).

The search for market reach, technological complementarity, and the reduction of innovation timespan are driving cooperative efforts. Various forms of R&D cooperation are evident (de Laat 2001) including joint ventures, research cooperations, joint R&D, technology exchange, minority investments, customer–supplier relations, and uni-directional technology transfers (licensing and second sourcing). These are illustrated in Figure 8.1, where we show how the demands on the firm's secondary capabilities increase as greater impact on the organization is sought through different forms of alliancing.

The degree to which there is mutual interaction between the partners will vary considerably between the different forms of cooperation. Technology transfer and exchange may well be a straightforward market transaction,

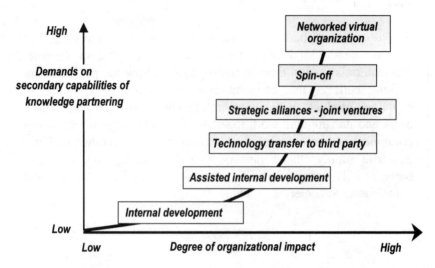

Figure 8.1 Different approaches to knowledge partnering and their impact on the organization and its secondary capabilities

whereas other forms (joint ventures, R&D alliances) will involve intense interactions and cooperation.

In general terms, a strategic alliance is a close, long-term, mutually beneficial agreement between two or more partners in which resources, knowledge, and capabilities are shared with the objective of enhancing the competitive position of both partners (Spekman et al 1998). In practice there are three basic forms of alliance:

- the joint venture where a new legal entity is established with joint ownership by partners
- an equity alliance where there is no new entity but a unilateral or bilateral equity holding between partners
- a non-equity alliance where there is no new entity nor equity exchange.

Reid, Bussiere, and Greenaway (2001) have a strong view about the role of alliances:

> the growing emergence of knowledge as a source of competitive advantage suggests that the rationale, formation rate, nature and structure of collaborative exchange are undergoing momentous change. The emergence of knowledge-based enterprises should portend an increase in alliance incidence. But also ... should firmly position strategic alliances as the optimal vehicle facilitating the exchange and recombination of knowledge-based assets.

GlaxoSmithKline research partnership philosophy

At GlaxoSmithKline, developing professional partnerships with others in industry, academe and government is fundamental to the way we conduct our business. We seek organisations engaging in breakthrough work to create new medicines, and we approach our collaborations with creativity and flexibility. We view partnership as an active alliance.

We bring to these collaborations an extensive history of successful partnership and the focused effort of an organisation committed to the highest quality science. Our collaborative research programs are driven by scientific curiosity and are characterised by shared input from each party.

We are committed to partnering with academic institutions. We have developed more than 800 early discovery research collaborations with colleges and universities around the globe, and we fund research for hundreds of masters-level, doctoral and fellowship students each year.

Our experience, expertise and enthusiasm for collaboration offers our partners the chance to fully realize their goals while allowing GSK to pursue its mission of helping people do more, feel better and live longer.

Source: http://science.gsk.com/about/partnership.htm, accessed 7 October 2004.

High-technology projects managed through alliances are full of uncertainties, not only in developing technologies but also in their combination and integration into products and services, putting in place production and operations, taking these products and services to market, market acceptance, and the actions of competitors. The key dimensions of successful alliances (and their implications for management) are:

- complementarity (such as avoidance of excessive redundancy)
- compatibility (for example in the infrastructure for communications)
- fit (such as in culture).

Despite good intensions at the outset, these projects are often medium to long term, and the strategic objectives of the collaborators may well change over the period of the project. This may result in one partner reprioritizing the technologies developed as part of the collaboration, and possibly even losing interest in the field. Even where the technology development is going well, the collaborator might make other strategic choices which impact on its ability to fulfil its initial intentions, and become unable to provide previously committed services.

Given this level of challenge in getting alliances to succeed in the short and long term, why would firms enter into such arrangements? The traditional approach of arms'-length contracts generally does not provide enough incentive for firms to enter into the deep collaborative relationships being sought (Gomes-Casseres 2003). The alternative of merger or acquisition may well not prove to be in the interests of the parties because of its inherent risks and costs. Also alliances often involve units from multiple partners, so an alliance in one of the many forms is the only feasible model.

The early choices made by firms in relation to the form of the alliance will have a marked impact on the future course of the collaboration. Many factors need to be considered in choosing the form of collaborative arrangements and setting them in place. These include the compatibility of the organizations and their strategic intentions, the commitments made by each partner, the quality of resources put into the collaboration, the degree of independence afforded to the venture and the means for avoiding direct competition with the partner organizations, the ownership of intellectual property, and the sanctions available for non-conformance. It is not unusual for initial cost forecasts to be wide of the mark, and one or more partners then may be either unwilling or not in a position to contribute further. Due diligence investigation following on from the initial negotiations can avoid problems later. But it is unlikely that the due diligence process will consider one particularly important factor, the cultural fit between partners. Nor is it likely to consider any differences in the business principles espoused by each partner and their compatibility, which includes ethical conditions.

No contract is precise enough to define all aspects of a developing relationship. Gomes-Casseres (2003) describes alliances as based on an "incomplete contract"—a phrase he borrows from the economics of law, as an agreement in which the terms cannot be completely specified and agreed at the outset. Where technology development is involved there will clearly be many aspects not specified within the contractual arrangements. Where the parties enter into agreements with a positive approach to resolving issues, these arrangements can be workable. But where a partner is either predisposed to mistrust others, or through concerns about the behaviours of the other parties feels unfairly treated, there will be a tendency towards lowered commitments, and then the possibility of the eventual breakdown of relations.

Three key principles for effective alliances

1 Define the purpose. Included in this should be specific metrics to track progress
2 Establish a formal alliance management process:
  - Map out the alliance based on the firm's strategic plans.
  - Identify and select partners—start with finance, strategy, assets, and capabilities, then move on to cultural fit and personal rapport.
  - Define the rules of engagement—how will the alliance be governed and how will it operate?
  - Establish metrics for success and a process for review—both at the firm level and for the partnership.
  - Have a clear exit strategy as part of the initial agreement.
3 Nurture the evolution of the alliance actively and deliberately:
  - Carry out regular joint reviews.
  - Ensure effective communications.
  - Involve multiple levels of management in the relationship.

Source: based on Kaplan and Hurd (2002).

Key questions

- What are the firm's current strategic objectives in partnering?
- How does the process operate for formulating and revising strategy on alliancing?
- Where are guidelines available within the organization to assist in partnership formation?
- How does the organization capture and share its learning from prior experiences in partnering?

In bringing together staff from two or more organizations into a joint venture or other collaborative arrangement, there is always the possibility that the participating organizations will reserve their highest-calibre staff for their own operation. This is more likely when one or other party keeps a research interest in the field of the joint activity. One way around this is to make new appointments to the venture rather than assign staff from the partnering organizations. This has its own risks and limitations. One in particular is the reduced likelihood of the parent learning from the venture, as the staff involved are not networked into the parent company. However, it is this very leakage into the parent which may be seen by other partners as opportunistic behaviour, taking unfair advantage of the joint activities.

Collaborations take up the time and attention of executives and managers in the partnering organizations as well as the joint activity. A joint venture can be particularly time-consuming. Not only will it have a board, normally comprising the partners in proportion to their involvement in, and financial commitment to, the venture, but it will also involve internal meetings between the executives of partner companies to oversee the venture. One reason in practice for the failure of ventures is under-management of the venture. Much attention is paid at the set-up stage but once it is up and running, the sponsoring companies pay little attention to the adequacy of management systems and the maintenance of the venture (de Laat 2001).

In contrast to joint ventures for new product or service delivery, joint R&D and research corporations are created to generate research results, not to jointly commercialize the results. Ideally, this research is either pre-competitive or leading to incorporation into non-competing product offerings from the partners, or if there are similar products, they should be in clearly differentiated markets. If the partners will be in direct competition, the management of the collaboration is more likely to be problematic. But the benefits of establishing a common standard, or of arriving at the market ahead of other competitors, may make this collaboration worthwhile (de Laat 2001). If there is the likelihood of direct competition, there is the possibility by staff of any of the partners of non-disclosure of relevant knowledge of technology advances to the parent.

Innovation at Telenor

Mobile telecom operators are forced to find new ways of revenue generation as the penetration of mobile phones increases. Cost reduction is not enough to sustain revenue growth. Telenor has sought to:

- develop new products and business models
- introduce new methods and culture
- accelerate learning across borders
- utilize networks and alliances.

Despite difficulties in generating revenues from data services, Telenor has worked on its own service, Content Provider Access (CPA), to develop messaging-based services. This is being expanded into e-commerce services based on electronic purse and PKI. To do this it is cooperating in development and service provision with a range of partners including suppliers, content providers, customers, and competitors.

Ease of use of the network by providers is seen as the key to future business development. To aid this Telenor is pushing for standards.

The culture changes to achieve more cooperation across the organization, greater flexibility, and innovative project-based working, are reflected in its new HQ building to house its 6000 staff. It is believed to be the largest fully mobile office complex in the world.

Given the converging market opportunities in their different business lines, the transfer of knowledge, technology, and functionality across the cooperating companies is imperative. Telenor is building its organizational structure to promote benchmarking best practices, information sharing, and intra-group improvement processes. It is building excellence in networking with other companies and organizations through such means as partnerships working on EU-funded projects. Bringing the results of R&D to actual revenue-generating business is a key challenge.

Source: Oddvar Hesjedal, executive vice president, Telenor Research and Development, Norway.

The sharing of tacit knowledge between partner firms enables recombination in ways which can lead to competitive advantage for the alliance, and is in many ways the rationale behind such endeavors. But beyond the knowledge sharing intended at the outset of the venture, there will always be leakage of knowledge in joint activities. So long as all partners feel that they are benefiting this will be tolerated. But if one or more partners feel that the others are gaining unfair advantage, there will be strained relations. The success of these ventures does, to a large extent, depend upon trust between partners. No formal contract, as indicated earlier, can cover all eventualities, and overall there need to be good working relationships at the operational level in order to achieve the end goal, and a degree of trust at executive level.

One way of reducing the leakage is to locate the joint activity on a neutral site some way from any partner premises. Good briefing in expected behaviour of the personnel involved is also clearly desirable. Channeling contacts with the parent organization can also minimize unwanted knowledge transfer. But as pointed out by Nonaka and Takeuchi (1995), the goal is not to limit information overlap, but rather to create a rich environment of diverse information, where the conscious overlap of knowledge activities and management responsibilities creates the conditions for serendipitous combination.

Strategic innovation partnering with Team Alinghi

Team Alinghi, the Swiss team that won the prestigious America's Cup yachting race in 2003, brings together sailors, boat builders, and scientists—close to 100 people who are among the finest specialists in their respective fields. The members of the Alinghi sailing team alone have taken part 47 times in the America's Cup, with 18 victories, and they have also won 67 world championship titles between them.

Alinghi has a single goal, according to Grant Simmer, its chief technical designer. At the end of the day, everything comes down to "winning that race." The traditional product development and innovation paradigm beset by slipping deadlines and delayed market introductions have no place in Simmer's performance-driven world. Alinghi must "come to market extremely quickly." The date of the race sets the pace for innovation, and there is absolutely no room for compromise or negotiation on delivery time. The stakes are high. Alinghi consistently prepares to take high risks for what amount to relatively modest gains in racing time. But that's perfectly acceptable in a world in which even a few seconds' advantage is often all that is needed to win the race.

According to Simmer, the Alinghi design team's position is clearly established at the cutting edge of knowledge when it comes down to designing and building world-class, winning racing yachts. Also scoring high in Alinghi's secret of success, however, is its ability to manage an innovation network consisting of other world-class boat builders and technology providers.

Alinghi has established a very successful collaborative relationship with the Swiss-based Décision SA boatyard and the Lausanne-based Swiss Federal Institute of Technology (EPFL). Décision SA has built two of Alinghi's racing yachts in the recent past. The firm specializes in integrating the newest research into composite materials in its boats. In periods of intense innovation, such as in the period preceding a major race, the boatyard in essence becomes a part of the extended Alinghi team.

The EPFL fulfills a slightly different role in the Alinghi co-innovation network; it provides Alinghi with a window on new technological innovation. Currently, the partnership is focused on three dimensions: optimization of composite materials and their processing, advanced numerical flow simulation, and innovative measurement systems. Alinghi specifies and defines research projects which are allocated to respective EPFL research teams.

For Team Alinghi, strategic partnering has paid off handsomely. After all, success has meant bringing the America's Cup trophy back to Europe for the first time in over 150 years. For a team that calls tiny, landlocked Switzerland its home, that is quite an accomplishment.

Source: Odenthal et al (2004).

The uncertainties of technology development make it particularly difficult to formulate precise contracts. Another reason that contracts may be problematic is that the partners may not wish at the start of the relationship to disclose in detail proprietary information on the technologies that they are contributing to the venture. If parties later feel aggrieved, to seek redress in law is usually unsatisfactory—it is time-consuming, costly, and does not have any guarantee of success. Arbitration may be a more effective way of solving disputes than use of the legal process.

However at the outset where technology is being developed it should be clear what intellectual property rights partners will have, and how they will be guaranteed access to the technology if a joint-venture company holds any jointly developed intellectual property (IP). Non-disclosure agreements are also important. These should be put in place before due diligence is undertaken, as part of the initial negotiations

The partners to any agreement are likely to bring different capabilities to the alliance. But since they are different, it is likely that there will be quite different perceptions of their value, and even the means for valuation. For alliances to survive, there has to be a perception over the longer term of equity in the benefits derived (Spekman et al 1998).

Not all agreements between partners are with the intention of knowledge internalization (Reid, Bussiere, and Greenaway 2001). Firms might be seeking access to knowledge which is embedded in a component or product for subsequent integration into their own product or service. They may have no real interest in acquiring specific knowledge about the technical aspects of the firm's offer, but only be seeking assistance in integration where problems arise. But they may seek a long-term commitment to product development from the supplier.

Key questions

- Is there a clear policy in relation to alliances, who is the "owner," and how often is it reviewed?
- Is there a register of management experienced in working in alliances, and what training and development is given to managers in preparation for partnership management?
- Where is the organization's expertise in negotiating and contracting for alliances?
- Where is the organization's expertise in valuing partner contributions to alliances?
- Does the organization have a culture suited to support its intended partnership working?

The larger the number of partners, the more difficult partnerships are likely to be to manage. It is always going to be more difficult to police the behaviors of partners, the more there are. Also where the number of potential partners is small, firms will have less opportunity to switch, and so will have greater incentive to find ways of accommodating differences.

If the partnership is a "one-off" there is less to restrain staff from behaving in ways that are an abuse of the intent of the agreement. Reputation is important in determining future partnerships, and given the dependence on such arrangements common to most companies, this is an incentive not to behave unethically. As the venture progresses, the partners will be committing to further investment, in for example production facilities. Such "advance commitment" means the partner becomes more tied into the venture and will have greater difficulty withdrawing (de Laat 2001).

When the success of the alliance depends on the exchange of knowledge, some consider that equity-sharing governance arrangements are to be preferred because they incentivize all parties to bring the relevant knowledge to the table (Dyer, Kale, and Singh 2001). There is greater incentive to make the arrangement work.

In addition to the advance commitment of resources, such as manufacturing facilities, as the venture progresses there is inevitably greater sharing of proprietary knowledge. Again, this is a factor that increases the cost of withdrawal. A "phased commitment" to share proprietary knowledge may be appropriate as a way of developing confidence in the commitment to the other parties.

The degree of interdependency, and in consequence the need for cooperative effort, will very much depend on the nature of the relationships put in place at the outset. For example in joint R&D the partners may co-develop the technology, sharing effort equally on all components. Alternatively the work may be divided into independent modules which are subsequently brought together. In the latter, failure to meet commitments will be apparent, and in the event of failure of the venture, each partner has its own development work to show for the effort. However in the case of the former, mutual commitment is much stronger, and breaking up of the partnership more problematic. Hence partners are more likely to work hard at maintaining relationships. Success is also more dependent upon cultural fit between partners.

It is the informal relationships that make alliances work. This is the case with organizations in general, but it probably more so with alliances and partnerships. Formal agreements provide a frame of reference, but it is the informal interfaces that make for progress (Spekman et al 1998). It is unclear just how much dependence alliances have on personal commitment and trust to ensure their functioning, and how much on legal agreements. Joint sharing of responsibility can be a source of tension for managers, who in the main would probably prefer independence in decisions. Certainly uncertainties generated by a lack of clarity of roles can be damaging to relationships, but this is likely to be an unavoidable state in alliances.

A process view of alliance management is advocated by Spekman et al (1998), which is seen to come out of a focus on the lifecycle of the alliance.

Table 8.1 An example of an assessment of capabilities to make a strategy of the acquisition of technology companies a success[1]

Knowledge acquisition trajectory	Organization culture, values, norms	People-embodied knowledge & skill sets	Managerial systems	Technical, physical systems
1. Knowledge sourcing				
Examples of secondary capabilities: • Organizational capabilities • Environmental intelligence • Knowledge scouting capabilities • ...and others	Collective aspirations Curiosity Team culture Risk taking	Analytical skills Technology Expertise Integration of disparate bits	Systematic proceeses Visioning Networking Timing	...
2. Knowledge integration				
Examples of secondary capabilities: • Technology integration • Transitioning • Common platform creation • ...and other	Openness to new opportunities Embracing culture	Multidisciplinary Innovative problem solving	Decisiveness Responsiveness Managing across multiple interfaces	Establishing common platforms "Docking to the mother ship"
3. Knowledge assimilation				
Examples of secondary capabilities: • Grafting new capabilities on to existing capabilities • Impedance matching • Performance metrics • ... and others	Change readiness Entrepreneurial skills High motivation	Knowledge sharing Absorption of new ideas through interaction and learning	Motivation & retention of staff Optimization of new capability deployment	...

"SOFT" ← → "HARD"

Each stage, while actually rather blurred at the edges, requires a different style of management. Spekman et al advocate an examination of the interplay of activities, people, and processes. In their six stages—anticipating, engaging, valuing, coordinating, investing, and stabilizing—they also propose that both the business lifecycle and the interpersonal lifecycle should be studied. Such a perspective will influence the people specification and the appointment of managers and other key players. The form of organization is likely to be very different from the more hierarchical and bureaucratic organization from which the alliance emerged, and Spekman et al suggest that as a result, the alliance manager needs to have a different mindset from functional or business unit management.

It is recognized that alliance evolution takes time, as the partners adjust to the assumptions of risks with the accumulation of trust, positive results, and relational quality (Arino, de la Torre, and Ring 1998). The greater the complexity of the alliance, the greater are the trust levels needed to make it work effectively. Trust accumulation is subject to time compression diseconomies (Garcia-Canal et al 2002), since there are limits to how quickly an alliance can develop. This leads to the suggestion that firms should initially start with a simple alliance so as to test out partners, prior to a more complex endeavour. But often alliances are undertaken to speed up the desired developments and against the background of competitive actions.

Garcia-Canal et al identify three stages of trust development. First is *psychological trust* between the managers involved in the early stages of foundation of the alliance, based on cognitive and emotional factors, their interpersonal relations, and their perceptions of the attitudes of counterparts. Second, based on the history of ongoing interactions between a wider group from the partner organizations, a level of *social trust* emerges. *Relationship capital* is a term used to describe the quality of relationships between social actors in the alliance, and it consists of the socio-psychological aspects of the alliance. Later, as the alliance starts to produce results, *institutional trust* develops, which is more based on the trustworthiness of the firms involved. While it is generally assumed that trust aids relationships and the

Note to Table 8.1

1 This case is based on Cisco, which has a team dedicated to making sure that acquisitions get quickly integrated into the parent organization. By taking an early investment in companies with technologies that have the possibility of becoming vital to Cisco's future, it can later gain control if the technologies emerge as being significant. In one year alone it digested 21 companies so as to reshape itself or plug holes in its product offering. Chambers, the CEO, recognized at an early stage that Cisco could not go it alone and keep up with advances in technology (Thurm 2000). Hence capability in acquisition and integration is vital.

functioning of alliances, it can have the downside of reducing the effectiveness of negotiators if they are too closely involved with those with
whom they are negotiating (Jeffries 2000).

From one case of a global alliance, Garcia-Canal et al (2002) suggest that
the accumulation of trust in the alliance can be accelerated by consensus
amongst executives on how best to share resources, abilities, and knowledge: the routines to be put in place, and a governance structure that allows
the proper development of relational rents (such as equity exchanges), the
creation of a supervisory committee, and ad hoc groups. The case they
explore is relatively simple as it only involves two partners, but the
outcomes would appear relevant to a larger partnership. The development of
a cross-border alliance presents more difficulties in trust development than
one within a single culture.

Another study looking at international strategic alliances is reported
by Cullen, Johnson, and Sakano (2000), based on a study of more than
70 experiences of Japanese international alliances. They stress the
need for non-Japanese managers to understand that their behaviours
and interactions serve as trust or commitment signals. They need to
consider how to signal the deeper, more emotional levels of trust and
commitment, and when to de-emphasize the more calculative commitment and a focus on monitoring mechanisms, such as contracts and
reports. Further, partners are advised to gradually reveal short and
long-term goals for the alliance in line with their partners' declara-
tions, as this is an important element in the trust-building process.
Training in cross-cultural behaviors is also recommended.

Reid et al (2001) see alliances in knowledge-based enterprises very
much from a learning perspective. They suggest two forms of performance measurement: counts of knowledge-based outputs, and longevity.
The former is represented in outputs such as patents, new products, and
new technologies. But longevity is also considered important based on an
assumption, supported by empirical evidence, that the potential for useful
outputs increases over time.

If rapid learning is one of the key benefits of alliances, it is imperative
that any evaluation methodology reflects this aspect of the relationship,
but patent count may not be appropriate, as many organizations do not
seek to patent. However care is needed in the choice of measures for
assessing alliance effectiveness. As pointed out by Inkpen (1997), measures can aid or impair knowledge creation. Certainly a lack of financial
performance cannot be directly related to a lack of learning, so a broader
set of measures would seem appropriate, tailored to the specific objectives
sought from the alliance.

Firms are well advised to include termination clauses in agreements, and also to identify and remain aware of alternative arrangements and alternative partners. Termination may be by mutual consent, following a breach of the agreement, the result of change in control of a partner, or failure to achieve milestones. The agreement should cover issues in relation to any licenses, technologies developed, assignment of data and regulatory filings/approvals, financial obligations, and survival of key provisions such as confidentiality and product liability indemnification.

Many of the areas already covered might be seen as risk factors within any alliance. Consideration of alliance risks should include both the *performance risk* and *relational risk* (Das and Teng 1999). Risk factors can be classified as those that affect alliance performance, and those that relate to the risk of unsatisfactory inter-firm cooperation (the relational risks).

Performance risk is present in any commercial venture, but relational risk is peculiar to forms such as alliances. For the purposes of risk assessment it is useful to classify resources as either property or knowledge. Resources are properties when there are clear property rights and the firm's ownership is absolute and protected by law. Knowledge, on the other hand, relies for its protection on other means (for example, it often is tacit and so not easily imitated).

Das and Teng (1999) identify four strategic orientations for managing risk:

- **A control orientation**, which usually relies on one or more of contractual control, equity control (a major shareholding), and managerial control (the firm's management in key positions).
- **A flexibility orientation,** with the emphasis on performance risk, where the alliance is free from rigid engagement (licensing, funded research, shared distribution) and long-term agreements. It has minimized sunk costs, is adaptable to the new situation, and able to recover investment should the alliance fail, because of clear exit provisions at the outset.
- **A security orientation,** which is likely where the contributions are mostly in the form of tacit knowledge, as firms are concerned about relational risk in terms of the loss of power through the transfer to other partners of the knowledge. In seeking security, firms might choose looser links than joint ventures, where knowledge is compartmentalized and flows restricted as far as practical. This should be made explicit from the outset.
- **A productivity orientation** applies where the major risk relates to high performance based on the combination of the knowledge of partners. In

order to minimize the risks of failure the partners need to focus on the productivity of knowledge and how they can effectively work jointly in its exploitation. Rapid learning is imperative, and means for improving absorptive capacity should be sought.

Each stage of alliance management will have its own risks—partner selection; structuring the alliance; operating the alliance; evaluating performance:

> Risks relate essentially to balancing the competing demands in each stage such as the demand for flexibility and the demand for rigidity, The risk is in ignoring any one of these opposing demands. The difficult task of managing risks at each stage of the alliance can be carried out only if managers first understand the complex nature of these risks.
>
> (Das and Teng 1999)

Key questions

- Does the organization map capabilities needs against partnership strengths in order to develop strategies for partnership formation and termination?
- Does the alliance strategy coverage match the organization's reach (for example in geographical spread, markets, technologies)?
- In what way does the organization review partnerships and how effective is the process?
- Does the organization have the capability to revive failing partnerships and make effective use of them?

Alliance, constellation, and networks

With the growth in alliances as indicted earlier, many companies now have tens if not hundreds of alliances. To treat each separately would result in less gain than is potentially available from treating them as a portfolio. Going beyond that, one might see them as a network in that each alliance partner is likely to be involved in multiple other alliances. This network can give access to wider resources than would be available otherwise to any one company. So rather than seeing alliances as separate, they can be viewed as an alliance network.

Das and Teng (1999) distinguish between *alliance networks* and *constellations*. While the network is a collection of alliances in which the firm participates without there being any formal agreement across the network, a constellation is a strategic alliance involving more than two firms. The relationships are then with all parties rather than on a one-to-one basis. Many constellations involve alliance partners spread geographically as well as across traditional industry boundaries.

Gomes-Casseres (2003) goes beyond this earlier definition by describing a constellation as a set of firms linked together through alliances and competing in a particular competitive domain. So he sees a common interest as tying the constellation together. In addition to the widely held view of the benefits of alliances, Gomes-Casseres adds "hedging bets and creating options for future actions" as a typical goal. These constellations in his view go beyond the alliance portfolio of a business unit or company to include a shared utility serving various clients, co-production, R&D consortia, a co-marketing network or franchising system, and a committee to set standards. The constellation is governed by a system of alliances rather than by full organizational integration through ownership.

Given the rapid increase in the extent of alliancing and the increasing dependence of firms on such arrangements to further their innovation strategy, it is imperative that those involved develop the firm's capability in managing these ventures, whatever their form. Reid et al (2001) point out that knowledge about the collaborative process develops over time, and is known to affect the outcomes of collaborative exchanges. But the firm can go beyond this more passive stance and accelerate the development of capability by instigating a deliberate strategy, including the creation of dedicated resources, knowledge management efforts, personnel training and development. Going further, Reid et al (2001) identified five capabilities which in their view matter most:

- the ability to develop and sustain valuable resources
- absorptive capacity
- combinative capability
- experience with alliances
- appropriate design for knowledge exchange.

Certainly to take advantage of alliance constellations this body of knowledge and expertise is essential.

How to make strategic alliances work: forming a dedicated alliance function

Make it responsible for:

- Knowledge management efforts as a focal point for capturing lessons learnt throughout the alliance lifecycle and ensuring their future application. This can include guidelines, templates, specifications, checklists, and evaluation forms. Also mapping existing and potential alliances can inform strategy; preparing formats for due diligence and cultural assessments; training programs to help capture and exchange tacit knowledge.
- Ensuring external visibility to enhance the firm's reputation as an organization with which to do business through alliancing and to provide an external interface for enquiries.
- Internal coordination, gaining the all-important access to internal resources for alliances by providing links across the organization as well as to higher authority when resources are not forthcoming. Also the alliance function can keep alliance partners appraised of strategic developments in the parent organization, and help the avoidance of internal competition within the parent through ignorance of the role of the alliance.
- The elimination of accountability and intervention problems by instigating the setting of standard metrics and a process of regular alliance evaluation and action where appropriate. The alliance function can also reconcile differences where they are becoming apparent.

Organize it such that it:

- has a logical fit with the organization and the nature of its principal alliances: for example by business unit, by geography, by technologies, by functions
- facilitates the exchange of information, including topic information
- is located at the appropriate level in the organization, which should provide access to strategy formulation in relation to alliancing.

Source: based on Dyer, Kale, and Singh (2001).

To view alliances as constellations is to take a more strategic perspective on their potential impact on the competitiveness of the business. But to take advantage of the constellation, the capabilities needed for success should be defined. This then enables the identification of gaps and redundancies. For its creation and ongoing existence the constellation requires a "unifying force" in the form of leadership, shared business strategies of common motivations, and a lack of internal competition. Another consideration for the firm is the alliance activity of competitors—with what purpose, with whom, and with what shared capabilities. The ideal position for the firm in a constellation is the control over key scarce resources essential to the constellation. This gives the firm considerable bargaining power relative to those whose capabilities are more readily available from other firms. Another important factor in success is the reputation of partners and the degree of "lock-out" of competitors.

Key questions

- Has the organization developed a centralized service to manage partnerships, and if so, how effective is it?
- Has the organization started to consider alliances as constellations and networks rather than individual projects or programs?
- In what way does the firm measure its relational capital and its power and influence over its strategic alliances?
- How does the firm monitor its reputation as an alliance partner, and is the methodology adequate?
- How does the firm benchmark its partnership working, and how does it use the information obtained?

Concluding remarks

Partnerships and alliances are a vital component of the modern organization. It is clear that many drivers are pushing firms in the direction of increased working in these modes. This extends throughout the innovation process, from idea generation to market launch and support. It applies to innovation whether it is institutional, evolutional, or revolutional. So it has become essential that executive management have a good understanding of the capability requirements of these forms of working. This gives them the opportunity to more effectively plan and resource such ventures.

We have identified a range of possible inter-firm relationships, and identified the potential impact on organizational functioning as well as the potential for knowledge generation. We have also identified many of important features in making partnerships and alliances a success. We have also seen that alliance activity ideally needs organizing. An important aspect demonstrated by the Cisco case is the need to learn from experiences and develop deep capabilities in profiting from alliances that are strategically seen as important in whatever form.

Finally Table 8.2 provides a framework and summary of key capabilities.

Table 8.2 The key capabilities needed for successful partnership building and alliance working

	Institutional, evolutional, and revolutional innovation whether in partnership, alliances, or other forms of collaborative inter-firm working
People-embodied knowledge and skills	Integrative capabilities Relationship building Sharing ideas and knowledge Cultural sensitivity Openness and capacity to learn from other companies and their staff
Management systems/organizational structures	Systems for partner selection Operational systems for the management of partnerships and alliances Management of staff in temporary organizations Consensus building Stakeholder management Management of diversity Political sensitivity Executive systems for review and control of the firm's partnerships and alliances Intellectual property management
Physical and technical systems	Systems for the rapid transfer of new knowledge acquired through partnership working—collection, dissemination, enhancement, and integration Systems for managing partnerships and alliances Integration of systems with main information system of the firm
Cultural values and norms	Tolerance for other cultures No sense of "a not invented here" attitude Sharing and cooperation are desired attributes "Give and take" Security conscious

CHAPTER 9

Creating organizations and networks to support innovation

Introduction

It is widely recognized that successful entrepreneurs and intrapreneurs demonstrate their strength in networking and using their network to gain business advantage. In networking one of their key strengths is an ability to form relationships with people of diverse backgrounds and a wide range of capabilities. They then exhibit great skill in using these networks to help solve the challenging problems they face in developing sustainable businesses. But more than this, entrepreneurs and intrapreneurs often need to form strong relationships with companies in the form of alliances and partnerships in order to achieve their ends. Clusters, based on common interests such as a shared commercial sector, seem to offer a more formalized grouping than do networks, and they offer certain attractions to the innovative firm. Entrepreneurs exhibit skills, not only in identifying the need to engage other individuals and businesses in appropriate forums, but also in exploiting these relationships at the appropriate time. Within any innovation team there is the need for strong networking skills, and recognition of the need to spend time fostering, maintaining, and capitalizing on networks.

In this chapter we examine both outputs from research and practice so as to answer some key questions about engaging with other businesses for innovation leadership:

- Is the firm well enough networked to achieve its strategic goals?
- Is the firm doing enough to develop network capabilities in support of its innovation efforts?
- In what ways is the firm leveraging the benefits?
- How well does the networking contribute to the innovation portfolio?
- Is the firm investing enough in future networks?

Networks and clusters: new ways of organizing

We all operate within networks of relationships, as do the organizations within which, or for which, we work. But there is a considerable difference between the networking of individuals and that of firms. In both cases the relationships formed can range from the casual and informal to the organized and contractual. At the informal end of the spectrum, relationships are based on personal contacts, whether or not the individual represents an employing organization. As the network becomes more formalized it may well be more based around organizational representation rather than individual membership or association. However, organizations such as professional associations provide services to individuals, and have constitutions and governance procedures, as well as clear rules for membership under their constitution.

There are many forms of business relationships, and definitions are not consistent amongst researchers, policy makers, and business leaders. According to Chen and Chang (2004), a business network encompasses the set of relationships of a firm—both horizontal and vertical, including strategic alliances, joint ventures, long-term buyer–supplier partnerships, and similarly collaborative relationships. Ebers (2001) points out that inter-firm networking "is characterised by recurring exchanges relationships among a limited number of firms that retain residual control of their individual resources yet periodically jointly decide over their use." The OECD (2004) goes beyond this all-embracing notion to define networks as "an organisational form of economic activities that may allow firms to cope with market failures that hierarchy (i.e. internalisation of transactions through acquisitions, mergers, etc) cannot correct."

Huggins (2000) suggests that two or more companies are bound together through some form of sustained interaction within which there is necessarily a degree of commonality. Jones, Hesterly, and Borgatti (1997) go even further in suggesting that inter-firm networks are "a select, persistent and structured set of autonomous firms engaged in creating products or services based on implicit and open-ended contracts to adapt to environmental contingencies and to co-ordinate and safeguard exchanges. These contracts are socially, not-legally, binding." Huggins does not always see the relationships as governed by contracts—some have a "dotted-line agreement." They may take the form of "hard" networks involving firms joining together to co-produce, co-market, co-purchase, co-operate in product, service or market development. Or they may be "soft" in that they seek to jointly solve problems, share information, or acquire new skills.

According to Oliver (2000), the main reasons for firms to establish inter-organizational relationships are:

- when mandated by higher authorities through law or regulations
- asymmetry, allowing one party to exercise power or control over the other
- reciprocity, when common or mutually beneficial goals can be achieved
- efficiency, when higher input/output ratios can be achieved
- stability, where they can rather better face the challenge of uncertainty
- legitimacy, where reputation is established or enhanced.

This contrasts somewhat with the results obtained from empirical work in the UK, where Glaister and Buckley (1996) reported the main factors as technology development, market power, market development, resource specialization, and large project size. In the case of industries subject to rapid technological change, "because advanced technological systems are not and cannot be created in isolation, innovating organizations must form horizontal and vertical alliances" (Ebers, 2001).

These networks are believed to exert a strong influence on the development of member firms. According to Simsek, Lubatkin, and Floyd (2003), studies in entrepreneurially intensive industries (such as biotechnology, fashion, film, financial services, and semiconductors) have highlighted the pervasiveness of networks. These authors point out that the behavior of firms is "embedded" in ongoing systems of inter-firm relationships. The network creates opportunities but at the same time causes constraints.

The combining of complementary resources is one of the most important reasons for forming business networks, and these resources can be either *mutually specific* or *co-specialized* (Chen and Chang 2004). Co-specialized resources will be further developed to meet the changing needs of the network's customer base. Over time firms in the network will tend to consolidate their co-specialized resources. Being increasingly recognized for having these specialist resources enhances the position of the firm within the network, and leads to new opportunities, since it is easier for partners to do business with this firm than look outside for alternatives; the transaction costs are significantly less.

There is much interest among policy makers and researchers in the role of clusters in improving industry effectiveness. *Clusters* is a term used to describe groups of firms that are specialized within a few related industrial activities while benefiting from co-localization in a geographical sense (Lorenzen 2002). The OECD (2004) views this geographic concentration of business activity as resulting in agglomeration economies, a more efficient division of labour amongst firms, offering the possibility of scale economies. The linkage between the firms is an important aspect of the cluster: "production processes are closely linked through the exchange of goods, services and/or knowledge, in particular the informal exchange of information, knowledge and creative ideas" (the untraded interdependencies) (Huggins 2000).

Porter (1990) defines regional clusters as "geographically proximate groups of interconnected companies and associated institutions in a particular field, linked by commonalities and complementarities." He sees regional clusters of firms as a generator of unique competitive skills that can be maintained by these firms for an extended period of time across global markets. He further suggests that firms with a common geographical background share certain knowledge resources which provide competitive advantage. He identifies four conditions as a prerequisite for successful cluster development:

- factor conditions (the quality of labour, capital and knowledge available)
- demand conditions (scale and quality of the home market)
- supplier industries (globally competitive suppliers, specialist services)
- business strategy (rivalry between local firms, but also a willingness to cooperate in research, sales and marketing).

In particular the combination of cooperation and competition is vital. Too much competition can be destructive, but on the other hand too much cooperation can lead to cartels. Firms are likely to seek a balance of long-term and dedicated supplier relationships, with a portfolio of shorter-term and flexible relationships (Lorenzen 2002). A strong cluster may well have the effect of attracting highly qualified customers to the locality, something which in turn will aid innovation.

There are numerous examples of successful clusters in industries as diverse as biotechnology, textile manufacture, racing car production, and IT. Various disciplines have been used to study clusters and their effects.

An OECD report (2004) describes the different backgrounds to networks and clusters. Clusters are an outcome of market forces, and often include competition between co-located businesses as well as, at times, simultaneous cooperation. On the other hand, networks are the result of agreements between firms, either contractual or informal, and hence membership is restricted. Networks are less spatially confined than clusters, which by definition comprise firms that are co-located. The features are summarized in Table 9.1.

Table 9.1 Distinguishing features of networks and clusters

Business networks	Enterprise clusters
Provide access to specialist services at lower costs	Attract specialist services to a region
Restricted membership	Open membership
Based on contractual agreements	Outcomes of market dynamics
Assist firms engage in complex production	Generate demand for more firms with related capabilities
Based on cooperation	Require competition
Common business goals	May have collective visions, including public interest

Source: based on OECD (2004).

While there are fundamental differences in this conceptualization, in practice clusters may create an environment in which networking develops between member firms. The OECD points out that "efficient networks are at the core of successful clusters." But clusters do normally have access to a wider range of support services in the form of government-sponsored initiatives, universities and colleges, government research establishments, and commercial support services. However, the outcomes of research focused exclusively on networking do have direct relevance to clusters, but do not cover all aspects of cluster development and performance.

Innovative networks can take different forms in several dimensions:

- **The type and variety of partners.** Functional links such as research, production, logistics, and marketing are increasing in importance relative to the more traditional links in the traditional supply chain. Networks involving firms of different sizes and public research organizations are also on the increase.
- **Innovation mode.** Many have a sectoral focus, but those that cross industry and technological fields are on the increase.
- **Geographic scope.** Electronic interaction is opening up the possibilities for extensive cross-border networking, but traditionally networks have been more localized. However, face-to-face contacts appear to be important in the exchange of tacit knowledge (van den Berg, Braun, and van Winden 2001). Cultural proximity appears important when the information is sensitive and perceived to be of high value.

- **Organization and relations between partners**—from loose to structured multi-actor partnerships. Even where the network has become formalized, personal relationships are important in holding it together.

(Source: OECD 2004)

Key questions

- To what extent is the firm involved in networks and clusters?
- What form do these networks take?
- Does the firm have a method for assessing the benefits and costs of networking?
- What stories tell of success in networking?

Networks and clusters: contributing to a firm's innovativeness

Interactions between network members help entrepreneurs make sense of their environment. Network members will use these contacts to assist in the innovation process, not only by offering advice and encouragement, but probably more importantly by giving support though access to supplies, capabilities, technology, and test markets. Empirical studies are reported as confirming that collaborating firms are more innovative than non-collaborating ones irrespective of size (OECD 2004). Networking is also believed to be a prerequisite for technological innovation for many SMEs, since it allows firms to cope with the increasing interdisciplinary nature of technical change, to reduce the risks of investing in novelty, and to link innovation to demand.

Particularly in the service sector, networking is a source of added value and flexibility. During early phases of new product or process development, cooperation is likely to reduce transaction costs and reduce the risk of loss of reputation. Members may share other risks involved in innovation. But because of the innovation dynamics in member firms, the relationships are likely to be in a constant state of flux.

As pointed out earlier, a key outcome of network membership is the degree to which member interactions can help individuals make sense of the complex world in which they operate. An important aspect of entrepreneurial activity is the rate of change being faced, and the need to constantly reassess situations and attempt to understand competing pressures in order to make reasoned decisions. Interactions within a trusted network can aid in sense-making by providing opportunities for discussion, interpretation, reformulation, and reassurance. For networks to meet these higher-level aspirations it is clear that there needs to be willingness among members to give as well as take from relationships. The frequency and intensity of interactions across and between members, the reach across diverse organizations, and the extent of perceived status differences will all impact on the value obtained by members. Trust, commitment, and acceptance of a set of norms governing behaviour are important features of networks—the unwritten "rules of the game." In addition the degree of shared understandings, perhaps concerning their beliefs about the types of issues perceived important, their understanding of these issues, and their views on how best to address them, will have an impact on benefits obtained.

Networks are seen as helping individual firms be more resilient in dynamic environments (OECD 2004). Firms in rapidly changing business environments need to continuously explore multiple contacts in order to cope with their evolving, but largely unpredictable, knowledge needs, and should accept that some of these contacts will at the end of the day be redundant. Networks aid flexibility in response to changing market needs, in that firms are better placed to benefit from "chances" (Huggins 2000)—firms are able to react by engaging in partnerships with others with complementary strengths and capabilities. Access to the resources in other firms such as specific know-how, technology, finances, and products can enable firms to concentrate on core capabilities but still be able to respond to market needs.

On the downside there is also the possibility that familiarity among network members will lead to blinkered thinking on the part of individual members.

Networks tend to be based around common interests. The status and standing of members are important influences. Invitations to join are inevitably based to some degree on similarities in socio-economic background, educational level, occupational and industry sector. This similarity has benefits in forming strong network ties, but the cognitive similarity which results can limit the challenge provided to the entrepreneur. According to Granovetter (1973), weak ties (that is, distant and infrequent relationships) are efficient for accessing novel information because they bridge otherwise disconnected groups and individuals.

From a study of clothing firms, Uzzi (1997) reported that the greater the number of strong ties, the more likely that firms were sealed from new and novel information or opportunities from outside the network. But there is some evidence to suggest that strong ties lead to greater entrepreneurial behaviour. Uzzi suggests that strong ties are more likely to promote in-depth communication as well as valuable and accurate information exchange. This information is likely to be relatively inexpensive, and probably as reliable as commercially available information. The interpretation gained through interaction with other members is likely to add value to the source information.

Simsek, Lubatkin, and Floyd (2003) conclude that weak reciprocity norms are more significant for radical innovation, whereas strong reciprocity norms are more significant for incremental innovation. Certainly diversity is a contributor to the development of novel ideas. Additionally, if strong ties into a network act as constraints on member firms, they are less likely to step outside the normal ways of working so as not to desta-bilize the network relationships. The sharing of best practice, knowledge, and experiences in new technologies and the use of complementary skills has the potential to lead to incremental change. Shared understandings between network members can result in communication economies, and hence serve to accelerate the rate of adoption of these incremental inno-vations. High cognitive similarities, however, tend to lead to compressed search times, consideration of fewer alternatives, and a push for "one best solution" (Simsek et al 2003).

Key questions

- Is there a firm or departmental strategy for networking?
- Who has responsibility for the strategy and how often is it reviewed?
- Is there an accessible register of networking activities and a regular review?
- Is there a balanced portfolio of network membership including long-standing as well as emerging networks, loose as well as tight-knit networks?
- Is the firm being adequately recognized for its contribution to key networks?
- How is network membership enhancing the firm's reputation?
- Is there a policy of time allowance for key individuals, and appraisal of personal contributions and personal development?
- Is there the means by which learning from networks can be captured and shared?

While reciprocity is an important feature of networks, the timing of reciprocation also has an impact. Breaking expected norms of behaviour will eventually result in deviant members being excluded. This may follow attempts by other members to apply sanctions, ranging from gossip and rumours through to ostracism. This can have a direct impact on the firm's reputation and business opportunities within the network. So a downside of membership of a strong network is the pressure to remain within the fold and the potential costs of defection. Clearly another cost is the time required to maintain the ties and to respond to the needs of other members. Doubts will arise about the risk of failing to gain reciprocal benefits.

Networks and clusters: realizing the benefits

Tallman et al (2004), in their review of research, focus particular attention on knowledge sharing between firms through the medium of untraded interdependencies: that is, knowledge that is exchanged without any formal agreement or payment. They focus on the role of knowledge stocks and flows. Economic geographers, according to Tallman et al, have emphasized the importance of knowledge exchange in determining performance—technology slipovers, informal exchange, and movement of people. A resource-based view of competitive advantage focuses attention on embedded, tacit, firm-specific knowledge resources, capabilities, or competencies in explaining comparative success, and it is the enhancement and exploitation of this tacit knowledge that networking needs to achieve to be seen as successful. Long-term networks are seen as particularly beneficial in allowing for in-depth insights into the operations of partners, thereby facilitating technology transfer of joint R&D. Short-term relationships transfer information amongst firms, allowing for close monitoring and learning from the mistakes of others (Lorenzen 2002).

Combinations of relationship-based contracting, institutional support, and social factors within a close community have long been recognized as providing the context for extraordinary economic success. The grouping of subcontracting firms can reduce transactional costs, thereby creating what are termed *agglomerative economies*. Trust development within neighbouring firms results in the lowering of transaction costs. But political, social, institutional, and other non-economic factors are as important as, if not more important than, technology spillovers (Saxenian 1994).

Untraded interdependencies involve the exchange of knowledge for which there is no means for valuation and no market mechanism. This exchange is often associated with more formal contractual arrangements, and being additional to transactions covered by the formal contract, it adds value to these relationships. It involves interpersonal interaction. The interdependencies include rules, accepted practices, and conventions. It is the exchange of tacit knowledge which might well have an impact on the collective competitiveness of firms in a cluster.

Once established, successful clusters become a magnet for additional firms, and hence there is an expansion in the knowledge base available to all members. The intense sharing of knowledge leads to common understandings of not only specific knowledge, but also the context of such knowledge.

These networks are dynamic in nature, and the informal understandings that exist contribute to the sharing of technical knowledge. Knowledge flows more freely as ongoing practice creates knowledge both about how the system works and about the context and meaning of such knowledge.

Agglomeration economies result from related economic activities in a locality. Lower input costs are a result, as is the development of common suppliers, specialist skills and know-how, and greater understanding of the working of the industry. Where the social relations are also strong, there will be a reduction in transaction costs. The network appears to be able to develop capabilities in excess of the addition of the individual firms. But knowledge that is codifiable and hence rather more procedural or simpler is more readily transferable.

Firms will also differ in the extent to which they can absorb this knowledge and take practical advantage from it. Cohen and Levinthal (1990) highlight a number of influencing factors, including the firm's stock of related knowledge (for example, as a result of a broad-based R&D effort). Tallman et al (2004) explain that *component knowledge*, consisting of specific knowledge resources, skills, and technologies relating to specific parts of an organization (for example, scientific, technical, engineering, and design skills in technology-based firms) is subject to discovery rather than creation by organizations. In the case of consumer industries this component knowledge would include knowledge of consumer behaviour, markets, and sales promotions.

This form of knowledge is transferable between informed individuals and organizations. Given the ease of transfer, leakage is also to be expected, and to take place fairly quickly. So within a tight-knit cluster protection of component knowledge is weak, but firms will vary in their ability to absorb and capitalize on this knowledge, so the originating firm can still gain competitive advantage even in a tight-knit network. This advantage, however, may be the result of systemic knowledge rather than technical know-how.

Architectural knowledge is in many ways the glue of the organization. It relates to the overall organizational system, and comprises structures and routines for coordinating and integrating component knowledge to deliver products or services, and also to enable learning and improvement. This makes each organization unique. It is difficult to replicate architectures and build architectural knowledge even if one achieves a degree of codification, because of the specificity within a context. Architectural knowledge can be an enabler of the absorption of ideas from outside, but it may also act as a strong barrier. It is likely in particular to make the absorption of alternative architectures very problematic.

Tallman et al (2004) describe a higher level of architectural knowledge within a network which enables this greater collective competitive edge. They include this as the development of "rules of the game," where firms understand the nature of the interactions, interdependencies, and common interests. It can facilitate exchange between firms. It also enables the cluster to develop a sense of identity. This higher-level architectural knowledge might actually aid firms in the absorption of new knowledge by a common set of organizing principles, and this might result in more tacit knowledge being absorbed.

Once component knowledge has escaped from the firm it can become available to the network, and will be absorbed rapidly by those firms with high absorptive capacity. It may be the source of competitive advantage to the network as a whole until it spreads more widely. Spreading beyond the cluster may take rather longer than spreading within the cluster, because of the lack of proximity of other firms. In the case of architectural knowledge, diffusion is nowhere near so rapid, if it diffuses at all. However, in order to gain competitive advantage component knowledge is only of practical use if it is related to the firm's architectural knowledge—the system comprising the totality of the component knowledge. Membership of a cluster can lead to new knowledge creating and diffusion through untraded interdependencies (Saxenian 1994, Jenkins and Floyd 2001).

So for firms to gain benefit from cluster effects they need to do more than just co-locate. They need to join in, becoming active members, contributing to as well as taking from, the relationships, and assisting in the development of the higher-level architectural knowledge. But to gain competitive advantage from membership the firm needs absorptive capacity and architectural knowledge which can accommodate changes readily. Otherwise membership will not result in the firm gaining competitive advantage.

While there are benefits to be derived by organizations of all sizes, the OECD (2004) reports that the propensity to engage in innovative networks, including both the density and diversity of linkages, decreases with the size of the firm. The size of the firm also influences in-house innovation processes, with smaller innovative firms collaborating as a substitute for internal activities, whereas for larger firms collaboration leads to increased spending on R&D. This lack of networking by smaller firms may be explained in part by the shortage of managerial skills available, SMEs' perception of dominance of networks by larger companies, and the period over which membership needs to be maintained to gain benefits.

Key questions

- Is there a good understanding of how benefits can be realized through network membership?
- Is there an acceptance of the potential benefits of network membership and a legitimization of the approach?
- Is there the means for the regular collection of evidence of the impact of network membership on technology transfer?
- Is there the means for the regular collection of evidence of the impact of network membership on new business development?
- Does the firm regularly review the form of relationships it has with partners and ensure their appropriateness?
- Are there internal mechanisms for sharing best practice in networking?
- Does the firm have measures of absorptive capacity in place, either formal or informal, and are there regular reviews?

Networks and clusters: incremental or radical innovation

We have seen that the networking behaviour to support radical innovation appears different from that in support of incremental innovation. The latter involves "innovation, venturing and strategic renewal activity within the bounds of the established premises, policies and customary views" (Simsek et al 2003). The focus is on improvements in functionality, appearance, or price, or in processes and procedures. In contrast radical innovation focuses on the new, and results in fundamental changes in organizational routines, approaches to products, processes, or markets.

In practice there is competition within organizations for the resources needed to support innovations, particularly management time and attention. A balance has to be struck between innovation that profitably exploits and develops current capabilities by extending their reach, and the much more risky development of novel features with the potential to disrupt, which may have much higher pay-off by setting the organization apart from competitors and ensuring its long term future.

Business networks can be viewed as information repositories (Chen and Chang 2004). To meet their needs members develop appropriate structures and routines for interaction. Since incremental innovation is to a large extent based on the use of existing information, competencies, and technologies, it can be facilitated by networking. Faced with radical innovation, however, networks need to regroup to access new knowledge. Highly embedded business networks are likely to experience similar difficulties to those experienced by large organizations when confronted with the novel.

Table 9.2 summarizes important aspects of networks in both incremental and radical innovation.

Key questions

- Does the firm have a good link between networking and technology strategy?
- Does the firm have appropriate representation in networks that are likely to result in radical innovation?
- Is the international spread of this networking adequate to capture key technology developments?
- Does the firm have adequate representation in clusters which are hot-beds of development in relevant technologies?
- Does the firm regularly review its organizational capability and structure to capitalize from breakthrough ideas and developments?
- Does the firm have an adequate monitoring system to review the effectiveness of its networking in support of its portfolio of innovations, both radical and incremental?

Table 9.2 Important aspects of networks in both incremental and radical innovation

Nature of innovation	Stage of innovation process			
	Opportunity search	Resource acquisition	Seeking legitimacy	Survival and performance
Incremental	More use of weak ties could open up more opportunities.	Strong ties enable asset-parsimony—networks can be exploited for efficiency gains.	Strong ties can assist in gaining legitimacy.	The network can create its own architectural knowledge which can be used for market responsiveness and competitive advantage. Transnational companies can transfer knowledge from the outside and act as catalysts.
Radical	Weak ties to diverse networks but early strong ties to key players. A balanced approach "Trusted" feedback vital.	Strong ties give access to brainpower with the exchange of fine-gained information and tacit knowledge.	Overcoming the "liability of newness"—establishing both cognitive and socio-political legitimacy. Lobbying may best be achieved through extensive weak ties. Strong ties may present a barrier. Weak ties with outsiders are important for building cognitive legitimacy and reputation.	Flexibility due to ready access to firms with complementary capabilities. Ready absorption of good practice from network members.

How networks develop

Since clusters have attracted much attention as a means for enhancing the economic performance of localities, it is unsurprising that there has been considerable attention given to their formation and support at a national and even international policy level.

Much of the research has been case study-based, focusing on either successful or unsuccessful networks or clusters to identify key success factors. Work done by van den Berg, Braun, and van Winden (2001) is an exception in that it sets out a conceptual framework. They identify three interrelated elements from a review of the literature, which they believe influence the growth of clusters:

1 Spatial-economic conditions:
   - strong local demand for the products or services, perhaps from a large corporation or government agencies
   - the quality of the transport infrastructure and accessibility of the locality, particularly internationally
   - the overall quality of life making it an attractive locality to live and work in, hence providing a pool of high-quality potential employees
   - "cultware"—the willingness of firms and individuals to cooperate and their motivation to be innovative.
2 Cluster-specific conditions:
   - the potential size of the cluster—the larger the cluster, the greater the economies of scale, the faster the penetration and adoption of all types of innovation, and the greater the pool of resources to quickly reconfigure to meet client needs
   - the presence of one or more cluster engines—termed as "spiders" in global and local networks or as 'flagships' of the cluster as a whole. A transnational company routed in the region can be an important disseminator of new knowledge, information and innovation from abroad into the region
   - the extent of strategic interactions such as long-term relationships at a high level between organizations
   - new firms locating within the cluster and the rate of start-ups to bring dynamism, innovation and job creation, including for attracting young talent.
3 Organizing capacity:
   - the local ability to mobilize and manage a cluster—vision/strategy formulation, gaining political/societal support, partnership building.

Policy recommendations for business networks

- Implement broad campaigns to introduce the networking concept to business—this is to create informed demand for network services so that it is participant-led rather than supply-driven.
- Provide a degree of public financial support for feasibility work, start-up activities, and network brokerage, but transfer responsibility for funding to participants as early as practical.
- Adopt realistic time-frames—this is years rather than months, although "early wins" for participants are needed to engender enthusiasm and encourage continuing membership.
- Ensure the presence of experienced network brokers with credibility in the eyes of participants.

Source: based on OECD (2004).

Factors determining network success

- A real sense of belonging to and ownership of the network.
- Involvement of executives with decision-making power.
- Removal of "free-loaders" and a trusting relationship.
- A relatively low level of direct market competition.
- A credible, trustworthy, and competent broker, and realistic expectations.
- A small group faced with common problems.
- Ground-rules emerging from experience.

Source: based on Huggins (2000).

A particularly important aspect of effective networking, referred to earlier, is the level of trust developed amongst member organizations. Lorenzen (2002) defines trust as a cognitive coordination mechanism. He contrasts this with the incentive-related mechanisms formed through contracts or reputation effects. He distinguishes between *dyadic*, *networked*, and *social trust*.

Dyadic trust is between two parties; networked trust he defines as between a small number of firms; social trust is mutual amongst a larger group of firms as typified in a cluster. Lorenzen sees social trust as essential for the effective working of the network. This is the means by which transaction or coordination costs are lowered. In rapidly changing markets firms experience difficulties in foreseeing contingencies and conflicts in relation to partner firms, and it is under these circumstances of high uncertainty that coordination is more rare. Even formal contracts are unable to cover all eventualities, and the more they seek to cover them, the greater the increase in costs. Under this uncertainly firms are more likely to act opportunistically, seeking to sink less effort into any venture. Because of a lack of information firms may then overestimate the risks involved in partnering.

It becomes important that expectations are aligned, so as to build mutual trust, which in turn will enable coordination. This trust is created and maintained through dialogue and a social learning process over an extended period. The network broker has a role to play in this. Reputation within a cluster also acts as a restraint on opportunistic behaviour. But again there are downsides—if social trust becomes so dominant that it leads to collusion, it will result in the cluster being closed to entry or change (Casson 2000).

Key questions

- Has the firm a clear vision for what it wants to achieve from networks?
- Has the firm identified those areas where networking is needed long-term?
- Does the firm review its contribution to the development of new networks in areas of strategic importance?
- Is there regular review of the resources devoted to the formation and maintenance of key networks?
- Does the firm have means for regularly reviewing its reputation and standing within networks?

The notion of stages in the development of networks is apparent in research by a number of investigators:

- Three phases from Larson (1992): pre-networking to establish relationships; creating conditions for relationship building; solidifying network relationships.

- From Gray (1987): problem solving involving identifying those with similar interests; direction setting involving the articulation of values, and a common purpose structuring phase.
- From Snow and Thomas (1993): formation, development, and testing.

Mutual economic advantage, reputation of potential partners, operational and strategic integration, a lead partner, shared power and legitimacy, and the assistance of a broker are all factors seen as explaining successful networks. In contrast some investigators suggest a cyclical process of repeated negotiations of mutual expectations, future commitments, and assessment of prior contributions in terms of fairness and efficiency.

Concluding remarks

The importance of the firm's networks as a source of innovation stimulus and support is without question. However, if benefits are to be derived there needs to be a balance struck between the time spent in developing and contributing to networks, and the time devoted to implementation within the parent organization. Clearly networks take different forms and will impact differently on the firm's innovative capability. The firm is advised to put in place mechanisms to manage network membership to ensure it is adequately and appropriately represented in those networks key to its future. It needs to decide in what types of networks it wants to take a lead role or one of influence, and ensure that it is well represented at an appropriate level.

Membership of networks can enhance reputations and also has the potential to damage them. But the real benefits will only be derived if there is an appropriate level of management intervention within the organization.

Table 9.3 The key capabilities needed for successful networking by members of the organization

People-embodied knowledge and skills.	Resource investigator skills and inclination. Personal competencies in building and developing networks with diverse membership. Personal competencies in maintaining networks. Maintenance of strong links across the parent organization. Strong architectural knowledge to provide linkage for ideas and new knowledge. Trustworthiness. Strong technical disciplinary knowledge as well as breadth of knowledge in relevant disciplines. Curiosity and learning capacity. Sensitivity to the needs of networks and the parent organization (e.g. weak ties vs. strong ties).
Management systems/organizational structures.	Development of staff relationship building capability. Ability to effectively monitor and control networking activity. Ability to leverage the benefits of networking. Organizing skills applied to networking set up, maintenance, and termination.
Physical and technical systems.	Clear governance structures for relationships with networks and clusters. Reward systems to support networking. Systems for evaluating the impact and cost benefit of networking. Systems for the rapid transfer of new knowledge acquired through networks—collection, dissemination, enhancement, and integration.
Cultural values and norms.	Culture supporting relationship building by staff. Acceptance of the value of outside relationships.

CHAPTER 10

Managing complex technology projects, programs, and portfolios

Introduction

At any one time organizations will have many projects underway. Some will be scoped to have major strategic impact, but many will be localized and focused on operational improvement. Not all projects will be aimed at bringing about innovation. But all need to be managed either as individual projects or within portfolios.

A project may be undertaken for internal clients and funded from organizational resources. It may be externally funded and undertaken for a specific client or a consortium. It may be publicly funded, for example as an EU Framework project which focuses on pre-competitive research and development.

All projects should have a sponsor. This may be the executive board or a subcommittee. For small projects it may be operational management. There also needs to be a governance structure to oversee the overall management of projects. This may be a specifically appointed executive committee or another ongoing decision-making body.

Many projects have a relatively high degree of certainty: the technology is known and reliable, the market already exists and is calling for the development, the processes for manufacture are already functioning. Others will have a high element of risk, being innovative in terms of technology, manufacture, and market place awareness. The aims and purpose of projects will also be highly variable. Here we are concerned with projects that are innovative and aimed at having high market place impact in terms of improving the competitive position of the firm, in some cases by disrupting that market place, particularly by introducing new technologies.

Since projects are one-off by their nature they contain uncertainties. Not only are there uncertainties within the project itself, probably more importantly there are uncertainties in their environment. The market place is constantly changing, and projects will sometimes become redundant because of these very changes. Customers, competitors, regulatory changes, displacement technologies will all have an impact. The underlying assumptions behind projects have to be constantly reviewed in an objective way so as to ensure their continuing value to the business.

The failure to hit targets for innovation projects can be extremely costly. An example of the possible impact of not being first to market when planning to be so is demonstrated in Figure 10.1. Not only is this project not going to yield planned return, the delay might have a devastating effect on cash flow. So effective project management is essential to delivering timely innovative new products and processes. In the case of incremental projects, project management is essential to progress from initial idea to market realization. These projects might have relatively low risk, but poor performance in the project can still impact severely on market position, as illustrated in Chapter 6. But while projects leading to radical innovation may need a different style of management, project management including the effective management of risks is still an essential element in the overall innovation process.

Companies with superior capabilities in managing innovation projects will demonstrate their superiority by outperforming competitors in getting new products and services to market, in the time taken, the quality achieved, the customer needs fulfilled, and the overall costs to the firm.

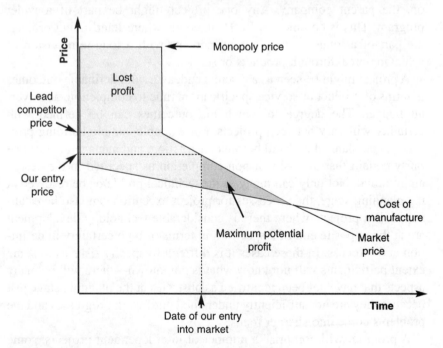

Figure 10.1 The cost of late entry into the market

Areas we address here include:

- Given the need to drive innovation forward at ever-increasing rates, what best practices can be applied to ensure project success?
- How can projects be time-compressed?
- How can risk be managed through project endeavors?
- What are the key capabilities needed to manage complex projects?

The nature of complex technology projects, programs, and portfolios

Organizations have to make choices about how best to manage innovation projects. For some the initiative will be just one more project within a portfolio. For others the organization's executive will prefer to set up a separate organization, as described in Chapter 6, to allow an innovation project to prosper without over-interference from, and over-dependence on, the parent company. Any one project might be part of a wider program. This is common in R&D functions where interlinking projects are part of a longer-term program, perhaps with a long-term vision of achieving breakthrough products or services.

A project might be seen as a discrete endeavor with definable outcomes in terms of product or service specification, time to completion, and overall budget. The degree to which the outcomes can be defined with certainty will vary between projects. For example, simple building projects can be planned in detail before construction, and management can be fairly certain that the risks of non-completion as specified in the design are minimal. Not only can many of the technical problems be resolved at the planning stage, the processes for project execution can also be established. But projects where there is considerable technology development are at the opposite end of a spectrum in terms of both certainty in definition and process. In these cases it is difficult to specify risks as to some extent participants will not know what is not known—there will be many aspects that have not been identified as obstacles at the planning stage just because they are not sufficiently understood until work progresses and the problems come into sharper focus.

A program will comprise a number of interdependent projects, some carried out in parallel, others in sequence. Program management is strategic in nature whereas project management can be purely tactical. It focuses on the achievement of intended strategic business results through the integration and coordination of multiple projects, compared with the project management focus on the tactics of planning and execution of the work output in one project. It is also often cross-functional. For example, the program may require the delivery of a new product to a customer, either internal or external. It is likely to consist of several technology development projects as well as coordination with projects in marketing and sales, and after-sales care.

Programs can also consist of a series of projects rather than projects undertaken simultaneously. Programs are then subdivided into projects in such ways that each project makes a worthwhile contribution as a stand-alone project. Even if the program is abandoned at some stage, the projects will in themselves have been worthwhile. If programs are subdivided into projects there is the opportunity to carry out more thorough reviews as projects near completion and "go/no-go" decisions are taken. Particularly where endeavors are such that they warrant a longer-term program, it is likely to be the case that they are of major strategic importance to the firm.

Where firms have considerable investment in R&D, portfolio management will sit above the management of individual projects or programs. Here there will be a concern to see a fit between the organization's overall strategy and the portfolio of innovations. We can expect to see a balance of short and long-term projects, more and less risky projects, linkages between projects so as to create and develop platforms for future products or services, attempts to optimize resource utilization across projects, and to maximize learning to create new business opportunities.

Projects might start their life in the corporate laboratory or in skunkworks designed to generate and germinate new ideas, but then be seen as best taken forward in a spin-out. As indicated in Chapter 6, this has the advantage of greater freedom for management to develop the innovation without the encumbrance of the more stable and often bureaucratic organization. Managers in the spin-out are also likely to be subject to different motivations than their counterparts within the more static parent organization. Some firms have a policy of seeking partners at the stage of spin-out so as to spread the risks in development. Others watch developments carefully with a view to bringing the spin-out back into the fold of the corporate enterprise if the development becomes more central to the firm's forward plans and there is a desire to gain greater control. Where the firm's intellectual property is no longer central to its future business focus, a joint venture may offer greater return than licensing or disposal, but of course will require more management attention.

It is likely that the firm will have a range of partners in any project. It may, at one extreme, contract out all its project work. It may contract out discrete elements. It will do so for a variety of reasons including spreading the risks, gaining access to specialist resources not normally employed by the firm, gaining access to technologies, gaining access to new markets, and benefiting from experiences gained elsewhere.

Whatever the approach taken to organizing innovation projects the principles of good project management are still applicable.

Features of high-technology development projects

All high-technology projects by definition have a high level of risk because of the uncertainties inherent in the development of any new technology. But the risks extend well beyond the risks associated with the development of technologies to include the market reaction to something new, the problems of creating an organization to produce and deliver the output of the innovation, the possible cessation of existing activities, and environmental, health, and safety aspects. One of the major areas for executive decision making is taking a holistic view in relation to the strategic direction planned for the enterprise and balancing the risks against the rewards to be achieved from success.

All projects have three basic elements—a performance specification, a scheduled time to completion, and a cost estimate. The specification for project outcomes is increasingly likely to include elements of lifetime costs and disposal considerations.

For innovation projects we can view the task facing project management as "a race against time" as they strive to outpace competitors. So a key issue facing the firm is to determine the means to achieve compressed project time in order to succeed. It may well subcontract work to firms who can provide access to off-the-shelf tried and tested technologies, or form alliances or joint ventures with other firms with the development expertise essential to the endeavor. To win the race to market the initiating firm will be seeking to learn quicker than rivals through any partnership it has set up.

If work is contracted out, some of the risk can be transferred through the contract. Cost and performance can be contracted out legally in many countries, but schedule compliance is not legally covered in countries such as the UK. Contract disputes are time-consuming and costly to resolve, so while it gives some comfort to project investors, a contract, however well formulated, may only offer partial protection against risk.

It is often the potential damage to the reputation of the contractor that is a greater deterrent to violation of contracts. Rather than depending on the contract to determine working relationships, a partnering approach to project working is to be preferred, where all parties engage with the over-all project objectives and see benefit from cooperating to resolve difficulties jointly. For the project owner the identification of those with whom strong relationships hold the key for success enables a clear focus in terms of relationship building and maintenance. A "no surprises" basis for part-nership working ensures that risks can be proactively managed. "What if" worst-case scenarios can be used to help identify risks and means for mitigation. Where work on innovative projects is carried out by contrac-tors and partners, the intellectual property issues need to be dealt with clearly from the outset.

Technology readiness is an important element is assessing project risk. How mature are the technologies being considered? The approach used by NASA, the US space agency, has ten levels of readiness. Often decisions have to be made about the relative importance of technological advance versus timeliness of delivery. The qualifications of those carrying out assessments are vital in the use of such techniques.

Often the integration of technologies causes major problems in achiev-ing project delivery. This is an area where problems are much less easy to predict, as are the outcomes. Integration is more than technological compatibility; it is the alignment of all the disciplines involved within the project to ensure a workable solution.

Understanding the risks in innovation projects is important if control is to be applied. This involves considerable detailed work. It has been argued that management should be at the activity level at which risk can be properly identified, and at the level at which defined outcomes can be properly delegated to competent teams. Probability impact assessments considering the level of risk associated with the program assess different types of risk such as high-probability outcomes and high-impact outcomes. One key consideration is how close a control the executive management seeks to have over project endeavors. As we shall see later, excessive control can stifle rather than foster innovative projects.

For long-term programs a high-level control regime is necessary based on major anchor milestones—points in time by which certain elements have to be completed. For extensive programs earned value management, with at least two reviews per annum, ensures that the proj-ect is achieving the necessary intermediate milestones by measuring schedule and cost variance. An alternative used on military contracts is "three-point estimating," with numerical values assigned to stage outcomes as pessimistic, most likely, and optimistic, along the lines of traffic signals.

Another strategic consideration is the incentivization of all parties.

As pointed out earlier, it is important that there is a clear governance structure. In many organizations an executive committee will be answerable for overseeing any sizeable projects, programs, and portfolios. This committee in turn may be answerable to the board of directors of the business or a business unit. Below this committee there has to be in place a formal structure with clear roles, responsibilities, and accountabilities. Innovation projects may be under the stewardship of a different committee from other investment projects with goals unrelated to the innovation portfolio, so as to separate out projects so different in nature that their management requirements are also dissimilar.

Key questions

- Does the organization have clear strategies for managing different types of project?
- How well equipped is the organization for tackling projects in a multi-disciplinary way?
- How does the organization prioritize projects and allocate resources?
- Has the firm identified the capabilities needed for successful innovation projects?
- How does the organization audit internal capabilities and those in the project supply chain, identify gaps, and take action?

The process of new product development

The lack of theoretical framework for innovation through new product development (NPD) is seen by Ernst (2002) as having two consequences. First, management cannot be certain that all relevant factors have been considered. Second, they cannot be sure that factors that have not proven significant will not in fact have an impact. As a result we have an incomplete picture of those factors that make NPD a success.

The greatest contributor to the field is undoubtedly Robert Cooper. His work extends back to the late 1970s. He has been a big advocate of a stage gate approach to NPD, and even from his early work reported that such a process, along with the use of market information along the entire process, would improve the probability of success. The latter is described as *market orientation*, not to be confused with customer integration into the NPD process. The NPD process can serve to bring a degree of uncertainty reduction. At each stage risks can be identified and probabilities of success estimated. This can then lead to strong commercial decision making at each stage. Even though the stage gate process advocated by Cooper is essentially sequential and in today's business environment this may no longer be the most appropriate method, the commercial rigor proposed has equal applicability in a less sequential approach to NPD.

The determinants of NPD success appear to be (Ernst 2002):

1   The quality of planning before commencing the NPD process. This includes a broad evaluation of ideas, technical and market feasibility studies, and a commercial evaluation. The benefits to the customer of the development and the target market need to be clearly stated.
2   The continuous assessment of the commercial viability and the axing of unprofitable projects.
3   The orientation of the NPD process to the needs of the market. While this is seen as based on good market intelligence, a strong understanding of customer needs and competitor offerings, it would imply that beyond this there is a good understanding shared by the project team guiding their actions.
4   The appropriate integration of customers into the NPD process. This will vary with the nature of the product or service under development. Integration at all phases in certain situations can prove more disruptive than helpful.
5   The use of cross-functional project teams with responsibility for the entire process and a strong commitment to success.
6   Strong project leadership by someone commanding authority within the enterprise, with a project champion/promoter at a senior level able to acquire resources (but it is important that this person is not so committed to any one project as to railroad it through the NPD process).

7　Relative autonomy of the project team but effective communications to stakeholders.

8　A conducive culture encouraging and rewarding risk taking, which might be manifest through such features as time for staff to devote to developing ideas, support for work on unofficial projects that might have already been stopped by management, and the availability of internal venture capital to assist the realization of creative ideas.

9　Commitment of senior management to all stages and aspects of the NPD process—but again this group needs to maintain objectivity. Beyond commitment, accountability is also seen as important.

10　A strategic approach including clear definition of objectives for the NPD program, a strategic focus for projects, and a long-term thrust.

A metastudy of new product performance by Henard and Szmanski (2001) brings into question some of the factors identified by Ernst (2002). First they found that functional diversity does not always result in greater product success:

> Although functional diversity can play a role in the tasks that lead up to new product development performance (e.g. idea generation) and can be effective for improving performance in limited situations, integration of more functional areas into the new project initiatives and heightened communication across these areas may not always represent a productive approach for directly improving the success of new products. Rather, integration in the selected contexts and under the selected conditions ... may be more advisable.

They also found that alignment of product, strategies, and processes to the environmental context is particularly important for high-technology markets. Delaying entry (in other words not being first to market), having less structure, having dedicated personnel, and selling more sophisticated products with clear advantages over competitor offerings, are all important. They stress that management perceptions of product performance can differ from objective estimates in a detrimental way, and also that differences in perception between senior and product management can be dysfunctional in that they can lead to inappropriate or ill-informed strategy development.

The stage gate process at Agilent

Stage 1: Idea generation
  Gate 1: Initial screen
  A gentle screen
  Does it fit with the vision or mission?
  Is there a strategic alignment?
  Is it technically feasible?
  Gate 2: Preliminary assessment
  Purpose is to determine market size, market potential, and likely market acceptance.
  A preliminary technical assessment is carried out.
  Assess development feasibility and costs and time to execute.
Stage 2: Definition
  Conduct market research to customer's needs and wants.
  Apply competitive analysis.
  Develop a detailed technical appraisal.
  Preliminary financial analysis, discounted cash flow.
  Gate 3: Decision on business case
  Finalize financial analysis.
  Refine target market definition, definition of market concept, desired product features.
  Develop plans for preliminary operations and marketing.
  Decide whether to "go to heavy spending."
Stage 3: Development
  Involves development of detailed test, marketing, and operations plans.
  Updated financial analysis.
  Legal/patent/copyright issues are resolved.
  Gate 4: Post-development review
  Check on progress and continued attractiveness of the product and project.
  Development work is reviewed and checked.
  Test and validation plans for next stage are approved.
Stage 4: Validation
  In-house product tests.
  User and field trials of the product.
  Trail or pilot production.
  Pre-test market, test market, or trial sell.

Revised financial analysis.

Gate 5: Pre-commercialization decision

Operations and marketing plans are reviewed and approved for implementation.

Review financial projections.

Confirm results from validation stage.

Stage 5: Commercialization

Involves implementation of both the marketing launch plan and operations plans.

Post-implementation review

Conduct a post-audit: critical assessment of project's strengths and weaknesses. What can we learn from this project? How can we do the next one better?

As an alternative to the stage gate approach Levine (2004a) proposes the *bounding box* approach. This is suitable for projects that do not easily fit into phases. This might be the result of overlaps or iterations within the process. This involves the setting of critical parameters such as delivery dates, cash flow, performance metrics, and then management by exception. It represents a "light touch" style of management by the executive or governance committee. While the project is maintained within the critical parameters, the project team are free to progress it. When it goes outside the parameters, the project is reviewed by the executive committee. The parameters may then be adjusted to allow the project to proceed.

Cooper, Edgett, and Kleinschmidt (2001), in examining best and worst performers in terms of new product development, identify a number of key differences which focus around a new product development strategy. This includes NPD goals, strategic arenas or areas of focus, and a product or technology roadmap. It takes a long-term view and includes *strategic buckets*—resources dedicated to NPD in specific areas of activity.

So we can see differences in perspective and managerial philosophy at work. One philosophy and set of practices is based on tightening management control through the application of strong process management. This is particularly suited to innovation effort that is primarily focused on continuous improvement and incremental innovations (referred to as institutional innovations in Figure 5.2). But there is a questioning of the suitability of a strong process management perspective for projects of a more innovative nature, and certainly those aimed at radical or revolutionary innovation, where goals and processes are highly uncertain at the outset.

Controlling time and cost in projects: earned value analysis (EVA)

The tight control of project performance is key for the success of innovation projects aimed at incremental change. Much emphasis in control is placed on planning and the control of time on the one hand, and on cost control on the other.

While assessing progress against a project plan, for example using critical path programming, it is possible to get an indication of program slippage, but this does not give any indication of the project performance in terms of costs against work achieved. Traditional approaches to cost monitoring do not take into consideration program slippage. Earned value analysis (EVA) can provide a useful method to get an early indication of slippage in terms of resource utilization as well as time over-runs, and gives the opportunity to take early remedial action. EVA is seen as presenting a more realistic picture of the project than other techniques, thus allowing managers to take more effective and early decisions when variances are indicated. It also encourages a review at an early stage when changes are proposed to the project scope.

EVA requires cost allocation to the activities in the project schedule as derived from a work breakdown structure. This cost can be expressed as either a financial measure or person-hours. The budget at completion (BAC) represents the overall planned resource. The budgeted cost of the work scheduled (BCWS) shows what is planned at any stage. By assessing the work completed at any time it is then possible to compute the budgeted cost of work performed to date (BCWP). By comparing the BCWP to the BCWS it is possible to derive a measure of the schedule variance, the schedule performance index (BCWP/BCWS = SPI). A negative schedule variance and an SPI ratio of less than 1 indicates that the project is behind schedule as defined by the budget.

By dividing the original duration by the SPI, an estimate of the reviewed project duration can be obtained. Then, by taking the actual cost of work performed (ACWP) and comparing this with the BCWP, it is possible to generate the cost variance (CV).

Going further, by comparing the BCWP to the ACWP the cost performance index (CPI) can be computed (BCWP/ACWP = CPI). A negative CV and a CPI less than 1 indicates that the project is subject to cost over-run. The estimated cost to completion (ECC) is obtained by adding the ACWP to the forecast of project completion costs (FCC). Comparison between projects in the portfolio is made possible on two indices, SPI and CPI.

Questions in applying earned value analysis

- How much work was scheduled for completion by the time of the measurement?
- What is the budgeted value of the work?
- How much of the scheduled work is actually completed?
- What is the actual spend?
- What is the schedule variance?
- What is the cost variance?

An example of EVA is presented in Figure 10.2. The budgeted cost of work scheduled (BCWS) is shown cumulatively over the project duration of 15 months, and forms the performance measurement baseline. The contract budget base (CBB) includes the management reserve (MR) or contingency that is additional to the budgeted cost to completion (BAC). The project is represented as a typical "s" curve with a slowish build-up, rapid progress during the middle phase, then a wind-down towards the end of the project period. In the illustration, the work competed by period 6 is behind schedule, resulting in the budgeted cost of work performed (BCWP) being less than the BCWS, and the actual cost of work performed being also less than budgeted.

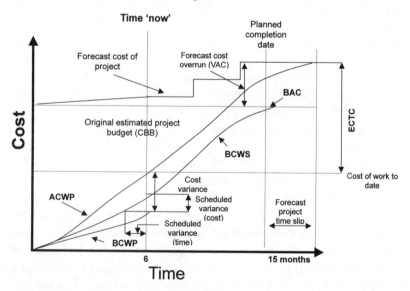

Figure 10.2 An example of EVA

The schedule variance and the cost variance can be seen from the diagram. At the rate of progress is also possible to see the estimate at completion (EAC), which is the sum of the ACWP and the estimate to complete (ETC). This shows the project to have slipped well beyond the planned end date on both schedule and cost. The variance at completion (VAC) is shown as well as the projected program delay.

The standard EVA approach has its limitations in that it does not take into account scope changes leading to additional work or omissions. But EVA can be applied in a more dynamic way to take into account this limitation. Additionally profit and overhead can be eliminated from calculations so as to ensure that actual costs are being considered, and to avoid the situation where comparisons are being made between projects that are bearing different overhead allocations and profit margins. Adjustments are also needed for any price fluctuations.

Key questions

- What are the firm's particular critical success factors for innovation?
- Is the NPD process codified and widely understood by the stakeholders?
- Is the organization clear about the conditions needed for innovation to prosper?
- Is the NPD process subject to continuous improvement?
- Is the firm clear about the type of projects that lend themselves to an NPD approach?
- What means does the firm have for monitoring and controlling breakthrough projects, and how effective are they?
- How does the firm assess the capabilities needed for project success and develop strategies for their development?
- Does the firm's executive have effective means for monitoring project performance?

One of the benefits of EVA in its basic form is its simplicity. But to be really useful it needs to be used more flexibly and with regular corrections for changes. This can be time-consuming, and the changes are open to question. Nevertheless by getting a better handle on earned value, the executive committee can be better appraised on progress and in a stronger position to take corrective action.

EVA seems particularly useful for innovation projects where both the end point and the processes are knowns at the outset, but it is of less value where it is infeasible to establish a work breakdown structure, in such cases as breakthrough projects. Here other forms of monitoring are required to ensure that executive management is satisfied with progress.

Accelerating innovation projects

In many of today's organizations, those with responsibility for innovation are under increased pressure to deliver, in terms of both the quantity of successful innovations, and the amount of resources expended on innovation activities. So boards and other stakeholders are charging executive committees and other responsible parties with shortening project durations and achieving a greater rate of success in terms of market place impact.

If we look at Figure 10.3 we can see the project curve with time and resources plotted on the x and y axis (curve A). The compression of project duration according to this curve requires an increase in resources. On the other hand an increase in time results in a lower resource requirement. If both time and resources are fixed and the project is to be time-compressed,

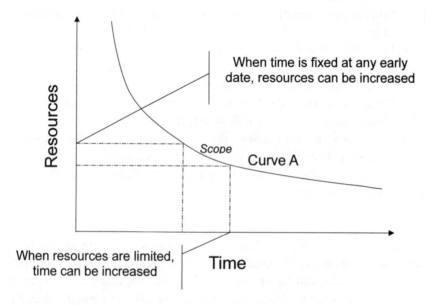

Figure 10.3 Making project tradeoffs

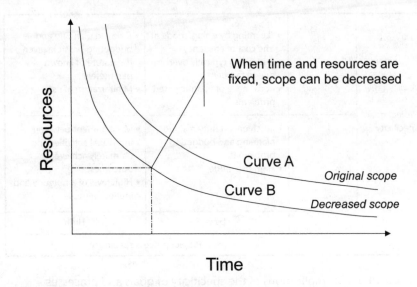

Figure 10.4 Time and resource constraints lead to a reduction in scope

the only option appears to be to reduce the scope (Figure 10.4, curve B). But this of course is a simplification of most project endeavors. The project process is far from being an exact science. At the planning stage durations are only estimates based at best on historic data. As projects develop, activities are required which were missed at the planning stage, and dependencies emerge which were not apparent earlier. Resources are unlikely to perform as predicted even if available at the time when they are actually needed.

In the case of high technology projects, particularly where these are dependent on the outputs from research and development, there are increased levels of uncertainty which add high unpredictability to planning, and lead to opportunities for resource sub-optimization. Even the goals may not be clearly specified, but rather emerge as the technology develops. The processes in highly innovative projects may also lack definition, as shown in Figure 10.5. So in many projects there is clearly the possibility of improving project performance.

While the systematic adoption of a NPD process can improve performance compared with a more ad hoc approach, and certainly best practice adoption has been shown to bring about benefits (Cooper et al 2001), here we examine two approaches that have been advocated to increase project performance: time compression through the adoption of *critical chain management* for projects, and time compression through *concurrent* or *fast track processes*.

Project goal specificity	High	• "Learning by doing" mode at the cost of efficiency • Budgeting typically overrun due to frequent occurrence of unanticipated problems	• Detailed planning and budgeting possible given the nature of known parameters • Minimization of risk
	Low	• Much uncertainty making planning and budgeting problematic • High-risk mode	• Misalignment between individual activities and ultimately achieved outcomes • High level of ambiguity and ineffectiveness
		Low	High
		Project process specificity	

Figure 10.5 The implications of the specificity of goals and processes

Critical chain management

This approach is based on an assumption that estimated project durations are often inflated, and that by the adoption of a rather different approach to planning projects, improvements can be achieved. In some organizations this is believed to be of the order of 25 percent. The approach is based on the theory of constraints promoted by Goldratt (1992). The approach focuses attention on bottlenecks and then seeks to reduce their impact.

The traditional approach to project planning is believed to lead to:

- Padded project durations by breaking projects down into elements which are each then given an inflated time estimate in order to have a high probability of success. The probability of completion within the time estimated may be as high as 90 percent. But if one assumes a skewed distribution as shown in Figure 10.6, 50 percent of activities could be completed at the 50 percent point on the estimate curve. Each activity, if included with 90 percent probability of completion on time, has its own built-in contingency. But if generous time estimates are fixed it is likely that the work will expand to fill the time allotted. This leads to time inflation because of the misuse of hidden contingencies, as well as an inability to bring forward activities to compress the overall project period.
- Many of the resources involved in a project endeavor are usually also engaged in other projects simultaneously. This is particularly likely to

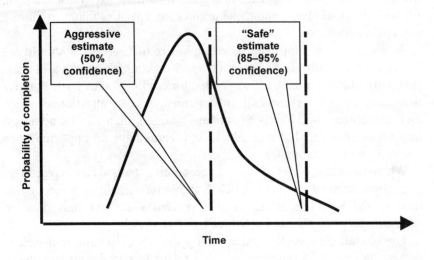

Figure 10.6 An estimate is not a single number: it is a range of possibilities, a statistical entity

be the case in organizations that have adopted matrix structures. Multi-tasking is seen as reducing productivity on any one project, adding further demands for time as people are constantly having to juggle their contribution to several projects and to readjust to each in turn as they move between them.

- Even where activities are completed ahead of schedule, it is very difficult to bring forward subsequent activities. These will have been planned with specified start and finish dates, and the necessary resources are likely to be engaged on other activities outside this scheduled time. So any saving gets lost as a result of inflexibility built in by a fixed schedule.

How might his traditional approach be improved? First, the duration times for activities are set as aggressive estimates. The buffer times normally attached to each activity are not eliminated, but rather aggregated into an overall buffer. Activities that are on the critical path for the project are identified, and it is ensured that they are protected, or ring-fenced, so that resources are readily available as and when needed. Resource buffers from the overall buffer are inserted into the critical chain so as to ensure the availability of resources at the appropriate times. The project resources are provided with estimated start times and activity durations rather than milestones. The importance of superior performance by all involved is emphasized. Buffer management is used to control the plan, particularly to accommodate those unforeseen activities that arise during any project endeavor.

Advocates of this approach also emphasize that resources should not be engaged in multiple projects, as multi-tasking is seen as a distraction particularly from the effort needed for completion of critical activities. The use of performance management is also questioned, since this encourages individuals to set lower targets than can be achieved in practice in order that individuals and teams have an opportunity to put in a good performance.

Where work is contracted out, cost accounting methods are replaced by throughput accounting—how much is the improvement in project cycle time worth? Suppliers are required to present alternative bids showing trade-offs between shorter cycle times, cost, and risk.

The overall philosophy underpinning the critical chain approach is that by finding and strengthening the weakest link in the project chain, improvements in project durations can be achieved. The principles can be applied at either the project or the portfolio level. By considering resource dependency as well as task dependency, decisions about when to accept new projects into the pipeline might well be made using different criteria, particularly ensuring the availability of critical resources. Fewer projects are likely to be in the portfolio, but completion times will be reduced, so more throughput should be achieved overall. But this will impact on the organization's decision process in relation to projects, and department heads may well not welcome this approach to allocation of project resources. Non-critical activities are delayed until near the point at which they become critical so as not to commit spending too early, and to have a positive impact on the project's cash flow. A more holistic approach to project management is advocated, one which requires training of project personnel in new ways of looking at projects and their management.

Performance is measured using several means: by comparing the percentage of the critical chain completed with the percentage of project buffer consumed; by comparing the percentage of the feeding chain completed with the feeding chain buffer consumed. The pace at which buffers are used is also a key indicator of the project's performance over time.

Another feature of this approach is an emphasis on recognizing performance problems that have systemic causes, and addressing these at a higher level than individual projects. If no solution is forthcoming, their impact should be included in project plans.

Fast tracking and concurrent engineering of projects

Fast tracking is a management technique used to ensure that projects are completed within the minimum time possible. It is normally achieved by undertaking non-dependent project activities simultaneously, and by ensuring that the time spent on dependent activities is minimized. Fast tracking is facilitated by information technology tools, making possible rapid communications and transfer of information between project members, and more rapid decision making.

Before fast tracking can be undertaken:

1 A realistic schedule is needed, with all activities clearly established.
2 Task dependencies must be understood.
3 The overall project requirements must be clearly understood and agreed by stakeholders.
4 Good relationships must exist with all stakeholders—project clients, executive management, sponsors, suppliers, and subcontractors.
5 Processes for tracking progress and managing risks must be in place.

Then consideration should be given to the reason for fast tracking. As it is more than likely to increase the overall project cost, it is necessary to be clear about the benefits sought and how they will be measured. The increase in costs arises in part due to the increased complexity resulting from time compression and the associated risks, additional costs of supplies and subcontracts because of the flexibility required of these suppliers, the costs of additional management attention and the impact on other projects which may lose access to resources, and early commitments to services or materials that then prove to be redundant.

Fast tracking may preclude some ways of working, such as competitive tendering for goods or services. It may involve close working with suppliers of services as well as products, where long-standing partnerships are likely to make the approach more sustainable. So fast tracking may be appropriate where there is a strong business need, for instance to be first to market when the competition is actively developing new directly competing products or services; if the project has to be brought to fruition quicker than initially expected, perhaps because competitor intelligence has identified new market entrants that plan to launch sooner than the completion date of the current project; or if the project is running late and time compression is needed to bring it back on stream.

One issue in fast tracking is the need often to compromise and make choices in relation to time, cost, or quality in order to reduce the overall project demands on resources and enable compression. Greater risk taking might be necessary, for example disregarding the need for thorough due diligence on contractors in order to speed up the appointment process. Normal company procedures may be too bureaucratic to support fast tracking which needs rapid decision processes and flexibility. However more thorough planning by highly experienced personnel can reduce the impact of these negative aspects.

Fast tracking does not always imply additional resources. In practice extra resources may not lead to a speeding up of project progress, as there are limits to the improvement of performance through the addition of resources— beyond a certain point additional resources just lead to confusion and bottlenecks. Smarter ways of working have to be sought and implemented.

Following the clarification of goals, the process for fast tracking comprises a number of steps:

1 Examination of the question of feasibility.
2 The identification of possible methods.
3 Analysis of alternatives and decisions.
4 The gaining of buy-in from all parties concerned.
5 The setting up of a system for monitoring and corrective action as needed.

First it is necessary to ask the question, "Do we have access to the skills and resources needed to manage the project if it is fast tracked?" The next step is to examine the project schedule and examine in particular those activities that are on the critical path, to ensure that time estimates are realistic and the logic is sound.

Hard dependencies are those tasks that depend upon completion of previous tasks before work can start. *Soft dependencies* are tasks that can be modified to remove dependencies. *Concurrent tasks* are those with no dependencies.

The concurrent tasks can be planned for completion in the shortest possible time so as not to hold up overall project completion. The soft dependencies can be examined so as to reduce their impact. The hard dependencies now need careful attention to see if organizational changes such as overtime working, shift work, outsourcing, or other means can reduce the lapsed time required. The hard dependencies that are on the project's critical path are the areas needing most attention, as time compression is vital on these activities.

In development projects, one way to fast track is to remove uncertainties in development by substituting existing, tried and tested sub-components. Yet another approach is to change the scope of the project to shorten the schedule. This may involve reduced project functionality, which may of course impact on customer satisfaction, but this is a factor to be weighed up in the decision process. Another approach is to encourage teams to work concurrently, for example researchers working more closely with manufacturing and marketing, with these two departments starting work on the project before research and design is complete. However, for this to be successful there has to be a good way of working agreed between departments, and good working relationships established and maintained.

Activities that were previously seen as sequential may be worked on concurrently, but redundancy will need to be built into components in order to accommodate the different needs of those on which they are dependent as they are finalized. This is particularly well illustrated in fast-track building construction, where early design of foundations before the superstructure design is finalized requires design for greater load-bearing capacity than may be required by the superstructure design when it emerges.

Information dependencies may well determine the shortest project duration. According to Denker, Steward, and Browning (2001):

> project inefficiencies occur when the structure of the information flow inherent in the project clashes with the information flow enabled by the project organization. Cycle time is often wasted by hold-ups for critical information missing because no prior analysis was made of the information dependencies inherent in the process.

By examining the information-dependencies of each activity on the master program processes can be put in place, and this ensures a timely decision process to support the project program, particularly where fast tracking is to be implemented. The elimination or minimization of interactions can also reduce the overall project duration. Denker et al (2001) advocate an approach termed a *dependency structure matrix* to aid the analysis and provide answers to two key questions "What information do I need to do my job?" and "What information do I owe others so they can do their job?"

They also advocate a review process based rather more on reviewing points at which assumptions have been clarified; small problem-specific reviews rather than large-scale reviews at stages in a generic process or to a predetermined schedule. This might well reduce the number of costly project reviews, again leading to time compression. One general point to take from this, however, is that reviews should serve a clear purpose and be kept to the minimum needed to satisfy executive management and other stakeholders that progress is satisfactory.

The fourth stage involves an analysis of alternative means for time compression. This involves an assessment of risks not only that the project will not achieve the required compression, but also the impact of project compression on customers, staff, suppliers, and other projects being undertaken at the same time.

The next stage involves getting the necessary agreement and support from relevant stakeholders for the preferred route. This is particularly necessary in relation to budget and scope changes.

During project execution it is essential that systems for monitoring and variation management are adequate to support this approach.

The application of the principles of *concurrent engineering* (CE) to NPD goes beyond time compression through parallel working. Ainscough, Neailey, and Tennant (2003) use the following description of CE: "the systematic approach to the integrated concurrent design of products and their related processes, including manufacture and support." So CE then is dependent on the organization's ability to undertake product development as a series of overlapping phases to deliver on time, goods and/or services meeting a customer need at a price customers are willing to pay. For this to be achieved a "right first time" approach is seen as essential.

Ainscough et al's self-assessment model (2003) covers six areas of operations, demonstrating their perspective on the integrated approach needed for effective concurrent engineering of NPD. These are:

- a formal NPD process
- teamwork including problem solving by cross-functional and cross-discipline teams
- information technology to support the process
- tools and techniques such as rapid prototyping, quality function deployment, failure mode and effects analysis
- supply chain management, including the involvement of suppliers in the overall process
- project management.

They advocate the use of self-assessment as a possible alternative to project reviews and audits because of its emphasis on continuous improvement: on not only the current state of play but also the gap between that and the ideal state.

Ottosson (2004) distinguishes concurrent engineering as the division of single tasks into smaller tasks to then be performed in parallel, with the same starting point. *Simultaneous engineering* he sees as meaning that design and process engineering are performed in parallel, with separate start dates for activities in a waterfall pattern. This approach is based on the use of analytical tools such as quality function deployment, Total Quality Management and design for manufacture and assembly. He sees these approaches as unsuited to more radical innovations. When the approach includes cross-department working to involve marketing and business development, he refers to the process as *integrated product development*.

Key questions

- How effective are the organization's approaches to prioritizing projects?
- What approaches to project compression have been applied effectively to priority projects?
- Based on the firm's experiences, is it clear under what circumstances project compression offers a workable solution and in what ways is it effective?
- How effectively does the organization incentivize project contributors?
- How effective are the innovation processes?
- How does the organization identify and manage the development of the capabilities needed for the time compression of projects?

Given that breakthrough and more radical innovations do not readily lend themselves to tight project management and compliance to a structured approach which may lend itself to a degree of time compression, how can these projects be more effectively managed so as to deliver what the organization needs of them?

One method might be to seek to develop a culture of achievement, but with a commercial edge to the organization and its ways of working. A *deliverables orientation* includes an organizationally integrated approach —so delivery is against the organizational needs, rather than against fragmented departmental objectives. This is an approach which allows for personal and team creativity, but it may not meet the tight time targets unless a clear focus is maintained.

Agile approaches combine some of the characteristics of the deliverables orientation alongside a much greater task focus. This approach recognizes that end goals are emergent in more radical innovations. It seeks to combine some of the principles underlying the management control approach with the need for responsiveness by the empowerment of individuals

A deliverables orientation for R&D and other functions involved in innovation projects

This approach involves the careful alignment of expectations throughout any project. In the case of R&D this might involve a focus on deliverables required rather than activities to be undertaken. This deliverables orientation focuses on the requirements of the business and the end goal of the overall project, rather than the narrower perspective of the R&D process itself and even its specific outputs. It involves constantly reminding participants of the overall objectives, and to some degree a move away from micro and short-term management.

The advantages of a deliverables approach to innovation management include:

- A clearer understanding of what is expected by management from R&D and other functions involved in the innovation process.
- The establishment of interim deliverables are a useful means of demonstrating progress to management.
- The impact of any changes to specification can be more readily highlighted.
- The agreement of SMART project aims makes performance more measurable and also improves general understanding of not only the R&D process but the contribution of other functions to the innovation.
- A multi-functional team can be involved in defining goals, and thus there is greater involvement of all functions in the innovation process from an early stage.

This approach is clearly based on a different philosophy from the critical chain approach, as it emphasizes performance management against the overall project objectives.

Accelerating development times under turbulent conditions: an agile approach

Vandenbosch and Clift (2002) criticize both the NPD process-driven approach and the time-compression strategies. They see these approaches as adequate in mature markets such as automotives and white goods where the emphasis is on avoiding unnecessary changes and uncertainty in the evolution of technologies and market needs, and where the efficient execution of a well defined process leads to clarity and stability in the development process. In more turbulent environments where technologies are developing throughout the period of the NPD process, there is a need for much greater responsiveness and hence flexibility. In some instances the development process involves change and adaptation to the original concepts. The project definition will change during development as organizations find it necessary to adapt to changing conditions, and an evolutionary process is required.

Time to completion is a key aim in such projects. Organizational learning is a key component in successful execution, and being faster to learn and absorb new knowledge is the key to beating off competition. The design process is radically different in that it allows for the development and testing of many possible solutions through the use of rapid prototyping, leading to constant adaptation as the ideal solution is sought.

Vandenbosch and Clift (2002) go on to explain a further development, which they describe as *flash development*. Here the process begins with a defined and known outcome, and effort is channeled to its achievement. In order to achieve a short time to market, management has to be willing to allow short cuts to be taken in development, and minimum time is spent on review processes. In addition to many of the features of other strategies—cross-functional teams, high levels of intra-team communications, customer involvement, and active senior management support, it proposes an number of other features:

- The team should be selected for its commitment to the task in hand.
- The team should focus on the task rather than question its validity.
- The objective is made clear and modifications are not tolerated without a very clear business case.
- Decision making is ongoing rather than at stage gate reviews, and decisions are communicated to team members.
- Decisions must be accepted by team members, who are required to adapt their work to fit, but a participative management style is adopted for consideration of how to adapt.
- Future resources are kept informed of progress well ahead of the time required.
- Traditional NPD process reviews are eliminated.

The latter changes are intended to reduce the "friction" present and lead to smoother project processes. So keys to success are:

- a shared view of the task brought about through a detailed business case
- concurrent working with clear communications on progress between units
- project decisions made in real time
- coordinated provision of resources.

> *Gorillas* are products that dominate a market, placing the company in an extraordinarily powerful position. Gorillas can be so strong that they force any potential competitor to search for a niche market instead.
>
> Geoffrey Moore of Intel

Managing a gorilla project will involve:

1 Flexible planning to engage leading edge technology development.
2 Timing to achieve first in the market place.
3 A mitigation plan to accommodate risks.
4 A well-managed communications system between stakeholders, but also protecting confidential information from the outside world.
5 A high priority within the project portfolio.

The writings of Ottosson (2004) add other dimensions to these more flexible approaches. He describes an approach he terms *dynamic product development*. Like the other approaches, a holistic view of projects is advocated, with a widely understood clear vision of the intended outcomes. A concept group also acts in the capacity of a steering group. It works on what is seen as the all-important concept development, but alongside product and production development. The first iteration of the concept is developed prior to project kick-off. The emphasis for the concept team is low development time, low costs, and good performance, at the same time as creative solutions for the new concept. The starting point is a "wish" rather than a "need" as in other approaches.

Rather than benchmarking competitive products, which leads to a more closed thinking process, the concept development team has a blank sheet of paper. Once a unique solution has appeared, benchmarking should take place. Early working models and prototypes are also used, and widely tested, including customer feedback at an early stage. The project teams, the composition of which will be changed to meet the specific project requirements at any one time, undertake execution.

Good communications between concept and project teams is essential, with regular progress meetings and the strict execution of follow-ups. Open and frequent communications are required.

The Pareto principle, or the 80/20 rule, is adopted iteratively in all activities. Decision aids are used extensively. Planning at the outset is kept to the minimum. Dynamic problem handling is used to adjust speedily to changing circumstances. Budgeting is also very limited. The project leaders have a key role to play in being well informed about changes, understanding how they might impact on the project, and managing the changes demanded in response.

A more entrepreneurial style of management is expected, with project leaders acting as coaches rather than adopting a more authoritarian style. The project leader is a member of the concept group, and uses this group as the sounding board prior to major decisions. Co-location in open offices is also seen as desirable at stages in the project where spontaneity is needed. "Management by walkabout" is preferred to "management by objectives" in order to get quick feedback and have a detailed understanding of progress and problems.

What lessons can be learnt from the experiences of controlled-chaos software development?

"SCRUM" was used by Nonaka and Takeuchi (1995) to describe a product development process used by the many innovative US and Japanese companies. It is an approach which has been adapted for use in systems development projects where development processes are not predictable and therefore are not capable of definition or repeatable. The approach relies upon constant measurement and control through intelligent monitoring.

Interaction with the environment throughout the development process is allowed and actively encouraged, leading in many cases to changes in scope, technology, functionality, cost, and schedule.

Large projects are broken down into manageable chunks which can be achieved in a short time by small teams. Work is partitioned into coupling packets to enable close monitoring of elements of work. There are small teams (with from one to seven members),

intensely focused, comprising the necessary skills for task completion, which should maximize both internal communications and the
sharing of tacit knowledge while minimizing overhead. There is
constant synchronization between chunks, a continuous search for
problems and solutions. There is continuous inspection, adjustments,
testing, and documentation of the product as it is built. Variables in
the system (risk, functionality, cost, time, and quality) are subject to
trade-offs as the project progresses.

Controls are measured, correlated, and tracked, and comprise the
following:

- Backlog—the work needed to complete the project/product.
- Objects—reusable components.
- Packets containing closely coupled objects but relatively
  independent of other packets.
- Problems needing solution to implement a backlog.
- Issues—concerns to be resolved before a backlog item can be
  assigned to a packet.
- Solutions—the solution to an issue or problem.
- Changes—activities performed to resolve a problem.
- Risk—associated with a problem, issue or backlog.

SCRUM sprints are set up—a short burst of activity to complete a
work chunk assigned to a team (one to six weeks in duration).

The final stage—closure—involves testing, developing training
materials, and completing final documentation. Outstanding work
(backlog) is assigned as part of newly formulated follow-on
chunks.

Given the complexity of many projects they cannot be done within the
boundaries of the traditional organization, so these approaches have to
often also cater for a distributed organization. This potentially puts a
strain on the organization's combinatory capabilities. Breakthroughs
are seen by many as coming not out of one firm's laboratories, but
rather as the result of joint efforts from loosely tied networks of
diverse organizations.

We have seen that there are fundamentally different approaches to
speeding up project delivery. Means which are based on a more "scientific" approach to managing including tighter performance management

of resources, removal of discretion over the use of contingencies, greater integration and focus, the imposition of "right first time" and strict quality standards including critical chain management, a deliverables orientation, and fast tracking. These may well be suited where projects at their outset have clearly definable goals and processes. But for many innovation projects this is just not the case. For these a less structured approach may work well and be the only practical means. Control systems need to be tailored to the particular environment, rather than adopt the more traditional methods used for cost accounting. This approach involves a different management style, greater empowerment, a clear vision but lower level of checking, emergent strategies and immediacy of decision processes, good communications, and team functioning.

Where organizations find themselves with a mix of project types within a functional area, this difference in styles required is likely to cause tensions and difficulties in operations. So organizations may well look at alternative means of organizing, where they have few breakthrough innovation projects in among many more incremental change projects. This may involve creating a separate entity to manage the highly innovative projects. It may involve joint venturing with partners more used to managing such projects, and who are prepared to share the additional risks which are inevitably involved. The organization may find ways within its overall project portfolio of managing the wide range of project types present within the organization. But accelerating projects does require a rather different mindset on the part of the stakeholders, and a culture which is supportive of the changes needed to bring about this different approach.

Key questions

- How effective are the organization's approaches to deciding project strategy?
- How are breakthrough projects identified?
- How are breakthrough projects managed?
- How is learning achieved throughout the project process?
- How are the tensions between more traditional project methods and breakthrough project methods managed?
- How does the organization identify and manage the development of the capabilities needed for management of breakthrough projects?

Portfolio management for overall performance improvement

Portfolio management of innovation projects is often compared to the management of a financial portfolio, where there is an emphasis on portfolio improvement by balancing the risk and return on individual projects so as to smooth out the effects of any single project on the overall endeavor. Cooper et al (2001) go on to suggest that portfolio project management is aimed at ensuring resource allocation is properly managed to achieve corporate new product objectives. It is a dynamic decision process which is constantly reviewing the active new products and the R&D projects that support them. The outcome of reviews may be acceleration of specific projects, termination or deprioritization, and the allocation or reallocation of resources. One key requirement for the approach to be successful is the agreement on criteria for the "go/no-go" decision and its application by a cross-functional team, hence reducing the politicization of the decision process.

Portfolio management has to address a number of problem issues which arise in many organizations. First, there is often strong resistance to killing off poorly performing projects. Second, project selection is not as objective nor as balanced as might be hoped. Projects are often not accepted on sound criteria, but rather based on power and politics within the organization. The criteria are not closely related to the organization's aims and key success factors; interdependencies between projects are not fully appreciated. Third, a portfolio approach demands that a new product strategy be in place for the business, and that strategic resource decisions are made explicit.

So portfolio management sets out to:

1 Maximize the value to the business of the portfolio of projects by relating their expected output to the company's key objectives. Low-value projects should be weeded out from the portfolio, since these use valuable resources and prove a distraction from the achievement of those projects critical to future operations.

2 Achieve a balanced portfolio in terms of parameters such as risk versus return, short-term versus long-term, and across the range of technologies and markets to be served. Projects will be aimed at maintenance/utility (supporting ongoing products and services to maintain current capabilities), growth/enhancement (aimed at keeping the firm in a solid competitive position), or transformation (these are breakthrough or gorilla projects, and aimed at market domination). They

also may be a mix of internally funded projects, client funded, and publicly funded, for example through the EC's various Framework programs primarily aimed at supporting pre-competitive research. They may also be sponsored by different groups within the organization, such as product/business development managers, operations, or executives relating to the overall strategy.

3 Through having in place a project portfolio governance structure representing relevant functions at executive level, ensure buy-in across the organization.

4 Gain a central oversight of innovation investments and progress tracking.

5 Align the portfolio to business strategy, which can be achieved by one of three approaches (Cooper et al 2001): top-down through having strategic buckets; bottom-up through effective gating and the application of appropriate criteria; or a combination of top-down and bottom-up by carrying out strategic checks.

6 Get an overview of resource utilization and means for accessing the required project resources.

7 Ensure that the impact on other parts of the organization's operations of agreeing specific projects is recognized and fully considered, including the financial impact, for example on cash flow.

8 Ensure that the organization is not over-committing, by focusing on priority projects and terminating those that are not in line with strategic intent so as not to spread resources too thinly.

9 Get different departments to share a common language.

10 Be the basis of improved communications of organizational priorities across the business.

11 Enable the central tracking of project outcomes.

The approach uses a range of practices and techniques to measure and increase the return on individual and aggregate technology investments, both existing and planned, and to identify, assess, and reduce risks. This variety of methods, used independently or in combination, includes the following.

- According to the study by Cooper et al (2001), **financial methods** dominate. These include net present value, return on investment, and other financial ratios. Project ranking is then based on financial indices.
- The second most used approach is described as **business strategy**. Essentially following the crystallization of the strategy, monies are allocated across different project types in "buckets." The basis of

allocation might be market sector, nature of innovation (radical versus incremental), technology area, or platform.

- **Portfolio maps** are also utilized. These position projects diagrammatically according to their position on a matrix with, say, probability of success against forecast financial return. Clearly where both forecast rewards and probability of success are high, projects are worthwhile. In contrast, where forecast success is low along with return on investment, the projects logically should be terminated and certainly needs serious review. The dimensions used on the axes will vary depending on business priorities.
- **Scoring models** involve rating projects on a number of agreed dimensions. These dimensions may be weighted and then summed to arrive at an overall score. Dimensions used include technological and commercialization capability, protectability, and synergy with other projects.
- Rather more simple is an approach using **check lists**, with projects being required to pass on all dimensions in order not to undergo more careful review. This approach seems to be used for individual projects within the portfolio rather than for the shaping of the overall portfolio.

Evaluating candidate projects

- Review of fit with strategic aims.
- Ranking by value and benefits, based on agreed and explicit parameters, possibly utilizing a balanced scorecard.
- Risk appraisal—particularly seeking high-value/low-risk projects.
- Review of resources needed and their availability, particularly paying attention to the management time taken up and the impact on mainstream operations,
- Fit with overall portfolio—particularly looking at the overall size of the pipeline and overall success factors.
- Establish a project charter—a specification of the project, its management, and control.
- Establish critical measures, milestones, and the process for review.

The better performing companies in the study by Cooper et al (2001) had an explicit portfolio method, with clear rules and management buy-in, with consistent application across the entire port-folio. A combination of methods was used for decisions, which did not exclusively rely on financial measures. The portfolio was more closely aligned to strategy.

Based on a survey of practices in IT portfolio management, Jeffery and Leliveld (2004) suggest an approach for examining portfolio management maturity in an organization. This has a broader applica-bility as it enables the review of the application portfolio management in any area of organizational activity. They suggest four stages of maturity: ad hoc, defined, managed, and synchronized.

Ad hoc companies make decisions in an uncoordinated way. This may be the result of autonomy granted to operating companies, country oper-ations, or departments within organizations. This is likely to be wasteful of resources if the duplication of effort is not stimulating competition.

Those companies at the *defined* stage will have a handle on the projects across the organization, their forecasted costs and benefits, and criteria for evaluation of proposals, but there will be weak links into budgetary cycles and weak feedback loops, as well as low overall organization-wide compliance. Decisions will be over-influenced by local issues and perspectives.

The *managed* companies have standardized processes that enable objective project selection related to business strategy. Financial metrics are used on a regular basis (probably annually) to review progress and align with strategy.

At the next stage, *synchronized* companies use evolving metrics to measure a project's value through its lifecycle. Each project is assessed on criteria such as the risk of delays, cost overruns, strategic misalignment, and end-user acceptance. The total portfolio is assessed on the extent to which it is focused on incremental versus radical or breakthrough inno-vation. Those responsible for the portfolio are in constant touch with senior executives to ensure continuous alignment.

Some of the companies in Jeffery and Leliveld's sample used the *balanced scorecard*. They will constantly be seeking answers to "what if" questions. They will also probably be consistently applying "after-action reviews." But they report a number of implementation hurdles to the introduction of portfolio management—the problems establishing accept-able metrics and measurement processes, the lack of commercial under-standing of many involved in the processes, difficulties engaging board members so as to gain strategic alignment, and resistance particularly from managers concerned about losing budgetary control.

Possible reasons for terminating projects

- No longer in alignment with the firm's strategy.
- The project benefits have changed and no longer fit with the agreed criteria.
- The project objectives now look unattainable.
- Displacement by new project opportunities which offer higher potential benefits.
- Technology changes have made the project obsolete.
- The window of opportunity in the market place has disappeared.
- More detailed feasibility studies do not confirm the earlier predictions.
- Other projects are taking greater urgency.

The introduction of a portfolio approach to managing projects does require the creation of an organizational structure for its management. Levine (2004a) advocates a *project portfolio governance council* to be responsible for key decisions affecting the portfolio. This would have representation from all relevant functions within the organization, at a level that enables effective decision making. This council must have clear responsibilities and accountabilities, with clear reporting lines. Below the council there may be a *project management office* to provide a service across projects. This office will be more concerned with tactical decisions and progress monitoring. It may prove infeasible to have one project office where projects are widely dispersed across the organization. However the governance or executive committee does need a support function in order for it to be effective.

In seeking to establish an innovative organization with a culture that supports development, senior management need to carefully consider their contribution and behaviours. Cooper, Edgett, and Kleinschmitt (2004), suggest a range of behaviors which distinguish better-performing companies, based on a study of more or less successful companies:

- Strong support and empowerment of project teams.
- Performance appraisal based on metrics related to NPD performance.
- A good understanding of the NPD process.
- An NPD process in which senior management have been actively involved in its design.
- Ongoing measurement and review of performance.

- A strong commitment to new products and product development.
- Avoidance of micro management of the process.
- Strong involvement in "go/no-go" decisions.

In addition they identified a number of practices which impacted NPD performance, including a climate and culture conducive to entrepreneurship, rewards for champions and project teams, open communications, risk aversion, resources made available for creative work, skunkworks and the encouragement of unofficial projects, and a time allowance for scouting.

Best practice portfolio management

- A portfolio which contains high added-value projects related to business needs.
- A good balance between long versus short term, high versus low risk, across markets and technologies.
- The breakdown of spending reflects business strategy.
- Proficiency ranking and prioritization of new product projects.
- A balance between projects and resources available.
- Alignment with business objectives and strategy.
- A formal and systematic portfolio management system.

Source: based on Cooper, Edgett, and Kleinschmitt (2004).

Key questions

- Are projects managed as a portfolio?
- How effective are the portfolio management processes?
- Does the organization have explicit methods for portfolio development and management?
- How is the portfolio related to the business strategy, and how often is it reviewed?
- Is the portfolio management approach at the appropriate level of maturity?
- Is there a suitable organization to support the portfolio approach?
- How does the organization identify and manage the development of capabilities needed for portfolio project management?

Two important elements in portfolio management are the information system, and the access of executives to information needed to support their decision making in a readily accessible format. The information system will ideally integrate data from the project management system, the accounting system, and the opportunity management system. At the operational level collaborative visualization and project management tools support more effective collaboration. Tools that allow for "what if" analysis are important aids to decision making.

Managing risk

All projects have an element of uncertainty due to the uniqueness of at least some aspect of the endeavor, whether in the technologies being deployed, the supply, the availability of internal capability, the funding, or potential acceptance by customers. This uncertainly is then a source of risk. But executive management and the shareholders to whom they are answerable do not welcome surprises. So an important aspect of the project manager's role is to manage risks in such a way that in the event of their coming to fruition, they can in the main be coped with within the project organization.

Where the events are such as to require either additional resources beyond those sanctioned or political support, communications between project management and sponsors should ensure that the changed circumstances are identified early on and executive management fully appraised of alternatives, so that decisions can be made with minimum overall loss to the project. But new products that do not push the risk envelope are unlikely to become market leaders, since competitors are probably also equally capable of their early development and a speedy response.

Project risks are defined as "undesired events that may cause delays, excessive spending, safety or environmental hazards, and even total failure" (Raz, Shencar, and Dvir 2001). Project risk management is the "planning, identification and preparation for project risks." It involves developing an understanding of the risk/reward ratio, then managing the risks or uncertainties that have the potential to directly impact on the new product development process.

Project risk management should not be restricted to narrow phases of the project, but really encompass the project's lifetime, particularly in the case of products where risks are present from definition to disposal. This may extend beyond the project manager's remit, to wider considerations of risk exposure by the risk management function in the firm.

Risk management essentially has three key components:

- risk identification
- risk analysis and assessment
- risk response and control.

The focus should be on what are seen as the more probable events, rather than possible but highly unlikely occurrences. Decisions have to be made on imprecise data, particularly since risk is concerned about something that may happen in the future. The quantification of every risk is both time-consuming and not necessarily helpful. Once a risk has been recognized, whether it has 60 percent or 80 percent probability of occurrence, it is necessary to develop strategies for coping.

Risk assessment must be based on the project scope and goals, so if these are not clearly specified it is not possible to assess risks with any credibility. Certainly unless it is possible to assess the impact of the changed circumstances on the project goals, it is not possible to determine whether or not to expend more resources in mitigating the impact of the risk.

Risks can fall into a number of categories:

- **Management risks.** The project is just beyond the managerial capability of the enterprise; the project is poorly defined; the project is not well supported by the executive.
- **Technology risk.** The technologies are not yet developed or not yet mature; integration of technologies is outside current experiences; supplies are vulnerable,
- **Resource risk.** This is caused by lack of competencies; high staff turnover; conflicting project demands on scarce resources.
- **Timing risks.** These include project over-runs causing funding problems; project compression leading to short cuts; and changes in market conditions.
- **Political risks.** These include changing personnel at senior level; changing strategic business goals; resource competition from competing projects; and changing business ownership.
- **External risks.** These include legislative changes; economic changes in the business environment; consolidation of competition; fashion changes; and climatic changes.

An example of the risks needing consideration at different stages in the product development life cycle is shown in Figure 10.7, based on Martinelli and Waddell (2004). They also use a dashboard system for assessing risks in what

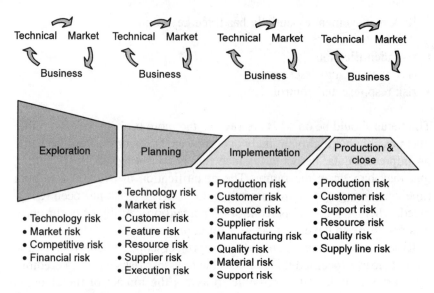

Figure 10.7 The iterative nature of risk

they term the *project strike zone* (Table 10.1). This is based on the identified critical success factors (CSFs) for the project, and the boundaries within which the team can operate without progressing the decision up to a higher authority. The control limits for each critical success factor are set, and regular reports highlight the state of play. This system has its uses in setting the authority level of project management and as a communications tool, and it gives the executive a role in overseeing progress against critical CSFs.

The process of risk management includes the documentation of decisions in relation to risk. Without this there is no reference point for actions when deviations occur, and also there is no means to allow for systematic learning to take place in the project team and beyond.

Clearly projects differ in nature along many dimensions—size, technological complexity, technology maturity, duration and resource concentration, locality, and dispersion of resources. The element of risk will also vary considerably. Routine projects which are in most ways similar to many earlier projects will have well-recognized risks. Projects with considerable novelty are likely to have many risks that are not apparent to the project team at an early stage, even when time and energy is spent on a systematic review. Project risk management should be tailored to the particular project and the extent of the exercise agreed at an early stage. Establishing the extent of effort put into project risk management and the budget allocation is a task for the executive with overall responsibility for the project—this of course requires a risk assessment exercise in itself!

Table 10.1 Example program strike zone

Program strike zone			
Critical success factors	**Strike zone**		**Status**
Value proposition:	**Target**	**Threshold**	
• Increase market share in product segment			
• Order growth within 6 months of introduction	10%	5%	green
• Market share increase one year after introduction	5%	0%	green
Schedule:			
• Product proposal approved	3/15/2003	3/30/2003	green
• Program plan approval	6/15/2003	6/30/2003	green
• Initial "power on"	10/1/2003	11/1/2003	red
• Product launch to market	4/15/2004	5/30/2004	yellow
Financials:			
• Program budget	100% of plan	105% of plan	green
• Program cost	$8500	$8900	green
• Profitability index	2.0	1.8	yellow

Das and Teng (1999) categorize projects on a matrix with technological uncertainty and system complexity on the axes, for the purposes of their study into the impact of risk management practices on project success. Using this matrix they suggest different project management strategies for different project types. They suggest four categories of technological risk:

- low tech (existing and well-established technologies, no development work, and design frozen before production starts)
- medium tech (mostly existing technology, limited development work, early design freeze)
- high tech (mostly existing technology but new application, development and testing takes up much time, and late changes are not uncommon)

- super high tech (well defined end objective but requiring that new technologies be developed, considerable flexibility required of project management).

They then looked at the use of five project risk management practices— systematic risk identification using a variety of means; probabilistic risk analysis including both risk of occurrence and consequences; detailed planning to reduce the impact of risks; methodical trade-off analysis to produce a risk response plan; and the appointment of a risk manager. They obtained 127 competed questionnaires in their survey. They found a very low level of project risk management practices reported.

Particularly interesting was the finding that on higher-risk projects systematic risk identification and detailed plans for uncertainty reduction were more commonly applied, but not probabilistic analysis, methodical trade-offs, or the appointment of a risk manager. The same was found for projects with greater technological complexity.

Das and Teng also found no correlation between the use of project risk management and project success in terms of meeting functional or technical specification. However there was an association between project risk management and meeting schedule and budget objectives. So from this evidence it would appear that a systematic approach to risk management is no guarantee of success. However, it is not possible to assess whether or not the neglect of project risk management would lead to poorer performance in terms of increased cost over-runs, penalties for failure to meet requirements, loss of reputation, or some other adverse impact.

Das and Teng conclude that:

> all risk management practices are positively correlated with meeting budget goals in highly uncertain projects.… Inherent in the planning of high technological risk projects is that it may not be possible to meet their objectives particularly within the desired schedule and budget constraints. Risk analysis coupled with contingency planning can highlight this early on and take into account possible changes in objectives and also in the option to terminate when basic objectives cannot be met.

They further point out an important need for project risk management to become part of the culture of any project management endeavor and a routine practice.

De Meyer, Loch, and Pich (2002) reported that managers studied over a five-year period consistently failed to recognize the different types of uncertainty in projects, each of which, they suggest, needs a different style of management. They point out that this is not surprising on novel or breakthrough projects. They propose an approach they call *uncertainty-based management,* built around four uncertainty types: variation, foreseen uncertainty, unforeseen uncertainty, and chaos.

Variations are classed as small changes to activities which have implications for budget and time, but which need to be monitored to be clear about the overall effects. *Foreseen uncertainty* arises from those factors identifiable and understood which may or may not happen, and for which contingency plans can be drawn up so that they can be catered for should they occur. *Unforeseen uncertainty* is that which cannot be identified during the planning phase of projects. There are inevitably such uncertainties in development projects where technologies, production processes, and market acceptance are all subject to unforeseeable events and reactions. *Chaos* in projects is where projects are so exploratory and innovative that they do not even start with clearly established goals.

The project team, based on past experience, data sources such as technology and market forecasts, or scenario planning, can establish uncertainty profiles. These profiles can then be used to assess the likely impact, and build contingency plans for those risks seen as most likely to impact. This is likely to be in the form of buffers in the program, or contingency budgets to allow for alternative means of expediting work. This is more difficult for unforeseen uncertainties and chaos. If crisis management is to be avoided on these projects, the project team must be constantly scanning for emerging trends which might impact on the project.

Organizational learning is an important element in coping with these uncertainties. Regular meetings of informed project team members are important for establishing the nature of such developments and their likely impact. Where projects are subject to chaotic conditions, as the project develops and opportunities and threats emerge, the project team and stakeholders have to be prepared to accept radical changes to the project, including the possibility of changes at the heart of the project such as the business model. It is this emphasis on learning which de Meyer et al see as distinguishing the projects mainly subject to variation and foreseen uncertainty from those subject to unforeseen uncertainty and chaos. The latter depend upon effective learning, whereas the former will be well served by good planning with built-in buffers and contingencies.

In developing contingency plans to cope with major occurrences which will impact the project, it is important to establish triggers—events that indicate a risk has been activated. This is something that needs a wide input from project stakeholders, and agreement at the top authority level for the project. However, increasingly company boards of directors are being required by legalization and good practice guidelines from bodies such as stock exchanges to report risks and means for mitigation. So they are expected to undertake due diligence at either regular intervals or stage gates, and consider actions to be taken.

One important issue is whether or not risk taking is to be valued in an organization. Russ Martinelli, manager of program management methods at Intel, states that risk taking is a core value at Intel, and Jim Waddell, former director of engineering at Tektronix, indicates that it is an expected behaviour on product development efforts (Martinelli and Waddell 2004). They believe that:

> good risk management by the program manager and the project team makes aggressive risk-taking possible by bounding the level of uncertainty through risk mitigation plans and actions.... By understanding and bounding the uncertainties on a program, the program manager is able to manage in a proactive versus reactive manner.

They go on to suggest that "good risk management practices allow program teams to move from product concept to product launch as quickly as possible by removing potential barriers well ahead of the points where they become impediments to time-to-profit goals." So the organization may set out to develop a culture of the importance of understanding the nature of risk and risk-taking within established parameters. Then it is possible to create a culture of "no blame," where risks which have been identified prove ultimately to be too high a price for the project to bear.

There is a need to have a general understanding of the organization's risk tolerance. In risk-averse industries, products will have redundancies built in. But the risk tolerance of the different stakeholders might well vary, so project management needs to carry out an ongoing dialogue with these stakeholders in order to be clear on what is acceptable practice at any project stage. This will enable project managers to find acceptable solutions to risk management—avoidance, acceptance, mitigation, or transfer.

Key questions

- How strong is the organization's culture in relation to risk taking?
- What impact does this risk culture have on the way people behave, and how satisfactory is this in terms of the firm's overall strategy?
- How effective is the risk management process—risk identification, analysis and assessment, and response and control?
- Are executives fully aware of the major project risks and measures for risk mitigation?
- What is the overall proportion of project budgets devoted to risk management, and is this provision appropriate?
- How effective is the firm's project risk organization?
- How does learning take place in relation to project risk management?
- How does the organization identify and manage the development of the capabilities needed for project and program risk management?

Concluding remarks

There is no doubt that project management capabilities are an essential enabler of innovation success. There is also room for improvement in many organizations. There are a number of approaches that can be used to time-compress projects where appropriate, but time-compression may not be the key to innovation success. It may be inappropriate to take short cuts at the expense of either functionality or quality.

The project management approaches suited to institutional innovation differ from those for radical innovation. The approaches to risk management will also vary between the different types of project. In the case of institutional innovation, there is greater predictability in both input requirements and outcomes than for radical projects. The latter may well be best served under a separate organization from the parent, in order to give some freedom to take risks while at the same time protecting the parent. But effective project management is still a prerequisite of success, in terms of delivery on time and within budgetary limits. The different types of project can benefit from different capabilities (see Table 10.2).

Table 10.2 The key capabilities needed for project management for different forms of innovation

	Institutional	Evolutional	Revolutional
People-embodied knowledge and skills.	Systematic working practices. Cost and time conscious. Awareness and understanding of market needs. Strong functional skills.	Ability to work cross-functionally. Resource investigation and exploitation. Spanning and crossing intellectual boundaries. Working outside the "rules".	Able to live with chaos and uncertainty. Scanning for ideas and solutions and absorption into workplace. Flexibility—breadth and depth of skills. Problem solving. Networking. Strong learning focus. Working in partnership.
Management systems/organizational structures.	Embedded NPD process. Strong management of the process. Prioritization, resource marshalling, and project planning and acceleration. Integration of technologies and disciplines as well as business functions. Benchmarking. Portfolio management. Risk management. Contract management.	Management of a mixed portfolio. Ring-fence and protect the more innovative and risky projects. Develop and argue the case for appropriate performance measures. Working to develop and protect assets superior to those of competition.	Ability to manage activities independent of mainstream organization. Entrepreneurial leadership. Alignment of strategies and processes to environmental conditions. Strong communications. The development and exploitation of wide external networks.
Physical and technical systems.	Project/NPD process information systems. Market intelligence. Technical support for the innovation elements of the process. Procurement systems.	Flexibility.	Access to systems for managing complex projects. Technical support from the parent organization.
Cultural values and norms.	Winning at getting innovation to market first. Acceptance of systems and processes for project working.	An innovative culture. Risk tolerance. Diversity appreciated. Open to ideas. Creativity and questioning of status quo appreciated. Pursuit of ideas encouraged.	Outward looking. Enthusiasm for and commitment to end goal. Performance rewarded. Proposed changes questioned but once agreed rapidly implemented.

CHAPTER 11

Measuring innovation performance

Introduction

The latter part of the twentieth century saw a burgeoning interest in the measurement of organizational performance. "What gets measured gets done" is a well-worn saying used by many management gurus as they encourage the use of a wider range of different measures, and particularly the adoption of performance management systems. Frameworks have been developed and have gained wide acceptance: for example, a 2003 study by Bain & Company of the use of management tools by business reported that 62 percent of the respondents across the world had adopted the widely accepted balanced scorecard first proposed by Kaplan and Norton in the *Harvard Business Review* (1992).

The measurement of intellectual capital has also attracted much attention, not only in business, but also from national governments which are seeking to ensure that firms invest in their future.

Information systems are making it rather easier to collect data and less costly. But is all this measurement really having the desired impact, and achieving the payback in terms of performance improvement that is generally assumed?

The measurement of innovation provides a special case within the framework of the overall information system. Much of what is being measured by such systems is the process and output of the organization's routine operations rather than its innovative endeavors, which are based on activities with high novelty and unpredictability. While innovation is vital to the ongoing well-being of the organization, it would appear that there is little agreement on how best to measure it, and then what to do with the information once compiled.

> When you can measure what you are speaking about, and express it in numbers, you know something about it; but when you cannot measure it, when you cannot express it in numbers, your knowledge is of a meagre and unsatisfactory kind.
>
> Lord Kelvin (circa 1870)

Even though on the surface it seems worthwhile to measure the outputs of innovation, such measurement is fraught with difficulty, in part because of the lapsed time between early investment in the development of ideas and the actual launch and success of a new product or service. Other factors also make innovation measurement problematic. Innovation in many cases is multi-disciplinary and multi-functional, and it is often unclear just how much contribution has come from each source within the enterprise and from its partnerships and alliances. Most organizations find that even the measurement of inputs is unclear, as time spent is not fully recorded and it is difficult to establish a monetary value. Spillover effects from the innovation process are rarely accounted for, but as we highlighted earlier, these may well have greater impact than the actual innovation itself. The list goes on.

Birchall and Armstrong (2004), in determining measures for an innovation survey, reviewed research by contributors such as Sivadas and Dwyer (2000) and Bean, Einolf, and Russo (1999), who examined the factors that contributed to an organization's successful development of new products and R&D benchmarking respectively. These researchers concluded that the measurement of the success of an innovation could be ascertained by collecting data that pertained to the following:

- **The total corporate expenditure on R&D.** Some researchers prefer a derivative of this indicator in that they adopt a ratio of the R&D spend to total revenue, whereas others insist that greater meaning can be ascertained if R&D spend is equated to the number of employees in general, or the number of employees engaged in R&D in particular.
- **New and improved products** launched in a given period were taken as being indicative of the output from the innovation process. This metric was given particular credence because of its relevance to the implementation stage of the innovation process.
- **The numbers of patents registered in a given period of time.** Of late this metric seems to have been taken as an indication of the inventiveness of an organization rather than a direct indicator of its ability to innovate. A patent that remains unexploited is merely a record of the legal entitlement of the organization to exploit. Ultimately patent registration is taken as the fertility of the organization to take ideas and progress them to a stage where they are ready for commercial exploitation. Bean, Einolf, and Russo (1999) particularly suggest that patents should be viewed against a measure of continuity and an ability of the organization to pursue particular methods of licensing and commercial cooperation.

- In this era of rapid advance and greater levels of complexity the virtues associated with the **employment of individuals who possess higher degrees** is being taken as an indicator of the organization's potential for innovation.
- The presence of **R&D divisions that are devoted to basic research, applied research, and or developmental research** is taken as being indicative of the expected success of an organization's innovation process. This indicator is not directly associated with outputs but it is recognized as an enabling factor.
- Following on from the previous observation, successful outputs have been associated with the **satisfaction of customers and the general image that the business maintains in the market place**.

While this seems to offer a rather straightforward set of measures from which to design an assessment regime, the authors themselves identify some of the limitations. It is also difficult to know what might be done to remedy a failing situation: for example, if the number of patents are not at the level of competitors, what can be done other than encouraging more patent applications and does this actually make the company more innovative? We earlier pointed out that the debate continues about how much innovation is serendipity-driven and how much of it can be influenced in a deterministic manner. It is rather easier to measure the impact of a clear innovation process than something that is believed by many to be far more likely to come about as the result of chance, and therefore is highly unpredictable.

Birchall and Tovstiga (2004b) report that few companies have comprehensive metrics that focus explicitly on innovation, beyond some well-known measures relating innovation activity to revenues. Even fewer, Hamel (2000) points out, have metrics that focus on radical innovation. Traditional performance metrics are decidedly weighted in favour of optimization rather than innovation, and generally encourage a "more of the same" environment for doing business. Innovation performance, Hamel argues must reflect the firm's ability to create wealth. Tidd, Bessant, and Pavitt (2001) argue, similarly, that innovation performance must relate the firm's innovative activities to its success in the market place. They do point out, however, that renowned assessments such as those used in conjunction with the Malcolm Baldridge award often fail to capture the true picture; a case in point is Florida Power and Light, one of the early winners of the prestigious award, which was nonetheless forced into receivership.

Neely (2004) talks about the "measurement crisis" which he sees to be the result of "drowning in data." He suggests that it is not that the wrong things are being measured, but that too much is being measured, and too great an attempt is being made to quantify features that do not really lend themselves usefully to quantification. The costs of measurement are increasing, but are organizations and their executives getting better value? Is measurement leading to improved decision making?

Key questions

- What innovation performance measures exist?
- How does the organization decide which innovation performance measures to adopt?
- How does one align measures to strategy?
- How does the firm ensure that appropriate measures, including those addressing the 'softer' side of innovation, are adopted for each level of decision making?
- How can the barriers to measurement be overcome?
- How is performance improvement driven through as a result of measurement?

Innovation performance measurement

This will be taken to include provisions for assessing the effectiveness of the innovation activity in terms of business success. A number of factors play an important role here and merit consideration. The first has to do with time. Truly successful innovations must pass the test of time. The real test of innovation success is sustained growth through continuous invention, adaptation, and commercialization. A second factor has to do with the fact that the outcomes of successful innovation may not be directly measurable, that is, successful innovation may exhibit qualitative *and* quantitative attributes. Hence, we may need to accept the fact that only certain aspects of a successful innovation outcome may be measurable and therefore quantifiable. Indeed, this second factor throws up the question regarding the very identity of innovation. Is it best thought of in terms of a process, that is, as the outcome of a manageable routine, or rather as a phenomenon that is largely serendipity-driven? The prevailing view on innovation has important implications for its measurability.

Source: Birchall and Tovstiga (2004b).

The purposes of measurement

We have argued elsewhere (Birchall and Tovstiga 2004b) that the prime purposes of measurement are to guide decision making, to enable audit, and to ensure the adequacy of governance. If the prime aim of innovation is to create new, better value for the customer or end user so as to gain improved return on investment, then the factors likely to provide that success are key areas for measurement. Clark and Fujimoto (1991), as early as 1991, demonstrated that the most crucial determinants of new product success are time to market, product performance, and development resources. Any measurement system should focus attention on the critical success factors in the particular business and its sector of activity. The overall targets for innovative efforts are likely to involve making trade-offs, for example reduced time to market may lead to a compromise on product performance.

As pointed out by Cohen, Eliashberg, and Teck-Hua (2000), industries focus on different success determinants. Mature industries are more likely to focus on total development costs. Start-ups with limited capital may also focus on overall costs. For high-tech industries new product evaluation is more likely to be based on product performance and time to market. But measures should not only assess the degree to which outputs achieve objectives (effectiveness metrics), but also the extent to which resource utilization meets that planned (efficiency metrics).

Measurement functions in performance control

- Identify deviations from plans in order to support corrective action by management.
- Stimulate learning about system functioning.
- Facilitate alignment and communication of objectives.
- The basis for performance related employee rewards.
- Assist staff in diagnosing problems and taking corrective action.
- Provide feedback to motivate staff and management.
- Inputs for the justification of decisions.

Source: based on Kerssens-van Drongelen and
Weerd-Nederhof (1999).

The nature of innovation performance measurement

> Everything that can be counted does not necessarily count; everything that counts cannot necessarily be counted.
>
> Albert Einstein

As we indicated earlier, innovation performance measurement is fraught with difficulty. It is both technically problematic and politically sensitive. The complexity of the innovation process, with its uncertainties, inherent time-lag between activities and demonstrable benefit, and the need to foster and develop creativity and risk taking during the process, compounds the difficulties in establishing suitable metrics. Outcome measures can be applied, but explanation for the outcome achieved is no simple matter. Many factors impact on the process of taking novel ideas to market, so that a direct link between specific isolated actions and organizational performance is tenuous to say the least. The very act of measuring performance will have an impact on behaviours, not always in the predicted ways, and not in all cases of benefit to the overall organization. Some areas are particularly difficult to measure, for example the value of inputs such as earlier intellectual property, and outcomes such as the advanced capabilities developed by the organization through carrying out the project.

In practice we find a variety of approaches taken to innovation performance measurement. These have come about as a result of the different views that exist on the nature and scope of innovation itself.

In Figure 11.1 we suggest a breakdown of innovation performance measurement in terms of the *scope* and *nature* of the measures. These relate to the three broad innovation clusters introduced in Chapter 5— *institutional, evolutional,* and *revolutional* innovation. For each cluster there are corresponding indicators of innovation performance.

The *scope* of the innovation performance measurement in a firm can either be focused on day-to-day operational aspects of innovation, or be strategic and futures-oriented. The former measurement is typically related to quantifiable indicators and measurable parameters, while measures related to the latter are largely non-quantifiable. Three main "innovation clusters" become apparent when we view innovation performance in this way. *Institutional* innovation (Mezias and Boyle 2002) is based on a rational, functional planned approach which tends to lead to incremental change. This approach lends itself to the application of metrics supporting performance management. In contrast, the *revolutional* approach requires a conscious effort to move away from established organizational systems and

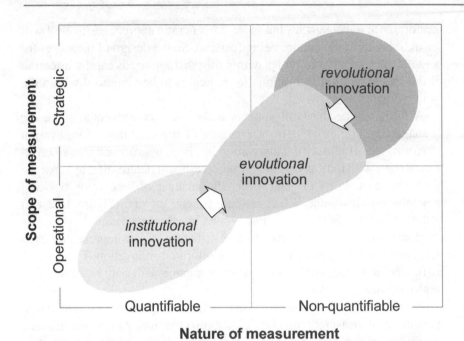

Figure 11.1 Innovation performance measurement clusters according to scope and nature of the measurement

procedures. As we have already indicated this approach fits uncomfortably within established organizations, as too many people are threatened and established processes suppress risky projects. Spin-offs, skunkworks, special project teams outside the normal organization avoid the control, coordination, and communication expected for internal projects. In this circumstance the traditional organizational metrics may not support the very behaviors being encouraged, so it is more difficult to design a system.

The third strategy (Mezias and Boyle 2002) is *evolutional*. It involves making organizational boundaries unclear, and encourages innovation by a process of "imperfect routine maintenance." Slack resources, promotion of risk taking, the highlighting of organizational change, characterize this approach, as do less precise routines, performance management, and control. Many projects are initiated and encouraged so as to result in some "winners." Search routines, which act both internally and externally to seek out developments and opportunities, are encouraged. When new areas are identified, resources are likely to shift from search to development.

Portfolio approaches to project review may be useful, but tight control is likely to discourage the creativity and individual initiative being sought. The latter stages in the innovation process are clearly amenable to performance management, but more bureaucratic approaches overall will be unlikely to fit the culture being fostered. So the design of measures for a range of innovative activities within the portfolio needs careful attention if the spectrum from institutional to radical is to be embraced within the single organization.

A further issue that still appears to be quite controversial in senior management circles concerns the degree of predictability of innovation performance. Traditionally, innovation has been approached in a stochastic manner, with returns on innovation investment determined by *after the fact* outcomes. In its extreme form, this manner of innovation tracking resembles a clustering of hits around a mean hit rate (Figure 11.2 (a)) which typically falls in the loss zone. In its more refined form this approach to innovation results in a distribution of hits represented by a frequency of hit curve as a function of return on innovation (Figure 11.2 (b)). Here also, we see that innovation is a game with only relatively few really significant hits.

Figure 11.2 (c) suggests a very different approach to innovation performance measurement; one that suggests that innovation performance might be approached in a significantly more deterministic manner than current practice would have us believe is possible. In this mode, innovation performance and its outcomes would be a predictable contributing factor to the business's bottom line profitability. It appears (Birchall and Tovstiga 2004b) that relatively few firms are prepared to think about innovation in this manner. The question the authors have raised with a number of firms[1] on this issue is, what would need to change in the way that organizations think about innovation and the way they practice innovation in order for innovation to become a largely predictable contribution to the business outcome? Our research has shown that companies are typically at a loss when it comes to providing an answer to this question.

A distinction can be drawn between regular *performance measurement* of a selected set of indicators, and *performance assessment*, which goes into more depth by examining a broader set of aspects on a less frequent basis (Chiesa, Coughlan, and Voss 1996). The latter is more typically the basis of an audit to examine in depth aspects of the process, and identify areas for specific improvement.

Kerssens-van Drongelen and Weerd-Nederhof (1999) distinguish two factors making up *operational effectiveness*—product (concept) effectiveness and process effectiveness. Operational effectiveness contributes to the achievement of operational goals. These goals should be related to the firm's overall strategy, and cover the short to mid-term. Product concept effectiveness is concerned with the fit with environmental constraints and

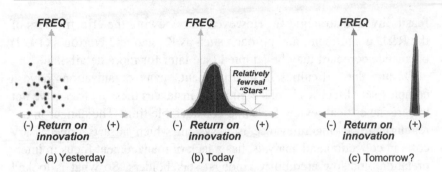

Figure 11.2 Innovation performance approaches in terms of frequency of hit and return on investment; progression of approaches

market demands (an external perspective) and fit with company competencies (an internal perspective). Process effectiveness includes speed, productivity, and flexibility. Strategic flexibility is described as "the proactive and reactive organizational potential for maintaining a dynamic fit between organization and environment … changing strategic goals … characteristics of people, means and organizational arrangements." Included in strategic fit are activities such as market scanning and forecasting, competence building, evaluating, and learning.

A distinction is drawn by Kerssens-van Drongelen and Bilderbeek (1999) between *feed-forward* and *feedback control*. The former sets out to ensure that the right organizational conditions (qualified people, equipment, coordination mechanisms) are in place to enable good performance. The latter is based on comparing actual performance with targets, and supports decision making and action. Feed-forward uses approaches such as organizational auditing, based on comparing those conditions found to pre-defined standards, or benchmarking against best practice elsewhere.

Kerssens-van Drongelen and Bilderbeek also contrast the R&D function with the R&D department. The latter is the organizational unit tasked with efficiently creating, sustaining, and exploiting the technological knowledge base needed by the company. In contrast the R&D function embraces, in their definition, not only technology processes but also product development. The R&D function may exist without an R&D department by comprising a multi-disciplinary team representing the skills needed to source technology, design and develop new products, establish manufacturing and operations, and develop the market. Much of this work is likely to be carried out on a project basis. These projects may well be subject to a stage gate process, and at each stage feasibility may be assessed in terms of market, economics, technical feasibility, and strategic fit. However, in reviewing the effectiveness of the R&D department, an approach such as Kaplan and Norton's (1992) balanced scorecard may be adopted (see later for more details).

Despite the difficulties in measurement, many organizations have a complex set of metrics in place. In many instances these metrics have not undergone critical review for some considerable time. The danger in not regularly reviewing relevance is a system which attracts unnecessary costs in collection and analysis, has a lack of management focus in interpretation, and low credibility amongst stakeholders. So what is looked for? Metrics should:

- measure and cover critical issues
- be simple and clear to all stakeholders
- not depend on complex, difficult to access data
- be valid and reliable and weaknesses and limitations recognized and understood
- be reasonably easy to evaluate
- be actionable.

Where companies rely on financial measurement to evaluate performance, they are more likely to favor short-term projects, since they have greater discounted cash flow returns on innovation investment costs (Kirchhoff, Merges, and Morabito 2001). The crucial objective becomes the maximization of returns on innovation investment. Monitoring focuses on keeping projects on track financially (Godener and Soderquist 2004). Christensen (1997) emphasizes the point that where these measures are applied to R&D, researchers can become focused on short-term, customer-driven projects which cause them to fall behind in new technology development and eventually lose market share to other firms.

Kirchhoff et al (2001) argue that:

the R&D process from project to project is too heterogeneous in nature to measure on any basis … this is especially true for technology areas where rapidly changing developments are driving whole industries. An additional argument is that until an industry is well developed, both the R&D outcomes and their timing are unknown, so financial models based upon discounted rates of return are unrealistic.

This is the basis of their case for the use of multiple metrics, both financial and qualitative.

As early as 1984, Cooper (1984) found a strong relationship between performance results and the strategies pursued by the firms he studied, showing that they can strive for different types of performance by employing different strategic thrusts. About the same time, Nystrom (1985) also found that different strategies relate to different new product development outcomes, technological, competitive, or financial. More recently, Hart (1993), in reviewing previous studies of NPD success and despite considerable research in the intervening years, states, "unfortunately, there is very little consensus amongst the major research studies on how best to define success; which dimensions of success to include and how to set about measuring these dimensions."

Hart (1993) identified a series of financial measures in use, which she grouped as *profit, assets, sales, capital,* and *equity.* But a reliance exclusively on financial measures would clearly have many weaknesses. Linton, Walsh, and Morabito (2002) point out that financial measures such as net present value are convenient, but this approach fails to consider differences in likelihood of success. Despite suggesting the use of call options, they go on to suggest that until a product is established, projections of rate of return are speculative, and that qualitative measures are important to capture the richness of projects. Many new product failures measured in purely short-term financial terms have later turned out to be successful because other by-products in terms of organizational, technical, and market developments have had a major impact on the firm's longer-term profitability. So it is important not to ignore long-term viability and organizational health when measuring performance. One particular aspect to consider is the potential the innovation offers for long-term profitability.

On a more practical level it is often actually infeasible to separate out the impact of an innovation on the organization's financial performance. Even where the innovation is developed within a separate business entity, there is likely to be a degree of dependency on the parent, and transfer pricing will distort "true" financial performance. Actual performance figures may be used, such as *average return on sales, profitability over the product's lifecycle, time to break even,* and *profit margin.* But less "hard" financial measures have been used to review the success of innovation: *profits reaching objectives set, profitability being acceptable, sales compared to other recent new products,* and *sales growth compared with industry average.* These have numerous weaknesses, including reliance on opinion and memory.

Non-financial measures identified by Hart (1993) are categorized by her as *design, activity, market, technological*, and *commercial*. These measures also are not free of criticism. One major weakness is that they do not appear to be related to the prime objective of the innovation. Also they are not easily operationalized, as for example *technological innovativeness, degree of novelty*, or *degree of patent protection*. Even where measures which relate product performance to the original expectations for the product, there is little to suggest that appropriate dimensions were adopted against which to assess performance. Activity-based measures were either based on the level of development activity (for example the regularity of product updates in relation to the competitive nature of the market) or measures of proficiency (such as direct measures—*the number of successful product launches, the rate of success, the number of failures*—and indirect—*the success of the program in relation to its objectives*). Hart's own empirical research on UK firms (1993) found that managers' success criteria fell into three clusters:

- beating the competition technologically, to market and with a techno-logical breakthrough
- reduced production costs/beating the competition on price, meeting objectives, and opening up new markets
- beating the competition to market, profit generation, and meeting objectives.

Godener and Soderquist (2004) identify a series of process management metrics concerned with *optimizing quality, lead time and cost*, and *progress accords to process-related goals*. Metrics include *development lead-time, total product quality, engineering productivity*, and *effectiveness of communication*; and motivational and behavioural factors such as *commitment, initiative*, and *leadership of human resources*. They identify knowledge management metrics—*knowledge creation, knowledge transfer, knowledge exploitation resulting in enhanced capabilities and intellectual assets*. In addition they report technology management metrics—*the efficient management of product technology for generating a continuous stream of new competitive products*. They focus management attention on product families, the renewal of underlying technology architectures/platforms, and the generation of derivative products; and also manufacturing flexibility. While they offer some interesting measures, there does appear to be the prospect of over-complication.

Key questions

- What aims have been identified by the firm for the measurement of innovation performance?
- How are measures related to strategic intent?
- How does the organization ensure that measures reflect short and long-term goals, have both an immediate and futures orientation, cover operational and process effectiveness, and are feed-forward as well as giving feedback?
- How does the firm ensure value for money from its measurement system?

The use of measures for innovation performance management

Dooley et al (2002), in examining NPD best practice, used Cooper's (1993) stage gate model: *customer requirements, product strategy, concept generation, concept selection, concept design, detail design and redesign, manufacturing and launch programs, product improvement,* and *disposal.* To this they added management and control aspects of the NPD process: *goals, metrics, project management, organizational context.* From a survey of 39 organizations they conclude that for many firms there is a mismatch between the best practices being implemented and those that are most likely to improve product and process success. In particular they stress the need to develop the human resources involved in NPD. Also they highlight that best practice was not being implemented at the "fuzzy front end" of the development process, despite this being recognized as a problematic stage. Much energy had been focused on the strategic implementation of NPD (project selection, goals, technological leadership, product strategy, and customer involvement). The authors believe that these are less significant in influencing NPD performance than the control of the execution (process control, metrics, documentation, and change control).

A worldwide study of innovation in 190 companies producing medical, electronic, automotive, and industrial products (Goldense 1999) concluded that despite pressures to reduce product lifecycles, manufacturers had "only a rudimentary idea of how to measure their new product development efforts." The results revealed that minimal use was made of common measurement systems across sectors, making benchmarking problematic; less than 40 percent of respondents measured NPD in relation to its contribution to the bottom line; responsibility for product development metrics was misplaced, in that it was generally at too low a level within the organization; and there was generally a lack of sophistication in the measurement tools used to capture the data.

Performance measures can encourage competition between individuals, teams, departments, and country divisions. On the other hand they can be used to encourage collaboration. The measurement system may enable benchmarking across internal divisions or with major competitors. Both may be intended to "raise the endgame" for those involved in innovation management. The measurement system may encourage openness and cross-project learning, or it may foster secrecy and team cohesiveness. It may support cross-functional working, or a greater focus on departmental or individual effort.

In a study of the performance consequences of non-financial measures, Said and HassabElnaby (2003) found that non-financial performance measures are associated with subsequent firm economic performance. Their use by firms is significantly associated with an innovation-orientated strategy, a quality-orientated strategy, the length of the product development cycle, industry regulation, and the level of financial distress (negatively). They found that the association between non-financial measures and firm performance is contingent on whether the use of non-financial measures matches the firm's characteristics in terms of its operational and competitive environment.

Werner and Souder (1997) surveyed a total of more than 100 sources which reported performance measurement techniques, and concluded that "the methods are so individually varied and uniquely designed for particular situations that they almost defy systematic classification." They distinguish between quantitative-objective measures normally based on R&D outputs, such as numbers of patents filed, and numbers of new products released, and quantitative-subjective metrics which are based on intuitive judgements. These measures can involve estimates of both past and future expectations. They introduce a system adopted at Alcoa Laboratories, where a panel comprising marketing, planning, and R&D staff collect past objective data and jointly estimate the expected future benefits of R&D accomplishments. Both Borg-Warner and DuPont are reported as estimating the annual business opportunities derived from R&D activities. Quantitative-objective metrics are reported as being most suitable for the later stages of R&D efforts, where outputs are more certain and definable. Qualitative-subjective metrics are more appropriate to early-stage R&D efforts, and are seen in some cases as the only method suitable, since so much uncertainty is a feature of early stages.

Qualitative metrics were also found to focus on the performance of individuals, teams, groups, or departments. Whereas quantitative metrics usually focus on technical processes, financial aspects, and numerical outputs, the focus shifts to assessing human performance as a measure of R&D effectiveness. These qualitative assessments are classified as one of self-evaluations, supervisory ratings, peer ratings, and external audits.

The actual process of conducting qualitative evaluations can itself result in improved information flows, networking, learning, and shared understanding. However, the development of appropriate measures is time-consuming, and for the process to work well there is the need for training. Werner and Souder advocate the use of integrated metrics, but point out, "Because R&D is fundamentally uncertain, its measurement will necessarily remain imperfect. Though metrics are often enlightening aids to decision-making, studied judgement remains the ultimate method for managing R&D."

Cohen et al (2000) report that setting a target on *time to market* has become commonplace as a response to increasingly shortened product life-cycles in many industries. Product performance targets normally relate to market share. From their analysis of the interplay between these two metrics and a third metric, *development costs*, they conclude that an overly ambi-tious time to market leads to an upward bias in intensity of resource usage, and a downward bias in product performance. Under the target performance development process, the coordination between marketing and R&D is easier, because of the separation of resource and time-to-market decisions. But an overly ambitious target leads to upward bias in intensity of develop-ment resources. It also can lead to delay in product launches. However this type of measure would seem more appropriate for institutional innovation than the more radical types of innovation.

Godener and Soderquist (2004) report a study into the use of R&D and NPD measures in three large electronics companies, where they found the measures were used to gain better coherence and relevance of product portfolios, reorienting projects before failure, deciding on corrective actions, supporting the launch decision, enhancing staff motivation, and facilitating well-balanced decision making.

Rather than taking either an approach focused on individual projects or one focused on a global assessment of inputs and outcomes from R&D and innovation investment more generally, Cooper et al (2001) argued the case for *portfolio management* as a means for ensuing maximum return from R&D investment, suggesting that "portfolio management is the manifestation of your business's strategy—it dictates where and how you will invest for the future." Construction of the portfolio requires decision makers to address issues such as maximization of value, the balance of activities, and the alignment to overall business strategy. The benefits come though active management of the portfolio. Not only are new projects weighed up against the existing portfolio, evaluated, selected, and prioritized, but existing projects may also be reprioritized and possibly more readily terminated. The process is likely to make decisions more transparent, involve a wider range of decision makers, and at more senior levels in the organization. Their research has found that strategic criteria are more widely applied in project selection and review, leading to a reduction in low-value projects and more effective project selection. Senior management also used the approach to achieve better balance between long and short-term projects, high and low risk. Better communication of the priorities across the organization was sought; and greater objectivity was claimed in project selection.

Innovation inherently links organizational learning and adaptation as much as it is about the interaction of technology, the market, and the enterprise. It is the organization's guarantor in coming to terms with a future that is inherently uncertain. Effective innovation measures must reflect the firm's performance in achieving an integration of key related management tasks related to competitive performance of the firm (Tidd et al 2001).

We are well aware that the measurement of innovation performance is a challenging area for both practitioners and academics, and it is clear that little consensus is apparent in the earlier research into the topic. We recognize that firms have to tailor the methods used for innovation performance measurement to their own unique set of organizational needs. So our own research (Birchall et al 2005) into the field, rather than looking at the overall range of measures in use, has focused on the challenges faced by executives in the design and application of metrics, and the importance attached to areas for measurement. This has revealed a range of challenges, many of which are inter-related.

In Table 11.1 we present dilemmas which became apparent from our own investigation. They have been identified from a review of the range of responses received to our survey, rather than from any particular individual responses. Executives may well not articulate these dilemmas when making decisions about individual measures or approaches. Many relate to the assumptions underpinning decision making in organizations, the nature of management actions, and its impact on behaviour. We believe that such a framework can provide practical assistance to executives in thinking through decisions, either in the design of an innovation performance approach tailored to the needs of the organization, or in an examination of the applicability of the existing approach.

Key questions

- How does the firm assess how well it is performing in innovation compared with leading businesses?
- How does the firm track the impact of innovation performance measurement on behaviour?
- How does the firm undertake reviews of the effectiveness of the measures being used?
- How does the firm distinguish between projects, portfolios, and overall innovation performance?
- How does the firm track the impact of spillovers on overall performance?

Table 11.1 The innovation performance measurement dilemmas facing executives

Dilemmas in the design and application of metrics	
Measurement focused on innovation as incremental change	Measurement focused on innovation as radical change
Measurement for control	Measurement for learning
Innovation process focus	Innovation outcomes focus
To support decision making in the short term	Looking at long-term impact
Framework based on simple metrics	Elaborate system based on fine-grained measurement
Emphasis on quantifiable metrics	Emphasis on qualitative attributes
Precise definition of costs of innovation	Broad view of impact
Internal focus in measurement	External (customer) focus
Measures designed for and tailored to the specific situation	Organization-wide measurement for comparison purposes
Narrow (departmental) focus	Organization-wide view
Project focus	Portfolio approach
Internal review	External comparisons
Stage-gate reviews	Standard review periods
Minimizing costs of administration	Quality, reliability, and validity of measurement
Quality of innovation process	Quality and quantity of outputs

Current practices in innovation performance measurement: the important measures

So as to better understand current practice in the field, we undertook a survey of innovation leaders (Birchall et al 2005). Respondents were invited to rate the importance of specific dimensions of innovation performance measurement. The statistical analysis of the results enabled the development of a set of five measurement scales, which we named *Futures focus, Market impact, Capabilities and image, Process*, and *Sustainability and overall effectiveness*. They are shown in Table 11.2.

The relative weighting given by the respondents to each of the constructed scales is presented in Table 11.3, from which we can compare the ranking of scales by firm types, the level of measurement, the stage at which measured, and the level of reporting. From this we can see that there is really considerable agreement amongst respondents on the relative weighting given to each scale. *Process measures* are consistently rated the most important, except where reporting is to the board level, where more importance is attached to *Sustainability and overall effectiveness*. *Market impact* is the second highest-rated scale, again except in the case of the board, where it slips to fourth place. *Futures focus* is placed third in importance by most groups (specialist suppliers, measurement at the level of the portfolio, the board, and operations management being exceptions). But we can see from Table 11.4 that *Futures focus* is considered important in all aspects of the use of measures (benchmarking, diagnostic purposes, allocating resources, compensating employees, informing markets, and setting future goals). Interestingly despite the importance attached to market image, it is only consistently seen as important for *Informing markets* and *Setting future goals*. Little importance is attached generally to *Sustainability and overall effectiveness* and it is only consistently seen as important for allocating resources and informing markets.

So particular importance is attached to the *Process* measures (indicators for budgeting processes, technology asset management. technical assistance, and project management). But the most broadly sought measure seems to be *Futures focus*, which is consistently seen as an important measure where importance is attached to benchmarking, diagnostic purposes, allocating resources, compensating employees, informing markets, and setting future goals.

We do have some indicators of the differences in importance attached by different audiences and for different purposes. This enables decision makers to examine their particular needs from measurement, and the

Table 11.2 The measurement scales

Futures focus	Market impact	Capabilities and image	Process	Sustainability and overall effectiveness
How important are indicators for Technology intelligence?	How important are indicators for Technology leadership?	How important are indicators for Image, brand and stock value?	How important are indicators for Budgeting processes?	How important are indicators for Sustainability, Resource use, Energy efficiency, Social and ethical issues?
How important are indicators for Market intelligence?	How important are indicators for Direct revenues from sales of services etc.?	How important are indicators for Idea management?	How important are indicators for Technology asset management?	How important are indicators for Societal responsiveness?
How important are indicators for Process intelligence?	How important are indicators for Innovativeness?	How important are indicators for Competencies and skills?	How important are indicators for Technical assistance?	How important are indicators for Project/Program portfolio management?
How important are indicators of Leadership, vision and mission?	How important are indicators for Product leadership and Customer satisfaction, Preference/Market share?	How important are indicators for Intellectual property management?	How important are indicators for Project management?	How important are indicators for Knowledge management?
How important are indicators for Knowledge, Know-how, Familiarity, Awareness and understanding?	How important are indicators for Cost efficiency?	How important are indicators for Strategy and portfolio drivers?		
How important are indicators for Technological options generated by R&D function?		How important are indicators for External partnerships and networking?		
How important are indicators for Radical innovation?				

Table 11.3 The relative ranking of the measurement scales

	Firm type				Level of measurement		Stage at which measured		Level of reporting		
	Science-based industries	Scale-based industry	Information-intensive sectors	Specialized suppliers	Information-intensive sectors	Information-intensive sectors	Information-intensive sectors	Information-intensive sectors	Specialized suppliers	Specialized suppliers	Specialized suppliers
Futures focus	3	3	3	4	3	4	3	3	5	3	4
Market impact	2	2	2	2	2	2	2	2	4	2	2
Capabilities and image	4	4	5	3	5	5	4	5	3	5	3
Process	1	1	1	1	1	1	1	1	2	1	1
Sustainability and overall effectiveness	5	5	4	5	4	3	5	4	1	4	5

Table 11.4 The Pearson product moment correlations between the importance of measures and the purpose of measurement

Importance for	Futures focus	Market impact	Capabilities and image	Process	Sustainability and overall effectiveness
Benchmarking	0.66**		0.32**	0.24*	
Diagnostic purpose	0.66**				
Allocating resources	0.55**		0.24*	0.37**	
Compensating employees	0.62**		0.24*	0.32**	0.23*
Informing markets	0.31**	0.24*	0.47**		
Setting future goals	0.65**	0.30**	0.45**	0.29**	0.25*

** Pearson product moment correlation is significant at the 0.01 level (2-tailed).

* Pearson product moment correlation is significant at the 0.05 level (2-tailed).

importance of measures in their particular context, and to devote their energy to ensuring that they have selected appropriate measures in these areas.

What is not being or cannot be measured?

In Table 11.5 we present the results of an additional question in our survey, in which we are looking at those areas important but not currently measured. This shows a considerable diversity of view around the non-measurable and non-measured.

Table 11.5 Areas considered important for measurement but not currently measured

---

Are there any important measurements of innovation performance that, in your estimation, are important but are not currently being measured, or perhaps cannot be measured?

Quality of innovations:
1 What would have happened if we hadn't spent the money on innovation
2 Platform leverage
3 Competitive position of our technology vs. competition
4 Savings in time from new technologies vs. what would happen if it wasn't adopted

Market related:
1 Barriers to innovation in the market place
2 Alignment with customer expectations
3 Diffusion time of new products
4 Effectiveness of marketing tools for new inventions
5 Percentage of dedication of sales representatives to innovation
6 Know-how to implement new technologies into the market place
7 Technical skills of sales to implement innovations
8 Developing technologies that start customer engagement
9 Direct customer input into innovation projects
10 Cost and time of access to customers
11 Customer perception of firm's innovations
12 Impact of innovation on company image
13 Impact of innovation on goodwill (marketing)
14 Impact both expected and actual as perceived by the business unit

Intangibles:
1 Difficult to measure intangibles
2 Creativity cannot be measured
3 Passion
4 Vision
5 Innovation cure
6 Entrepreneurial spirit

7 How innovation performance changes the company culture/organizational culture/ cultural change
8 Paradigm change—attempts to change
9 Risk taking
10 Build up of knowledge to be used for various purposes (not clearly allocated) kinds of purposes
11 Contribution of necessary (but not easily output-quantifiable) kinds of purposes
12 Innovation in management, such as organization structure
13 Innovation in procedures (such as change or improvement in work flow)
14 Human assets
15 Motivation of R&D personnel
16 Under-utilized know-how
17 Annual value of stock of knowledge
18 Confidence measures
19 Informal innovation network within the company and partners

Contribution of R&D:
1 How effective are we?
2 Real time efficiency in R&D
3 Contribution of R&D to bottom line
4 Benchmarking of R&D process compared with competition
5 Actual allocation of resources to innovation process
6 Risk adjusted pipeline value
7 Number of innovations doesn't say anything about success of R&D team

Decision-making ability:
1 Measuring the amount of mandatory innovation for the company to continue being a presence in the market
2 Risk associated with innovation push by the company as opposed to the risk-free innovation that results from market pull
3 Expertise in differentiating core technologies and techniques
4 Ability to change/split/merge to focus on innovation
5 The right balance between incremental RT&D (to support existing business) and the radical R&D
6 Technical feasibility of very innovative ideas
7 Number of ideas not put into the system for the lack of resources
8 Risk taking
9 Number of people who don't understand the process
10 Long-term impact of short-term decisions
11 Conversion—effectiveness of strategy process
12 Senior management sentiment to innovation over time
13 Ability to change our minds

Inadequacy of measurement:
1 Very poor at measuring successes
2 Radical innovation
3 Innovative design limited to a very few countables
4 Driver of incremental revenues
5 Balance—relation between sustaining engineering, value generative plant extension, and value adding

While these areas are obviously of importance to organizations, they may well be areas where measurement is impractical, and even if possible not feasible because of difficulties in data collection or costs of the process.

Firms may well be advised to steer clear of considering these as areas to include within their frameworks, but even if they are considered for inclusion, they may wish to consider very carefully whether or not to expend effort in these areas.

Frameworks for innovation performance measurement

Innovation and its management have been described in various ways. It has been described in terms of a routinized process with specific inputs, activities, and outputs. Alternatively, innovation has been described as a complex phenomenon. The particular view taken on innovation will largely determine the measurement possibilities and limitations.

As we emphasized earlier, innovation has increasingly come to be recognized as a highly complex and diversified activity. Traditional measurement has focused on macro-level indicators of input and output. Chiesa, Coughlan, and Voss (1998) stress the need for going beyond mere indicators of performance; they argue for looking closely at innovation capability and the process itself.

Performance measurement systems, according to Kerssens-van Drongelen and Cook (1997), consist of:

1 Metrics (performance aspects/indicators) organized in a certain structure.
2 Measurement methods.
3 Standards to measure performance against (norms).
4 Frequency and timing of measurement and reporting.
5 Reporting format.

These researchers point out that the purpose of the measurement procedure is a combination of the subject to whom the procedure has to apply, and the function the procedure has in the performance control processes of that subject. The metrics may be quantitative, such as the time to market in months, qualitative, such as that the time to market was "poor," "satisfactory," or "good," or semi-quantitative, by assigning numeric values to qualitative indicators anchored to definitions or behaviours, for instance on a five-point scale. Composite scales may be constructed by straight summation of item scores or by giving weightings to the items prior to summation. Scoring may be based on objective data such as the number of patents, or subjective, based on judgement, for example the future net present value. Scoring may be based on the judgement of one or more personnel with direct involvement, or on outsider opinion in the form of an "expert" panel. The latter is likely to be less biassed, but may lack the detailed knowledge needed for informed judgements.

Kerssens-van Drongelen and Bilderbeek (1999) distinguish four time spans for measurement:

1 Performance in the distant past.
2 Performance in the recent past.
3 Expected performance in the near future.
4 Expected performance in the far future.

They suggest that in the balanced scorecard (Kaplan and Norton 1992), the traditional financial indicators are based on past performance, the customer and business perspective focuses on the more immediate, and the learning and growth indicators are futures-oriented. As output measures for R&D endeavors they propose measures in five areas: quality, innovativeness, timeliness, cost, and quantity. The evaluation might take place at different levels in the organization: an individual, a group, a major design, an entire program, or a larger organizational segment. It might focus on the executive committee, the program board, a department, or a team. While the overall purpose is likely to be to improve or sustain organizational performance, the following four reasons are cited:

- to characterize—to gain an understanding and provide baselines for future assessment
- to evaluate—compare with plan
- to predict—the basis for new plans
- to diagnose problems, determine corrective action, and monitor.

The purpose might be to motivate employees, demonstrate to employees how they contribute to performance, communicate performance expectations, provide management information, identify performance gaps, support decision making, as the basis of rewards, or to stimulate learning.

We now provide an overview and briefly review a sample of innovation frameworks currently used by companies. These frameworks serve to illustrate the diversity of approaches being advocated, based largely on the objectives set for the innovative efforts. The frameworks provide a schema against which specific measures, such as those covered in Table 11.2, can be located. The following frameworks are included:

1 Arthur D. Little's innovation process model.
2 The balanced scorecard framework.
3 The Lucent value creation model.
4 The phenomenological approach to innovation.

1. Arthur D. Little's innovation process model

The Arthur D. Little innovation framework shows innovation as a process that consists of a number of sub-activities, ranging from business strategy visioning through to post-launch activities. The entire process is linked by continuous feedback loops representing learning and the development of new knowledge. Two specific external sources of inputs representing customers and network partners contribute to the overall process at a variety of intersection points. The basic assumption of the framework is that innovation is a more or less manageable process, with intervention opportunities at the individual activity level. It also assumes that inputs and outputs of each of the individual activities may be measured on at least two levels: on the level of *individual development projects*, and on the level of the *aggregate or portfolio of projects*. Outputs are compared with inputs; from this a yield can be determined which in turn is an indicator of performance. The key assumption in this process-type view of innovation performance is that the right inputs and outputs are being used for the yield analysis.

2. The balanced scorecard framework

Kerssen-van Drongelen and Bilberbeek (1999) propose its use in measuring the success of innovation projects. The basis of their scorecard is four perspectives: financial, internal business, customer, and innovation and learning (see Figure 11.4).

This approach takes a holistic view, relating outputs to strategy. It is particularly appropriate in organizations that have adopted the balanced scorecard more generally for performance review, as managers will be familiar with the principles and approach.

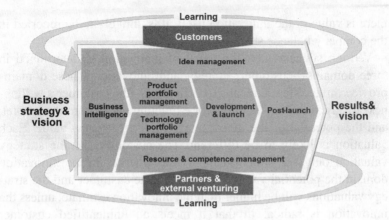

Figure 11.3 Arthur D. Little innovation process model
Source: Arthur D. Little. Used with permission.

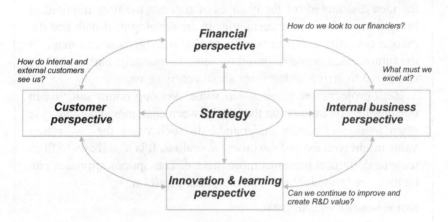

Figure 11.4 The balanced scorecard for assessing a project

Valuing innovation—an "options" approach

According to Verloop (2004), at the end of the day, the market is the ultimate arbiter of success in the innovation process. The value to the customer will depend upon many aspects, but might include the current operating costs of living with the problem which is being solved, the unfulfilled need being met, or the status enhancement the project outcome gives to the end user.

The innovation process generates new options that the company may or may not ultimately exercise at some time in the future. While there is value in the innovation itself, it is unlikely to be reported in the company balance sheet.

Verloop suggests that the value of innovation is determined in three domains—customer, strategy, and innovation. These domains provide three different means for valuation—the customer's willingness to pay, the firms' strategy for extracting value from the market, and the potential of the innovative idea to create new value. Each valuation is likely to be different. The customer and the strategy valuation only set limits on the value, whereas in the innovation domain the potential value is estimated. The customer and the strategy valuations will be higher than the innovation estimate, unless the innovation is radical in that it meets an unidentified customer demand. The strategy value sets the target for the innovation.

The option value of an innovation reflects the business value of the idea discounted for the chances of success, the time required to bring it to market, the uncertainties in the development path and the market conditions, and the decisions that management can make in the future. Each domain should be valued separately, and the values compared to arrive at decisions about continuance.

Each project creates an option value. Verloop points out that in outside-the-box innovation the link between customer and strategy is often weak and poorly understood. In such cases the innovation value might well exceed the other two values. It is also likely to fluctuate as definition becomes more precise. The options approach can be used for individual projects or for the portfolio.

Source: based on Verloop (2004).

3. The Lucent value creation model

Lucent Advanced Technology Division's framework is clearly oriented to portfolio management. It is useful is assessing the contribution of each project in a way that is designed to be understood by executives and managers.

According to Kirchhoff, Merges, and Morabito (2001), the prerequisites for the R&D management system (VCM) are:

1 A focus on managerial decisions concerning the current allocation of R&D funding and its eventual return in terms of revenues and profits—this focuses attention on future value creation.

2 Information to enable the setting of baseline operations and objectives.
3 It should be easily understood across the organization and meaningful to the users.
4 It links R&D to corporate and functional strategies.
5 It includes the critical corporate value creation factors associated with all the objectives of the technology commercialization process.
6 It has the desired cultural effect.

A portfolio management approach demands uniform measures of critical elements across projects. It also treats all budgets as corporate investments; all projects are interrelated for planning and budgeting; technologies should fit competency-based synergy and end product development strategic goals; and technology commercialization projects support the corporate strategy.

The portfolio value metric (PWM) measures the expected (future) financial impact of projects in terms of a benefit–cost ratio. It also incorporates an assessment of risk.

The qualitative metrics cover:

1 **Strategic initiatives.** Projects are rated based on their contribution to one or more of eight strategic initiatives. Combined with the PWM this can show the project's contribution to the financial objectives of the strategy.
2 **Market categories.** The market categories are the current and expected markets. Anticipated contributions are again assigned. Also each market category is evaluated for its place in the market lifecycle (future, emerging, widespread, or legacy). This enables an assessment of the potential continued life and profitability of new products entering a market.
3 **Intellectual property.** Nine future-oriented IP categories are used to define contributions. A lifecycle measure is also applied.
4 **Business units.** This assignment enables a view to be taken regarding the business units most likely to benefit from any one development.

An important aspect of the use of the system is the visual display of the data which at any one time might include 500 projects. (The source for all the above is Kirchhoff et al 2001.)

Criticisms of decision support systems

Despite recognizing that graphic decision support systems, such as Lucent's VCM, are reasonably compatible with the way managers actually make decisions, Linton, Walsh, and Morabito (2002) criticized the decision process as not being replicable in a systematic modeling manner as offered by management science techniques. A further criticism is that, despite good intentions, the technique can also add complexity to decision making when the number of projects is high. They propose a technique, data envelopment analysis (DEA), which they claim can sort through projects objectively in order to identify those that are "efficient" and can be automatically accepted, those that are above or below the threshold and can be accepted or rejected without further consideration, and those that need management consideration. For these projects a more subjective decision-support tool such as VCM is considered useful.

Linton et al (2002) illustrate the approach as applied at the Advanced Technologies Group of Bell Laboratories. The aim is the advancement of technologies into commercial application in the short and medium term, including process and management innovations to support current products and processes. The measures used include required investment; discounted anticipated cash flow for the next four years (pessimistic, most likely, optimistic); stage of the product lifecycle; and stage of the intellectual property lifecycle. This results in three input measures (discounted cash flow of investments, lifecycle stage of intellectual property and lifecycle stage of product) and three outputs (discounted pessimistic cash flow, discounted most likely cash flow, and discounted optimistic cash flow). The interdependence of multiple projects is flagged on each project and considered separately.

4. The phenomenological approach to innovation

This asserts that innovation is, for the most part, a serendipity-driven phenomenon that largely defies precise definition. Some aspects of innovation, indeed, are very difficult to measure, even when possible. This view is in line with the phenomenological view of innovation. This interpretation of innovation subscribes to the view that while we may observe certain outcomes of the innovation phenomenon, we really do not understand the mechanisms that drive the phenomenon, since they are much too complex, and inextricably link a multitude of factors that eventually lead to what we refer to as innovation. Moreover, this view acknowledges that a significant part of innovation involves tacit knowledge that is difficult to grasp and almost impossible to quantify. Hence innovation, according to this interpretation, may at best be described in qualitative terms and qualitative measures only.

Van de Ven et al (1999) describe innovation as neither sequential nor orderly, but rather as a nonlinear dynamic system consisting of a cycle of divergent and convergent activities that may be repeated over time and at different organizational levels, provided enabling and constraining conditions prevail. Innovation in the view of this group of researchers is most aptly described as a journey that is responsive to a system of dynamic constraints and resources. Ven de Ven et al specify some of the soft factors of the innovation phenomenon that do not readily lend themselves to measurement. These include:

- development of the organizational culture for innovation
- learning amongst innovation team members
- leadership behaviours of top managers or other important innovation stakeholders such as investors.

A framework for measuring innovation embedment—the case of the Whirlpool Corporation

In seeking to embed innovation as a core competence, the Whirlpool Corporation set about a wide range of activities that "assimilate, incorporate, internalize and imbue the entire fabric or lifeblood of an organization with the mind-set and skills of innovation." The measurement system was designed to enable a comprehensive assessment of progress in embedment and to support midcourse adjustment.

1 **Business results measures:**
   - Revenue from projects due directly to the innovation effort.
   - Revenue from projects shaped by the innovation.
   - Revenue from projects not using innovation tools or methods.
   - Capital expended on innovation projects versus that planned.
2 **Embedment measures** (journey goals and measures and mainly qualitative):
   - Time spent on innovation projects by region.
   - Number and type of ideas at each stage in moving through the innovation pipe.
   - Understanding of innovation at all levels in the organization.
   - Proportion of staff involved in innovation activities.
   - Staff perceptions and reactions to experiences of innovation.

- The impact of strategic communications about innovation both internally and externally.

3 Individual measures:
- Numbers of staff able to describe how innovation has changed their job.
- Job descriptions including innovation.
- Identification and removal of barriers to innovation in any work group.
- Records of the use of innovation tools.
- Proportion of appraisals with innovation goals.

These measures were not without problems, particularly surrounding the definition of innovation. Different areas of the business used definitions such as: creates distinctive and innovative solutions valued by customers; creates real and sustainable competitive advantage; creates exceptional value for shareholders; represents significant opportunity for new revenue growth; a new category of product or service with minimal cannibalization of existing business; significant market share; average sales value improvement. Definitions were tailored to the specific need of the business unit. But in order to enable comparisons of performance across the corporation standard definitions are being introduced.

A questionnaire with scaled responses to items along with space for comments and random sampling methods is used quarterly to test progress.

Measures are applied at executive committee level, to the innovation boards and to individuals.

Source: based on Duarte and Tennant-Snyder (2003).

Tom Kelley (2002), associated with Ideo, a US design consultancy specializing in product development and innovation, sees innovation involving both process and phenomenological approaches. His view on innovation is:

innovation is part golf swing, part secret recipe.... [But] it's not a matter of simply following directions. Our "secret formula" is actually not very formulaic. It's a blend of methodologies, work practices, culture, and infrastructure.

Some of these elements lend themselves readily to performance measurement; others, particularly those steeped in the soft areas such as culture, demand indirect assessment.

Making innovation performance reviews pay

There is no point in having any measurement process unless the organization can gain benefit from such measurement. Earlier we referred to Neely's (2004) comment about the measurement crisis caused by executives receiving too much data. He goes on in the same piece to suggest that much attention has been given to deciding aspects such as which measures to use, how to measure soft aspects, how to align measures to strategy, and how to overcome barriers to measurement. But he then goes onto suggest that, instead of focusing exclusively on the design and implementation of systems, we really need to address the issue of how to make measures pay. He offers some practical advice:

- "Think in terms of performance planning, not performance review." Performance reviews are always backward-looking and tend to lead to defensiveness on the part of those responsible for delivering the outcomes, as they set about explaining and justifying their prior behaviours. But in practice it is more important to focus on what to do next so as to deliver the desired outcomes.
- "Ask for answers not for data." Rather than presenting raw data to review teams, those responsible should be required to present analysis, interpretation, and action plans. Executives can then focus on questioning the soundness of the reasoning, and provide new insights and ideas for possible actions.
- "Build the capability of the performance analysts." Neely suggests the need for specialists in performance analysis. Rather than taking a functional perspective they should be encouraged to look at systems and understand their workings.

In a later article with Kennerley, Neely (2004) goes on to argue that the decision making on what measures to use and which to ignore can lead the executive team to gain greater insights into the assumptions they have about how the organization functions. The use of strategy (or success) maps can aid this process by bringing together all the key objectives of the organization with their inter-linkages onto one straightforward map. Measures can be defined for each objective which are clearly specified (purpose, relationships, targets,

Capabilities for strategic advantage

means for calculation, frequency, who measures, using what data, and who will act in what ways). Then each measure should be assessed to ensure that it will deliver the behaviors being sought.

An important outcome of the review process is the challenge it provides and the opportunities for double loop learning. Collison and Parcell (2005), based on experiences at BP, introduce the concept of "learning before," "learning during," and "learning after." This is an approach to projects which requires those putting in bids for funding to provide evidence that they have taken on board lessons learnt from earlier projects. "Learning during" is ensuring not only that the project itself learns from interim reviews, but also that other projects can gain access to lessons being learnt. Finally the end-of-project review has to make available insights to future projects.

Key questions

- How effective are the firm's measures of innovation processes?
- How effective are the firm's innovation measures of market impact?
- How are radical innovations identified and measured?
- How well developed and appropriate is the innovation measurement framework?
- Have the assumptions underpinning the measurement framework been clarified, debated, and consensus reached?
- How has the organization supported the implementation of the framework?
- How effective is the organization at learning from innovation performance reviews?

Concluding remarks

Organizations are faced with big challenges when designing performance information systems. We have identified a number of these, such as defining the purposes for measurement; the selection of frameworks for both portfolio and project evaluation, and for institutional, evolutional, and revolutional innovation; the costs versus the benefits; alignment of measurement with strategic thrust; the measures to adopt; introducing a performance culture; using measures primarily for performance review or action planning; and evaluation or learning. Faced with a plethora of measures there is the need to adopt a measurement framework with careful selection of the most pertinent measures related to strategic intent. But there is also the need to consider the adoption of standard measures to enable benchmarking.

There are clearly no straightforward answers to the dilemmas faced by those responsible for reviewing innovation performance, but the advice given by Kennerley and Neely (2004) seems particularly pertinent. First, attention should be focused on what to do rather than explanations of why what was planned has not worked out. Second, executives should be presented with not data but rather analysis, so they have an opportunity to develop an understanding of processes and appropriate ways forward. Finally, to do this there is a need for people with skills in analysis. If these practices are adopted it is likely that many of the objections to measurement and its use to support decision making and action planning will be overcome.

Table 11.6 summarizes the key capabilities that are needed in order for innovation performance management to be successful.

Note

1 This research is based on data collected in the latter part of 2004 from executives and managers involved in innovation activities employed in business organisations. All 79 respondents were in positions of some authority in relation to innovation—as executives responsible for R&D within the business or a business unit, in a support function, or in business development. The data collection and analysis are described elsewhere (Birchall et al 2005).

Table 11.6 The key capabilities needed for successful innovation performance measurement

	Institutional	Evolutional	Revolutional
People-embodied knowledge and skills.	Measurement capability. Performance analysis. Responsive to feedback.	Self direction of "slack" time. Able to balance feedback on performance with risk taking. Able to live with ambiguity in feedback from measurement.	Able to focus based on measurement.
Management systems/organizational structures.	Design of information systems. Consensus building. Decision-making focus. Taking a strategic view. Clarity of purpose. Analytical. Conceptualization. Communications.	Adept at the politics of measurement. Able to respond to measures. Conceptualization.	Sensitivity to the limitations of measurement. Able to balance qualitative and quantitative measures. Balancing of intuitive with evidence-based measurement.
Physical and technical systems.	Innovation performance measures integrated into the overall information system. Measures aid decision making. Formalized periodic review of system quality and effectiveness. Portfolio and project support.		Metrics suited to entrepreneurial activities. Project focus. Soft measures well covered.
Cultural values and norms.	Management by the use of measures. Culture of performance management. "No-blame" culture.	Tolerance of slack in the system. Thriving on the challenge of the results of measurement and on ambiguity.	

Strategic capabilities portfolio analysis: Diagnostic methodology

Introduction

The purpose of the strategic capabilities portfolio analysis methodology developed by Birchall and Tovstiga (Birchall and Tovstiga 2002b, 2004a; Tovstiga and Birchall 2002) is to guide the manager through the process of identifying, mapping, and strategically evaluating the organization's portfolio of capabilities from a competitive perspective. The primary objective of the methodology is to guide the thinking process behind the strategic evaluation; it is to help the manager and his or her team articulate better questions. The real value contribution of the methodology lies in its systematic approach to a strategic exercise that can be very complicated.

A firm's portfolio of knowledge-embedded capabilities is a dynamic entity that must be managed in the context of the firm's rapidly changing environment. An appropriate strategic capabilities analysis must therefore address both where the firm stands today and where it should be moving towards, competitively speaking. It should also provide a comparative assessment of where the firm stands relative to its competitors. The methodology presented here addresses these issues in a systematic manner.

A unique feature of this methodology is its degree of tacitness analysis. Tacit knowledge is universally acknowledged to be a very important component of capabilities, yet it cannot be identified or assessed by conventional means. In the past, this has always presented a serious problem; critical insights into some of the most strategically relevant features of the firm's capabilities were simply not available. The authors have devised and integrated into the methodology an algorithm that provides a very broad estimation of the degree of tacitness of a capability. This measure is used as an indicator of the firm's position of strength with respect to a particular capability; the greater the degree of tacitness, the more the capability represents a unique competitive feature of the firm.

Figure A.1 presents a schematic overview of the methodology.

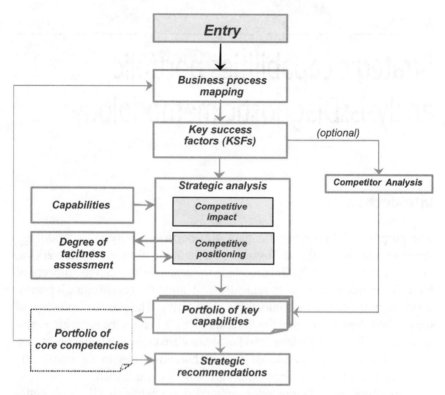

Figure A.1 Schematic overview of a methodology for assessing the strategic impact of the firm's portfolio of capabilities

The methodology in a nutshell

The analysis begins with a mapping of any one of the firm's business processes. The objective is to do this from a value-creation perspective. Implicit here is the premise that knowledge must both contribute to, and be an outcome of, the firm's value generation process. The relative importance of the firm's business processes is therefore determined on the basis of their net knowledge generation. One of the core business processes is then selected and examined in terms of its key success factors. Capabilities that deliver on these key success factors are then identified and prioritized according to importance. A set of important capabilities is subsequently selected and classified according to competitive impact (maturity) and competitive position (firm's position of strength with respect to the particular capability). These dimensions provide the coordinates for the mapping of the capabilities in a coordinate framework showing competitive impact and position. A strategic analysis, resulting in strategic recommendations, is then carried out on the basis of this mapping. A stage-by-stage description of the methodology is presented in the following sections.

Stage 1: Business process mapping

The first stage of the methodology focuses on breaking down the firm's business activities in terms of its business process value chain. A business process is understood to be any activity or group of activities that takes an input, adds value to it, and provides an output to an internal or external customer (Kaplan and Norton 1996). The objective of this first stage of the methodology is to map out a process value chain for the firm in question. Processes are identified according to their contribution to the overall value created. One of the important processes is selected for detailed analysis.

Stage 2: Key success factors

Key success factors can be thought of as being common to the firm's industry. They are just as relevant to the firm's competitors and strategic partners. That is to say that key success factors are characteristic of the market place within which the firm is competing. In retrospect, they are the variables a historian would pick to best discriminate the winners from the losers in an industry. Key success factors indicate, as their name implies, the critical criteria that the firm's particular competitive strategy must fulfil in order to succeed (Roos et al 1997). Aside from this, key success factors are a constant reminder of what factors need constant monitoring. Generally there is no limit to the number of key success factors a firm can identify. If the firm enumerates too many, however, it could be a good idea to prioritize them and concentrate only on the most important ones. Having too many factors to concentrate on would otherwise dilute the focusing effect that should be the prime directive of key success factors.

Examples of key success factors include the ability to:

- deliver superior value through products and services
- carry out competitive manufacturing and commercial process reviews
- attract superior talent, employees with critical expertise and skills

- grow the business through competitive pricing and marketing image
- establish and maintain long-term relationships with satisfied customers
- establish long-term relationships with parties in the distribution channels
- run efficient operations that cut costly red tape procedures to a minimum
- employ satisfied and competent employees
- access and absorb new and critical sources of knowledge and technology.

Key success factors must be identified within the context of the firm's industry. Ongoing monitoring and assessment of the business environment provides the firm with the requisite understanding of those key success factors that determine the firm's current and emerging competitive playing field. The choice of key success factors on which the firm focuses should reflect a clear understanding of the firm's changing competitive environment. It is helpful to think about current and future developments in terms of the industry's specific dynamic timeframe and scope, stakeholder profile and overall macroeconomic context when selecting key success factors. Key success factors relevant to the core business process are then identified and selected in this stage of the methodology.

Stage 3: Identification of capabilities

The challenge in implementing a competitive strategy is in identifying and developing those capabilities that constitute the critical building blocks of the firm's core competencies. These, in turn, will most impact the important key success factors of the industry. The firm's capabilities are drawn from the large and diverse array of fundamentally knowledge-based discrete activities, skills, and disciplines embedded in the organization. The key success factors identified in the previous stage are derived from the firm's external competitive environment. The firm's capabilities are the internal competitive activities with which the firm intends to fulfil and deliver on the key success factors.

Business processes depend on an entire range of capabilities. These can range from "supporting" to truly "core" in terms of strategic impact, as shown in Figure A.2.

The objective of this stage of the diagnostic is to compile a list of capabilities that support the core process selected in the earlier business process mapping stage of the methodology. Capabilities are selected on the basis of their impact on the key success factors identified earlier.

Stage 4: Competitive impact and positioning of capabilities

Competitive impact and the degree of control of the firm over the capabilities selected in the previous stage are assessed in this stage of the methodology.

Competitive impact

A capability can be classified as emerging, pacing, key, or base, as shown in Table A.1.

Similarly, a firm's degree of control over any particular capability is related to its ability to exploit that capability. The firm's degree of control

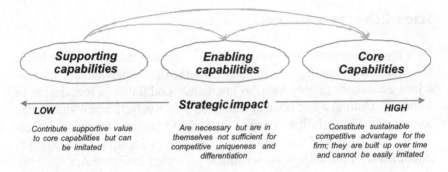

Figure A.2 Strategic positioning of the firm's capabilities

Source: adapted from Leonard-Barton (1995).

Table A.1 Classification of capability according to competitive impact

Competitive classification	Competitive impact of capability
I. Emerging	Has not yet demonstrated potential for changing the basis of competition.
II. Pacing	Has demonstrated its potential for changing the basis of competition.
III. Core	Is embedded in, and enables, products and processes. Has major impact on value-added stream (cost, performance, quality—and enables a proprietary position).
IV. Base	Necessary (enabling) but confers only minor impact on value-added streams; common to all competitors; commodity status (base).

can be high, neutral, or weak. For example, a capability may be controlled by a supplier if it is embedded in a bought-in component; or it can be controlled by a partner, as in the case of distribution by an intermediary. The situation in which critical capabilities are subjected to a high degree of external control requires careful review and perhaps restructuring of the strategic partnership. External recognition of the firm for its competitive capabilities, on the other hand, is a measure of a strong strategic positioning of the firm in its industry.

The decision tree schematics shown in Figures A.3 and A.4 provide a classification scheme for identifying the *degree of control* (that is, competitive position) and *competitive impact*. The outcome of the capability-by-capability analysis is used to map the firm's *capability portfolio*.

Stage 5: Degree of tacitness

Tacit knowledge embodied in capabilities, as we showed earlier in the book, can exist to varying degrees, ranging from the barely perceptible, subconscious awareness (highly tacit) to just barely codifiable (a low degree of tacitness). Getting a grip on, and managing effectively, the tacit knowledge component of capabilities remains one of the greatest managerial challenges. The degree of tacitness of the capabilities identified in Stage 3 is examined with the help of the schematic presented in Figure A.5.

Stage 6: Strategic analysis

The outcome of the strategic positioning exercise is displayed in the strategic mapping framework shown in Figure A.6. The objective of this final stage of the methodology is to formulate strategic recommendations on the basis of the capabilities portfolio determined in the previous stage. The matrix scheme in Figure A.6 suggests some broad outlines for strategic action.

Depending on where the capability is positioned in the overall mapping, possible strategic action might (broadly) focus on:

- **Scanning** (emerging at all levels of competitive position). Recognizing that capabilities can originate from a very diverse set of sources, this management action focuses on casting a very wide scanning net. It further involves developing and nurturing environmental scanning capabilities so as to detect strong or weak signals indicating both threats and opportunities.

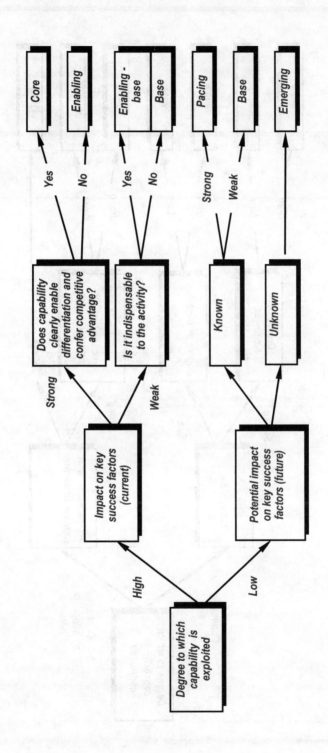

Figure A.3 Assessment of the competitive impact of the firm's capabilities

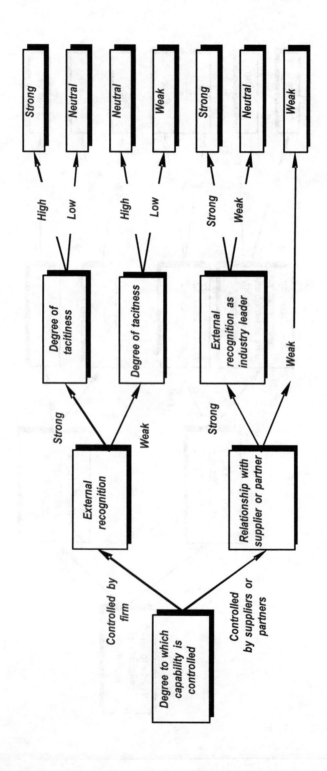

Figure A.4 Assessment of the degree of the firm's control over its capabilities

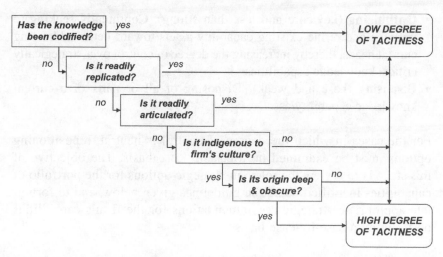

Figure A.5 Degree of tacitness ordering scheme

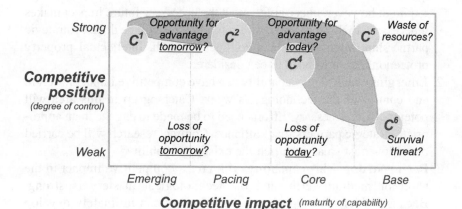

Figure A.6 Strategic capabilities portfolio framework showing a typical capabilities mapping outcome and strategic analysis

- **Protecting** (pacing to key/core and strong). Protecting against each eventuality, whether external (competitive factors) or internal (mismanagement of knowledge resources) that threatens the integrity of the capability portfolio , in either an active or a passive way.
- **Enriching** (pacing to key/core and strong). Nurturing the business environment most conducive for the growth of current capabilities, via in-house capability building, formation of strategic alliances, or acquisitions.

- **Optimizing** (key/core and less than strong). Continually seeking to improve and refine existing capability assets toward better addressing current needs, thereby increasing the degree of control over strategically critical knowledge capabilities.
- **Disposing** (base and weak). Disposing of all or parts of a current knowledge capability/asset.

For the cases in which the degree of control is neutral, repositioning options must be examined on a case-by-case basis. The objective of this stage is to review the relevant strategic options for the portfolio of capabilities identified using the guidelines given below, and to formulate appropriate strategic recommendations for the firm's capabilities portfolio on a case-by-case basis.

1. **Emerging/strong.** This capability can have competitive impact in future, and control of technology is strong. Optimization of the capability in question is in order to reinforce the potential competitive advantage required; however, uncertainty about the necessary future impact makes it necessary to do so at low cost. Preferably this will be done in strategic partnership, internally, or via contract research. Intellectual property protection measures need to be considered.
2. **Emerging/weak.** This capability can have competitive impact in future and control of the technology is weak. Catching up in this area will potentially be necessary. Efforts need to be made to engage in an appropriate strategic partnership or alliance. Contract research will be carried out at low cost so as to enrich the existing capability.
3. **Pacing/strong.** This capability will have a competitive impact in the short or medium term, and the technological mastery is strong. Because of its strong position, the company can ultimately develop some competitive advantage thanks to this capability. It can optimize by accelerating the development in order to come ahead. Those capabilities developed ahead of competitors will need to be protected. Joining a strategic alliance with partner firms can potentially shorten the introduction schedule. Furthermore, investment will be required for research into use of the capability in new products and new markets.
4. **Pacing/weak.** The capability will have a competitive impact in the short to medium term and mastery of the capability is weak. Enriching the portfolio by rapidly acquiring the capability will be a necessity. If the internal development period is too long, acquiring licenses or a joint development may be viable alternatives. It is necessary to

continue scanning the research efforts of competitors, changes in customer needs, and potential technology sources as well new uses for the technology.

5. **Key/strong.** The capability has a strong competitive impact and the mastery of it is strong. It is necessary to continue to improve and to exploit the capability. The development of synergies with other capabilities should be investigated. The company will also attempt to market its technology externally, via licensing, where there is no commercial risk involved in doing so. Protection can be achieved through successful early launch of resulting products or through appropriate business strategy.

6. **Key/weak.** The capability has a strong competitive impact and its mastery is weak. The core process is in danger. Does the possibility exist for enrichment by catching up quickly by way of an appropriate acquisition or by introduction of a substitute capability?

7. **Enabling-base/strong.** This capability no longer has any competitive impact on the business but it is necessary to the activity. The firm's mastery over it is strong. It is necessary to maintain the capability and to harvest it. Options include seeking new uses for it, or potentially disposing of it to third parties positioned in a different core process, for which the capability may still have some pacing or key character.

8. **Enabling-basic/weak.** The capability has no more competitive impact but it is necessary to the activity and mastery over it is weak. The associated core process is endangered. Is enrichment via catching up quickly through an appropriate acquisition, or through introduction of substitute capability, a possible option?

Stage 7: Debriefing

The methodology process can be quite involving and complex. Critical assumptions are made throughout; these need to be scrutinized and challenged at each of the stages. It is well worth the effort to review the outcome of the strategic assessment at the end of the process using the following guidelines:

1. Does the final outcome (strategic positioning matrix) make sense? Is the resulting portfolio of capabilities plausible?

2. What are the critical assumptions that the analysis is based on? How valid are they; how sensitive to variation are they? How would the outcome change if you were modify these assumptions?

3. Indeed, how, if at all, might the outcome be expected to be different if another group, representing different functional backgrounds in the firm, had carried out the same exercise?

Summary

Ideally, the exercise is carried out as a multidisciplinary exercise on an ongoing basis. The objective of the exercise is to identify and assess, strategically, the firm's portfolio of capabilities. Early in the exercise, one of the firm's core processes is selected as a basis for further analysis. The resulting portfolio of capabilities, of course, relates only to this particular core process. The firm, on the other hand, undoubtedly has any number of key processes in its value chain. Thus, to build a more complete picture of the firm portfolio of core capabilities, one would need to repeat the assessment process for each of the key business processes.

From the integrated and collective set of capability portfolios that support the firm's core business processes along its value chain, complementary and synergistic clusters of these ultimately constitute the basic aggregate of the firm's core competencies. To qualify as truly "core," competencies must:

- make a disproportionate contribution to customer-perceived value
- represent a unique source of competitiveness
- provide unique opportunities for new business ventures.

As pointed out earlier, core competencies must also clearly transcend any single business process, as indeed they may transcend any single business unit within the corporation.

Case study: BP Amoco and capabilities development

The oil exploration and production (oil E&P) industry is experiencing a period of fundamental change. Large players in the industry are redefining themselves through radical shifts in strategies. These are resulting in strategic combinations and alliances among asset oil E&P firms, alliances between oil E&P firms and service providers, and varying other types of outsourcing arrangements.

Much of the R&D in the oil E&P industry, for example, is being shifted from oil companies to major contractors. Major players in the industry have increasingly realized that their central R&D capabilities cannot even come close to matching the innovative potential of a well-managed outsourcing system, except in the few areas that are core to the firm. This realization has to no small extent been impacted by the drastic downsizing measures introduced by many of the large established firms in the 1980s. Service firms such as Schlumberger, on the other hand, are boosting staff, research spending, and technology development capabilities. Alliances, partnerships, and integrated, life-of-the-field management arrangements are rapidly becoming the industry norm.

Oil E&P firms, with fewer technical people and faster exploration-to-production schedules, are increasingly relying on service companies such as Schlumberger to deploy their technologies and broad arrays of competencies. New business models are emerging that are providing one stop shops that offer integrated solutions to established oil E&P firms to manage their field from cradle to grave. These initiatives are achieving new levels of reduced cost and revenue enhancement for all parties. Even more importantly, the new initiatives are also resulting in an unprecedented exchange of knowledge across the industry.

In a typical situation, for example, a strategic team is formed between a large E&P firm and a manufacturer of drilling equipment. The oil E&P firm agrees to purchase its equipment from the manufacturer. On one level, the drilling equipment manufacturer becomes an extension of the oil E&P firm by assuming responsibility for equipment selection and operationalization; at a deeper level the teaming agreement results in a considerable exchange of experiential, project, and operational knowledge between the two partners.

The cost savings to both parties can be substantial. Strategic teaming has brought operating cost down considerably, by the exchange of knowledge that now takes place between an oil E&P firm and equipment provider from the early design specification phase, throughout commissioning, and ultimately during operations. Industry specialists suggest that real cost savings to the oil E&P firm's bottom line achieved through this continual exchange of knowledge is significantly more than can be achieved through the simple price negotiations in traditional buyer/seller relations.

Winning through knowledge

BP Amoco CEO John Brown believes that all firms competing in the global information age face a common challenge: deploying knowledge more effectively than their competitors do. Brown goes on to point out that he is not referring only to knowledge already residing in the firm. Rather, he has been quoted as saying, "Any organization that thinks it does everything the best and need not learn from others is incredibly arrogant and foolish."[1]

BP Amoco is today a highly profitable oil E&P company. It has a strong position in essentially all of the world's strategically important oil and gas regions. Its exploration and development costs are now among the lowest in the industry. Yet organizationally, BP Amoco is much smaller and simpler than it was in the late 1980s. Before its recent merger with Amoco, BP had 53,000 employees—down from 129,000. Rather than being mired in procedures and divided into a multitude of baronies, BP Amoco now has an abundance of teams and knowledge networks across the firm in which people are eager to share and exchange knowledge.

What is BP Amoco doing differently now? What are the supportive capabilities it is developing to achieve successful sourcing and internalization of new knowledge? It has built a strong platform of supporting capabilities such as learning, strategic teaming, and relationship building with external partners, to maximize the strategic impact of its existing capabilities portfolio.

Learning on all levels

BP Amoco has developed a formidable learning capability. Learning is viewed at BP Amoco to be at the heart of the firm's ability to adapt quickly and seamlessly to changes in its rapidly moving competitive environment. Furthermore, it forms the foundation of its knowledge acquisition capability; it is at the root of recognizing and deploying new knowledge rapidly and fully. BP Amoco is currently applying a learning process known as an After Action Review.[2] This is a team-based learning process that is applicable to any event that offers the opportunity to capture and apply lessons learnt, to drilling operations, refinery maintenance, or even management meetings.

BP Amoco learns not only from its own people but also from contractors and from partners such as Shell. All sources of knowledge are considered to be crucial. The key to reaping big returns, BP Amoco's people have learned, is to leverage knowledge by replicating it throughout the company so that each unit is not learning in isolation and reinventing the wheel many times over.

Virtual team networking is BP Amoco's sophisticated computer network, which allows its people to work cooperatively and share knowledge quickly and easily regardless of time, distance, and organizational boundaries. It allows users to work together as if they were in the same room; the PCs feature videoconferencing capability, electronic blackboards, scanners, faxes, and groupware. Furthermore, the firm's virtual team networking PCs are connected to an intranet which features sites for sharing technical data on various specific topics such as muds used as drilling lubricants, sharing contacts, programs, and processes available to reduce the amount of pipe that gets stuck in wells.

BP Amoco also uses its virtual team networking capability to share knowledge with its contractors and outside suppliers. A recent development in the Andrew oil field in the North Sea is a case in point: The virtual team networking network was used by BP Amoco and its outside partner firms to figure out radical ways to cut the cost and time of projects. Partners briefed each other in places as far removed as Alaska and Columbia on how they made critical decisions. In other work, BP Amoco is using the network to improve the way it works with Shell in the Gulf of Mexico and Brown & Root in the North Sea. BP Amoco estimates that the virtual team network produced at least US$30 million in value in its first year alone.

Sharing capabilities through strategic partnering

BP Amoco is also developing capabilities that are focusing on forging distinctive relationships with external strategic partners. These are transforming contractual relationship management into genuine knowledge-sharing collaboration. This process begins with a mindset that focuses not so much on looking only at technology for a solution, rather looking at the firm's relationship with its outside contractors. Traditionally, outside contractors were looked upon and treated as adversaries. Rather than continuing the practice of playing them off against each other, BP Amoco began treating them as allies, offering them a financial interest in the project's outcome, and generally establishing a collaborative environment for working together to challenge costs, seek the best value, and innovate. Knott (1996), with reference to the Andrew oil field project, notes that:

> Delivering against targets became an established trademark of Andrew's team behaviour. Before the project began, BP had acknowledged that to improve business ventures beyond the benefits gained from technological advances alone, the necessary partner for technology lay in the cultivation of a positive behavioural attitude. This was sought and identified from the outset through the responses of the alliance contractors during selection, and was encouraged throughout the project at an individual level with continuous coaching of leadership skills and the active promotion of teambuilding.

A joint collaborative effort with Schlumberger, the oilfield services firm, to develop a special device called a logging tool further illustrates the point. BP Amoco was experiencing difficulties drilling horizontal wells. Schlumberger had critical knowledge in this area. BP Amoco proposed to Schlumberger a collaborative effort involving:

- bringing BP Amoco scientists and Schlumberger scientists together for joint development of the tool
- sharing development costs
- using BP Amoco wells for testing the tool.

A group of BP Amoco scientists ended up going to Schlumberger's research laboratory to work with its researchers on developing a prototype. When completed, the prototype was tested and modified until it proved to be successful in the field. Schlumberger was then asked by BP Amoco to build the tool and to make it available to BP Amoco before offering it to anyone else in the world.

BP Amoco has refocused its technology people from technology invention to technology application. Their mission is to source and access the best technology wherever it resides inside or outside the firm, to apply it quickly, and thereby cut cost and time to market. BP Amoco understands that it cannot expect to possess more than a fraction of the world's best technology, and that its people's ability to combine and apply externally sourced technology is what really endows real competitive advantage.

Notes

1 The discussion of BP Amoco's knowledge sourcing practices is based largely on Prokesch (1997).
2 BP's application of After Action Reviews (AARs) is described by Collison and Parcell (2001). The AAR process was developed by the US army for individuals and teams to learn and capture knowledge immediately from success and failures with just four questions:
    1 What was supposed to happen?
    2 What actually happened?
    3 Why were there differences?
    4 What can we learn?

REFERENCES

Aaker, D. A. (1992) *Strategic Market Management*, 3rd edn, Wiley.

Ainscough, M., Neailey, K., and Tennant, C. (2003) "A self-assessment tool for implementing concurrent engineering through change management," *International Journal of Project Management* **21** (6), pp. 425–32.

Andriessen, D. (2003) *Making Sense of Intellectual Capital: Designing a method for the valuation of intangibles*, Oxford: Butterworth-Heinemann.

Angle, H. L. and Van de Ven, A. H. (1989) "Suggestions for managing the innovation journey," in A. H. Van de Ven, H. L. Angle, and M. S. Poole (eds), *Research on the Management of Innovation*, New York: Ballinger/Harper and Row.

Arino, A., de la Torre, J., and Ring, P. (1998) "Learning from failure: towards an evolutionary model of collaborative ventures," *Organizational Science* **9** (3), pp. 306–25.

Arthur, W. B. (1999) "New economics for a knowledge economy: the law of increasing returns," in R. Ruggles and D. Holtshouse (eds), *The Knowledge Advantage*, Oxford: Capstone.

Atuahene-Gima, K. and Ko, A. (2001) "An empirical investigation of the effects of market orientation and entrepreneurship orientation alignment on product innovation," *Organizational Science* **12** (1), pp. 54–74.

Bahrami, H. (1996) "The emerging flexible organization: perspectives from Silicon Valley," in P. S. Myers (ed.), *Knowledge Management and Organizational Design*, Boston, Mass.: Butterworth-Heinemann, pp. 55–75.

Bain & Company (2003) *Management Tools 2003*, Bain & Company.

Barney, J. B. (1991) "Firm resources and sustained competitive advantage," *Journal of Management* **17** (1), pp. 99–120.

Barré, Bertrand (2001) *Vision oblique*. Les presses du management.

Barton, D. Leonard (1995) *Wellsprings of Knowledge*, Cambridge, Mass.: Harvard Business School Press

Bean, A. S., Einolf, K., and Russo, M. J. (1999) "Benchmarking your R&D: results from the IRI/CIMS annual R&D survey for 1997," *Research Technology Management* **42** (1), pp. 24–35.

Birchall, D. W. and Armstrong, M. (2004) "Market understanding as a determinant of innovation success in SMEs," *EBS Review* **18**, pp. 17–29.

Birchall, D. W. and Tovstiga, G. (2001) "The strategic potential of the firm's knowledge portfolio," in A. A. Thompson Jr and A. J. Strickland III (eds), *Crafting and Executing Strategy*, Boston, Mass.: McGraw-Hill Irwin.

Birchall, D. W. and Tovstiga, G. (2002a) *Future Proofing*, Oxford: Capstone.

Birchall, D. W. and Tovstiga, G. (2002b) "Assessing the firm's knowledge portfolio: a framework and methodology," *International Journal of Technology Management* **24** (4), pp. 419–434

Birchall, D. W. and Tovstiga, G. (2004a) "The strategic potential of a firm's knowledge portfolio," in S. Crainer and D. Dearlove (eds), *Financial Times Handbook of Management*, 3rd edn, London: Financial Times/Prentice Hall.

Birchall, D. W. and Tovstiga, G. (2004b) *Innovation Performance Measurement: Striking the right balance*, London: Grist.

Birchall, D. W., Tovstiga, G., Hillenbrand, C., and Chanaron, J. J. (2005) *The Measurement of Innovation Performance.* Henley-on-Thames: Henley Management College.

Birchall, D. W., Tovstiga, G., Morrison, M., and Gaule, A. (2004) *Innovation Performance Measurement: Striking the right balance*. London: Grist.

Bogner, W. C. and Thomas, H. (1994) "Core competence and competitive advantage: a model and illustrative evidence from the pharmaceutical industry," in G. Hamel and A. Heene (eds), *Competence-Based Competition*, Chichester: Wiley.

Bower, J. L. and Christensen, C. M. (1995) "Disruptive technologies: catching the wave," *Harvard Business Review* (Jan–Feb), pp. 43–53.

Brand, S. (2000) "Is technology moving too fast? Our technology Visions 21," *Time*, July 3.

Brockhoff, K.(2003) "Customers' perspectives of involvement in new product development," *International Journal of Technology Management*, **26** (5/6): pp. 464–82.

Buckman, R. (2001) Presentation given at the Henley KM Forum, Henley Management College, January 22.

Calato, R., Garcia, R., and Dröge, C. (2003) "The effects of environmental turbulence on new product development strategy planning," *Journal of Product Innovation Management* **20**, pp. 90–103.

Carr, N. G. (2004) "Bridging the breakthrough gap," *Strategy and Business enews*, Booz Allen Hamilton, http://www.strategy-business.com/press/atricle/04402?pg=0

Casson, M. (2000) *Enterprise and Leadership*, Cheltenham: Edward Elgar.

Chandler, A. D. Jr. (1990) *Scale and Scope: The dynamics of industrial competition*, Cambridge, Mass.: Harvard University Press.

Chen, C.-J. and Chang, L.-S. (2004) "Dynamics of business network embeddedness," *Journal of American Academy of Business* 5 (1/2), pp. 237–42.

Chiesa, V. and Barbeschi, M. (1994) "Technology strategy in competence-based competition," in G. Hamel and A. Heene (eds), *Competence-Based Competition*, Chichester: Wiley.

Chiesa, V., Coughlan, P., and Voss, C. A. (1996) "Development of a technical innovation audit," *Journal of Product Innovation Management* 12, pp. 105–36.

Chiesa, V., Coughlan, P., and Voss, C. A. (1998) "Development of a technical innovation audit," *IEEE Engineering Management Review* 26 (2), pp. 64–91.

Christensen, C. M. (1997) *The Innovator's Dilemma*, Boston, Mass.: Harvard Business School Press.

Christensen, C. M., Johnson, M. W., and Rigby, D. K. (2002) "Foundations for growth: how to identify and build disruptive new businesses," *MIT Sloan Management Review* 43 (3), pp. 22–32.

Christensen, C. M. and Overdorf, M. (2000) "Meeting the challenge of disruptive change," *Harvard Business Review* 78 (2), pp. 67–76.

Christensen, C. M. and Raynor, M. E. (2003) *The Innovator's Solution*, Boston, Mass.: Harvard Business School Press.

Clark, K. B. and Fujimoto, T. (1991) *Product Development Performance: Strategy, organization, and management in the world auto industry*, Boston, Mass.: Harvard Business School Press.

Cohen, M. A., Eliashberg, J., and Teck-Hua, H. (2000) "An analysis of several new product performance metrics," *Informs* 2 (4), pp. 337–49.

Cohen, W. M. and Levinthal, D. A. (1990) "Absorptive capacity: a new perspective on learning and innovation," *Administrative Science Quarterly* 35, pp. 128–52.

Collins, J. (2001) *Good to Great*, London: Random House.

Collins, J. (2002) "How great companies tame technology," *Newsweek*, April 29, p. 53.

Collison, C. and Parcell, G. (2001) *Learning to Fly*. Oxford: Capstone.

Collison, C. and Parcell, G. (2005) *Learning to Fly: Practical knowledge management from leading and learning organizations,* 2nd edn, Chichester: Capstone.

Cooper, R. G. (1984) "How new product strategies impact on performance," *Journal of Product Innovation Management* **1**, pp. 5–18.

Cooper, R. G. (1993) *Winning at New Products: Accelerating the process from idea to launch*, 2nd edn, Reading, Mass.: Addison Wesley.

Cooper, R. G., Edgett, S. J., and Kleinschmidt, E. J. (2001) "Portfolio management for new product development: results of an industry practices study," *R&D Management* **4**, pp. 361–80.

Cooper, R. G., Edgett, S. J., and Kleinschmidt, E. J. (2004) "Benchmarking best NPD practices—I," *Research Technology Management* **47** (1), pp. 31–43.

Covey, S. R. (1994) "The strange attractor," *Executive Excellence*, August, pp. 5–6.

Cristiano, J., Liker, J., and White, C. (2000.) "Customer-driven product development through quality function deployment in the US and Japan," *Journal of Product Innovation Management* **17** (4), pp. 286–308.

Cullen, J. B., Johnson, J. L., and Sakano, T. (2000) "Success through commitment and trust: the soft side of strategic alliance management," *Journal of World Business* **35** (3), pp. 223–41.

Das, T. K. and Teng, B.-S. (1999) "Managing risks in strategic alliances," *Academy of Management Executive* **13** (4), pp. 50–63.

Day, G. S. (1997) "Maintaining the competitive edge: creating and sustaining advantage in dynamic environments," in G. S. Day and D. J. Reibstein (eds), *Wharton on Dynamic Competitive Strategy*, New York: Wiley.

Day, G. S. and Schoemaker, P. J. H. (2000a) "Avoiding the pitfalls of emerging technologies," in G. S. Day and P. J. H. Schoemaker (eds), *Wharton on Managing Emerging Technologies*, New York: Wiley.

Day, G. S. and Schoemaker, P. J. H. (2000b) "A different game," in G. S. Day and P. J. H Schoemaker (eds), *Wharton on Managing Emerging Technologies*, New York: Wiley.

De Geus, A. (1995) "Organizational principles of long term corporate survivors," paper for Santa Fe Institute Conference on Complexity and Strategy, London.

De Geus, A. (1999) *The Living Company*, London: Nicholas Brealey.

De Laat, P. (2001) "Research and development alliances: ensuring trust by mutual commitments," in M. Ebers (ed.), *The Formation of Inter-Organizational Networks*, Oxford: Oxford University Press.

De Meyer, A., Loch, C. H., and Pich, M. T. (2002) "Managing project uncertainty: from variation to chaos," *MIT Sloan Management Review* **43** (2), pp. 60–8.

Denker, S., Steward, D. V., and Browning, T. R. (2001) "Planning concurrency and managing iterations in projects," *Project Management Journal* **32** (3), pp. 31–40.

Dierickx, I. and Cool, K. (1989) "Asset stock accumulation and sustainability of competitive advantage," *Management Science Quarterly*, **35**, pp. 1504–11.

Doering, D. S. and Parayre, R. (2000) "Identification and assessment of emerging technologies," in G. S. Day and P. J. H. Schoemaker (eds), *Wharton on Managing Emerging Technologies,* New York: Wiley.

Dooley, K., Subra, A., and Anderson, J. (2002) "Adoption rates and patterns of best practices in new product development." *International Journal of Innovation Management* **6** (1), pp. 85–104.

Drew, S. and Turner, I. (2004) "Resource analysis," in *Core Commentary 6 (Strategic Direction)*, Henley Management College.

Drucker, P. F. (1999) "Knowledge-worker productivity: the biggest challenge," *California Management Review* **41** (2), pp. 79–94.

Duarte, C. L. and Tennant-Snyder, N. (2003) *Strategic Innovation*, Hoboken, NJ: Wiley.

Dussauge, P., Hart, S., and Ramanantsoa, B. (1992) *Strategic Technology Management*, Chichester: Wiley.

Dyer, J. H., Kale, P., and Singh, H. (2001) "How to make strategic alliances work," *MIT Sloan Management Review* **42** (4), pp 37–44.

Ebers, M. (ed.) (1999) *The Formation of Inter-Organizational Networks*, Oxford: Oxford University Press.

Economist (2004a) "Southern comfort, eastern promise," *Economist*, December 11.

Economist (2004b) "Access all areas," *Economist*, August 5.

Economist (2005a) "Survey of nanotechnology," *Economist*, January 1.

Edvinsson, L. and Malone, M. S. (1997) *Intellectual Capital*, London: Piatkus.

Ernst, H. (2002) "Success factors of new product development: a review of the empirical literature," *International Journal of Management Reviews* **4** (1), pp. 1–40.

European Industrial Research Management Association (EIRMA) (2002) *Assessing R&D Effectiveness,* Working group report 62, Paris: EIRMA.

Evans, P. and Wurster. T. S (2000) *Blown to Bits*, Boston, Mass.: Harvard Business School Press.

Foster, R. and Kaplan, S. (2001) *Creative Destruction*, New York: Currency/Doubleday.

Fulford, B. and Huang, P. (2004) "Honda takes to the skies," *Forbes Global*, November 15.

Garcia-Canal, E., Duarte, C. L., Criado, J. R., and Llaneza, A. V. (2002) "Time compression diseconomies in accelerated global alliances," *Management Decision* **40** (7/8), pp. 745–55.

Gibbons, M., Limoges, C., Nowotny, H., Schwartzman, S., Scott, P., and Trow, M. (1994). *The New Production of Knowledge*, London: Sage.

Gilbert, C. (2003) "The disruption opportunity," *MIT Sloan Management Review* **44** (4), pp. 27–32.

Glaister, K. W. and Buckley, P. J. (1996) "Strategic motives for international alliance formation," *Journal of Management Studies* **33**, pp. 301–32.

Godener, A. and Soderquist, K. E. (2004) "Use and impact of performance measurement results in R&D and NPD: an exploratory study," *R&D Management* **34** (2), pp. 91–110.

Goldense, B. L. (1999) "Manufacturers don't measure R&D well," *IEEE Solutions* **8**, pp. 13–14.

Goldratt, E. M. (1992) *The Goal*, 2nd edn, Croton-on-Hudson, NY: North River Press.

Gomes-Casseres, B. (2003) "Competing in alliance constellations: a primer for managers," paper for Sixth International Conference on International Management, Carnegie-Bosch Institue, Carnegie Mellon University.

Goodman, R. A. and Lawless, M. W. (1994) *Technology and Strategy: Conceptual models and diagnostics*, New York: Oxford University Press.

Gotzsch, J. (2003) "Managing product expression," in unpublished DBA, London: Brunel University.

Govindarajan, V. and Trimble, C. (2004) "Strategic innovation and the science of learning," *MIT Sloan Management Review* **45** (2), pp. 67–76.

Granovetter, M. S. (1973) "The strength of weak ties," *American Journal of Sociology* **78**, pp. 1360–80.

Grant, R. M. (2002) *Contemporary Strategy Analysis*, 4th edn, Oxford: Blackwell.

Gray, B. (1987) "Conditions facilitating interorganizational corroboration," *Human Relations* **38**, pp. 911–36.

Groenveld, P. (1997) "Roadmapping integrates business and technology," *Research Technology Management* **40** (5), pp. 48–56.

Gruner, K. and Homburg, C. (2000) "Does customer interaction enhance new product success?" *Journal of Business Research* **49**, pp. 1–14.

Hall, R. (1997) "Complex systems, complex learning, and competence building," in R. Sanchez and A. Heene (eds), *Strategic Learning and Knowledge Management*, Chichester: Wiley.

Hamel, G. (1994) "The concept of core competence," in G. Hamel and A. Heene (eds), *Competence Based Competition*, Chichester: Wiley.

Hamel, G. (2000) *Leading the Revolution*, Boston, Mass.: Harvard Business School Press.

Hamel, G. and Prahalad, C. (1994) *Competing for the Future*, Boston, Mass.: Harvard Business School Press.

Han, J. K., Kim, N., and Srivastava, R. J. (1998) "Market orientation and organizational performance; is innovation a missing link?" *Journal of Marketing* **62** (4): pp. 17–33.

Hart, S. (1993) "Dimensions of success in new product development: an exploratory investigation," *Journal of Marketing Management* **9** (1), pp. 23–41.

Hayes, R., Wheelwright, S., and Clark, K. (1988) *Dynamic Manufacturing: Creating the learning organization*, New York: Free Press.

Helleloid, D. and Simonin, B. (1994) "Organizational learning and a firm's core competence," in G. Hamel and A. Heene (eds), *Competence Based Competition*, Chichester: Wiley.

Henard, D. H. and Szymanski, D. M. (2001) "Why some new products are more successful than others," *Journal of Marketing Research* **38**, pp. 362–76.

Hintermeier, D. (2004) "Sprit gespart mit Drachenkraft," *Handelsblatt*, October 22, p. 5.

Huggins, R. (2000) "The success and failure of policy-implanted inter-firm network initiatives: motivations," *Entrepreneurship and Regional Development* **12** (2), pp. 111–36.

Inkpen, A. (1997) "An examination of knowledge management in inter-national joint ventures," in P. W. Beamish and J. P. Killing (eds), *Comparative Strategies: North American perspectives*, San Francisco: New Lexington Press.

Jaworski, B. J. and Kohli, A. K. (1993) "Market orientation: antecedents and consequences," *Journal of Marketing* **57** (3), pp. 53–71.

Jeffery, M. and Leliveld, I. (2004) "Best practices in IT portfolio management," *MIT Sloan Management Review* **45** (3), pp. 41–50.

Jeffries, F. L. (2000) "Trust and adaptation in relational contracting," *Academy of Management Review* **25** (4), pp. 873–83.

Jenkins, M. and Floyd, S. W. (2001) "Trajectories in the evolution of tech-nology: a multi-level study of competition in Formula One racing," *Organization Studies* **22**, pp. 945–70.

Jones, C., Hesterly, W. S., and Borgatti, S. P. (1997) "A general theory of network governance: exchange conditions and social mechanisms," *Academy of Management Review* **22**, pp. 911–45.

Kanter, R. M. (1983) *The Change Masters*, New York: Simon & Schuster.

Kaplan, N. J. and Hurd, J. (2002) "Realizing the promise of partnerships," *Journal of Business Strategy* **23** (3), pp. 38–43.

Kaplan, R. S. and Norton, D. P. (1992) "The balanced scorecard: measures that drive performance," *Harvard Business Review* **70** (1), pp. 71–80.

Kaplan, R. S. and Norton, D. P. (1996). *The Balanced Scorecard*, Boston, Mass.: Harvard Business School Press.

Kauffman, P., Ricks, W., and Shockcor, J. (1999) "Research portfolio analysis using extensions of quality function deployment," *Engineering Management Journal* **11** (2), pp. 3–9.

Kelley, T. (2002) *The Art of Innovation*, London: HarperCollins Business.

Kelly, K. (1998) *New Rules for the New Economy*, New York: Viking/Penguin.

Kennerley, M. and Neely, A. (2004) "Measuring and managing the right things" in S. Crainer and D. Dearlove (eds), *Financial Times Handbook of Management*, London: Pearson Education.

Kerssens-van Drongelen, I. C. and Bilderbeek, J. (1999) "R&D performance measurement: more than choosing a set of metrics," *R&D Management* **29** (1), pp. 35–46.

Kerssens-van Drongelen, I. C. and Cook, A. (1997) "Design principles for the development of measurement systems for research and development," *R&D Management* **27** (4), pp. 345–58.

Kerssens-van Drongelen, K., Nixon, B., and Pearson, A. (2000) "Performance measurement in industrial R&D," *International Journal of Management Reviews* **2** (2), pp. 111–144.

Kerssens-van Drongelen, K. and Weerd-Nederhof, P. C. (1999) "The use of performance measurement tools for balancing short- and long-term NPD performances," *International Journal of Innovation Management* **3** (4), pp. 397–426.

Kessler, E. H. and Chakravarthy, A. K. (1996) "Innovation speed: a conceptual model of context, antecedents and outcomes," *Academy of Management Review* **21** (4), pp. 1143–91.

Kirchhoff, B. A., Merges, M. J., and Morabito, J. A. (2001) "A value creation model for measuring and managing the R&D portfolio," *Engineering Management Journal* **13** (1), pp. 19–23.

Klein, J. A. and Hiscocks, P. G. (1994) "Competence-based competition: a practical toolkit," in G. Hamel and A. Heene (eds), *Competence-Based Competition*, Chichester: Wiley.

Knott, T. (1996) "No business as usual—an extraordinary North Sea result," BP.

Kok, R. A. W., Hillebrand, B., and Biemans, W. G. (2003) "What makes product development market oriented? Towards a conceptual framework," *International Journal of Innovation Management* **7** (2), pp. 137–62.

Larson, A. (1992) "Network dyads in entrepreneurial settings: a study of the governance of exchange relationships," *Administrative Science Quarterly* **37** (1), pp. 76–104.

Leonard-Barton, D. (1995) *Wellsprings of Knowledge*, Cambridge, Mass.: Harvard Business School Press.

Levine, H. (2004a) *Components of a Project Portfolio Management Process: Part two—managing the pipeline*, Sciforma Corporation.

Levine, J. (2004b) "E-republic of Estonia – If it works, you can break it," *Forbes Global*, December 20.

Linton, J. D., Walsh, S. T., and Morabito, J. (2002) "Analysis, ranking and selection of R&D projects in a portfolio," *R&D Management* **32** (2), pp. 139–49.

Lorenzen, M. (2002) "Ties, trust, and trade: elements of a theory of coordination in industrial clusters," *International Studies of Management and Organization* **32** (4), pp. 14–35.

Maira, A. N (1998) "Connecting across boundaries: the fluid-network organization," *Prism*, Arthur D. Little (first quarter), pp. 23–35.

Martinelli, R. and Waddell, J. (2004) "Program risk management", *Project Management World Today*, http://www.pmforum.org/pmwt/archives/pmwt04/pmwt04-910.htm.

McDermott, R. (1999) "Why information technology inspired but cannot deliver knowledge management," *California Management Review* **41** (4), pp. 103–18.

Mezias, S. J. and Boyle, E. (2002) *Organizational Dynamics of Creative Destruction: Entrepreneurship and the emergence of industries*, Basingstoke: Palgrave Macmillan.

Mezias, S. J. and Glynn, M. A. (1993) "The three faces of corporate renewal: Institution, revolution, and evolution," *Strategic Management Journal* **14**, pp. 77–101.

Miller, W. L. and Morris, L. (1999) *Fourth Generation R&D*, New York: Wiley.

Mintzberg, H. (1988) "The structuring of organisations," in D. Asch and C. Bowman (eds), *Readings in Strategic Management*, Macmillan.

Mohr, J. J. and Shooshtari, N. H. (2003) "Marketing of high-technology products and innovations," *Journal of Marketing Theory and Practice*, Special edn, pp. 1–12.

Montoya-Weiss, M. M. and Calatone, R. J. (1994) "Determinants of new product performance: a review and meta-analysis," *Journal of Product Innovation Management* **11**, pp. 397–417.

Neely, A. (2004) "Performance measurement: the new crisis," in S. Crainer and D. Dearlove (eds), *Financial Times Handbook of Management*, Harlow: Pearson Education.

Nevis, E. C., DiBella, A. J., and Gould, J. (1995). "Understanding organizations as learning systems," *Sloan Management Review*, Winter, pp. 73–85.

Nonaka, I. and Takeuchi, H. (1995) *The Knowledge-Creating Company: How Japanese companies create the dynamics of innovation*, New York: Oxford University Press.

Nystrom, H. (1985) "Product development strategy: an integration of technology and marketing," *Journal of Product Innovation Management* **2** (1), pp. 25–34.

Odenthal, S., Tovstiga, G., Tambe, H., and Van Oene, F. (2004) "Co-innovation: capturing the innovation premium for growth," *Prism*, Arthur D. Little (first semester), pp. 41–55.

O'Reilly, C. A. and Tushman, M. L. (2004) "The ambidextrous organization," *Harvard Business Review*, April, pp. 74–81.

Organisation for Economic Co-operation and Development (OECD) *The measurement of scientific and technological activities*, <www.oecd.org/dataoecd/35/61/2367580.pdf>.

OECD (2004) "Networks, partnerships, clusters and intellectual property rights: opportunities and challenges for innovative SMEs in a global economy," in *Promoting Entrepreneurship and Innovative SMEs in a Global Economy, 2nd OECD Conference of Ministers Responsible for Small and Medium-sized Enterprises (SMEs)*, 2004, Istanbul: OECD.

Oliver, C. (2000) "Determinants of inter-organizational relationships: integration and future directions," *Academy of Management Review* **15**, pp. 241–65.

Orr, D. (2003) "Nice digs," *Forbes Global*, November 10, p. 30.

Ottosson, S. (2004) "Dynamic product development—DPD," *Technovation* **24** (3), pp. 207–18.

Paap, J. and Katz, R. (2004) "Anticipating disruptive innovation," *Research Technology Management* **47** (5), pp. 13–23.

Partovi, F. Y. (1999) "A quality function deployment approach to strategic capital budgeting," *Engineering Economist* **44** (3), pp. 239–61.

Partovi, F. Y. and Corredoira, R. A. (2002) "Quality function deployment for the good of soccer," *European Journal of Operational Research* **137** (3), pp. 642–57.

Penrose, E. T. (1959) *The Theory of the Growth of the Firm*, New York: Wiley.

Pietersen, W. G. (2002) *Reinventing Strategy*, New York: Wiley.

Polanyi, M. (1967) *The Tacit Dimension*, New York: Doubleday.

Porter, M. E. (1980) *Competitive Strategy*, New York: Macmillan.

Porter, M. E. (1985) *Competitive Advantage*, New York: Macmillan.

Porter, M. E. (1990) *The Competitive Advantage of Nations*, New York: Free Press.

Prahalad, C. K. and Hamel, G. (1990) "The core competence of the corporation," *Harvard Business Review* **68** (3), pp. 79–82.

Prahalad, C. K. and Hamel, G. (1994) *Competing for the Future*, Boston, Mass.: Harvard Business School Press.

Prahalad, C. K, Hamel, G., and Penrose, E. T. (1959) *The Theory of the Growth of the Firm*, New York: Wiley.

Prensky, M. (2004) "Capturing the value of 'generation tech' employees," *Strategy and Business enews*, Booz Allen Hamilton.

Priem, R. L. and Butler, J. E. (2001) "Is the resource based view a useful perspective for strategic management research?" *Academy of Management Review* **26** (1), pp 22–31.

Prokesch, S. E. (1997) "Unleashing the power of learning: an interview with British Petroleum's John Brown," *Harvard Business Review* Sept–Oct, pp. 146–68.

Quélin, B. (1997) "Appropriability and the creation of new capabilities through strategic alliances," in R. Sanchez and A. Heene (eds), *Strategic Learning and Knowledge Management*, Chichester: Wiley.

Quinn, J. B. (1985) "Managing innovation: controlled chaos," *Harvard Business Review* **63** (3), pp. 73–85.

Quinn, J. B. (1999) "Strategic outsourcing: leveraging knowledge capabilities," *MIT Sloan Management Review* **40** (4), pp. 9–22.

Quinn, J. B. (2002) "Strategy, science, and management," *MIT Sloan Management Review* **43** (4), p. 96.

Raz, T., Shencar, A. J., and Dvir, D. (2001) "Risk management, project success and technological uncertainty," *R&D Management* **32** (2), pp. 101–9.

Reid, D., Bussiere, D., and Greenaway, K. (2001) "Alliance formation issues of knowledge-based enterprises," *International Journal of Management Reviews* **3**, pp. 79–101.

Roos, J., Roos, G., Edvinsson, L., and Dragonetti, N. C. (1997) *Intellectual Capital*, London: Macmillan.

Rothwell, R., Freeman, C., Horlsey, A., Jervis, V. T. P., Robertson, A. B., and Townsend, J. (1974) "Sappho updated: Project Sappho Phase II," *Research Policy* 3, pp. 633–43.

Rumelt, R. P. (1994) "Foreword," in G. Hamel and A. Heene (eds), *Competence Based Competition*, Chichester: Wiley.

Sahal, D. (1981) *Patterns of Technological Innovation*, Reading, Mass.: Addison-Wesley.

Said, A. A. and HassabElnaby, H. R. (2003) "An empirical investigation of the performance consequences of nonfinancial measures," *Journal of Management Accounting Research* 15, pp. 193–223.

Saxenian, A.-L. (1994) *Regional Advantage: Culture and competition in Silicon Valley and Route 128*, Cambridge, Mass.: Harvard University Press.

Schein, E. H. (1992) *Organizational Culture and Leadership*, 2nd edn, San Francisco: Jossey-Bass.

Schoemaker, P. (1995). "Scenario planning: a tool for strategic thinking," *MIT Sloan Management Review* 36 (2), p. 25.

Schumpeter, J. A. (1934) *The Theory of Economic Development*, Cambridge, Mass.: Harvard University Press.

Schumpeter, J. (1939) *Business Cycles: A theoretical, historical and statistical analysis of the capitalist process*, New York: McGraw-Hill.

Senge, P. M. (1990) *The Fifth Discipline: The art and practice of the learning organisation*, New York: Doubleday.

Shapiro, C. and Varian, H. R. (1999) *Information Rules*, Boston, Mass.: Harvard Business School Press.

Simsek, Z., Lubatkin, M. H., and Floyd, S. W. (2003) "Inter-firm networks and entrepreneurial behaviour: a structural embeddedness perspective," *Journal of Management* 29 (3), pp. 427–42.

Sivadas, E. and Dwyer, F. R. (2000) "An examination of organisational factors influencing new product success in internal and alliance-based processes," *Journal of Marketing* 64 (1), pp. 31–40.

Snow, C. C. and Thomas, J. B. (1993) "Building networks: broker roles and behaviours," in P. Lorange, B. Chakravarthy, J. Roos, and A. van de Ven (eds), *Implementing Strategic Processes: Change, learning and co-operation*, Oxford: Blackwell, pp. 217–38.

Spekman, R. E., Forbes III, T. M., Isabella, L. A., and MacAvoy, T. C. (1998) "Alliance management: a view from the past and a look into the future," *Journal of Management Studies* 35 (6), pp. 747–72.

Swink, M. L., Sandvig, J. C., and Mabert, V. (1996) "Adding 'zip' to product development: concurrent engineering methods and tools," *Business Horizons* 39 (2), pp. 41–50.

Tallman, S., Jenkins, M., Henry, N., and Pinch, S. (2004) "Knowledge, clusters and competitive advantage," *Academy of Management Review* **29** (2), pp. 258–72.

Teece, D. J. and Pisano, G. (1998) "The dynamic capabilities of firms: an introduction," in D. J. Teece and J. Chytry (eds), *Technology, Organization and Competitiveness*, Oxford: Oxford University Press.

Teece, D. J., Pisano, G., and Shuen, A. (1990) "Firm capabilities, resources and the concept of strategy," *CCC Working Paper 90–8*, Berkeley, Calif.: University of California.

Thompson, A. A. and Strickland, A. J. III (2001) *Crafting and Executing Strategy*, 12th edn, Boston, Mass.: McGraw-Hill Irwin.

Thurm, S. (2000) "At Cisco Systems, real work begins after a deal closes," *Wall Street Journal,* Wednesday, March 1, p. A1.

Tidd, J., Bessant, J., and Pavitt, K. (2001) *Managing Innovation: Integrating technological, market and organisational change*, 2nd edn, Chichester: Wiley.

Tovstiga, G.. (1998) "Profiling the knowledge worker in the knowledge-intensive organization: emerging roles," *International Journal of Technology Management* **18** (5/6/7/8).pp. 731–44.

Tovstiga, G. and Birchall, D. W. (2002): "Strategic knowledge sourcing, integration and assimilation: a capabilities portfolio perspective," Chapter 6 in N. Bontis (ed.), *World Congress on Intellectual Capital Readings*, Boston, Mass.: Butterworth-Heinemann.

Tovstiga, G. and Birchall, D. W. (2004) "Capturing opportunity from disruptive innovation: the firm's strategic capabilities revisited," paper for Fifth European Conference on Organizational Knowledge and Learning, and Capabilities (OKLC 2004), Innsbruck, Austria: University of Innsbruck.

Tovstiga, G. and Fantner, E. J. (2000) "Implications of the new networked economy for e-business start-ups: the case of Philip's Access point," *Internet Research* **10** (5), pp. 459–70.

Treacy, M. and Wiersema, F. (1995) *The Discipline of Market Leaders*, Reading, Mass.: Addison-Wesley.

Tripsas, M. (2000) "Commercializing emerging technologies through complementary assets," in G. S. Day and P. J. H Schoemaker (eds), *Wharton on Managing Emerging Technologies*, New York: Wiley.

Tushman, M. T. and Nadler, D. (1986) "Organizing for innovation," *California Management Review* **28**, pp. 74–92.

Tushman, M. T. and Nelson, R. R. (1990) "Introduction: technology, organizations, and innovation," *Administrative Science Quarterly* **35**, pp. 1–8.

Ulrich, D. and Smallwood, N. (2004) "Capitalizing on capabilities," *Harvard Business Review* **82** (6), pp. 119–28.

Uzzi, B. (1997) "Social structure and competition in inter firm networks: the paradox of embeddedness," *Administrative Science Quarterly* **31**, pp. 439–65.

Van de Ven, A. H., Polley, D. E., Garud, R., and Venkataraman, S. (1999) *The Innovation Journey*, Oxford: Oxford University Press.

Van den Berg, L., Braun, E., and van Winden, W. (2001) "Growth clusters in European cities: an integral approach," *Urban Studies* **38** (1), pp. 185–205.

Van der Heijden, K. (1996) *Scenarios: The art of strategic conversation*, Chichester: Wiley.

Van der Meulen, B. and Lohnberg, A. (2001) "The use of Foresight: institutional constraints and conditions," *International Journal of Technology Management* **21** (7/8), pp. 680–93.

Vandenbosch, M. and Clift, T. (2002) "Dramatically reducing cycle times through flash development," *Long Range Planning* **35** (6), pp. 567–80.

Verloop, J. (2004) *Insight into Innovation: Managing innovation by understanding the laws of innovation*, Amsterdam: Elsevier.

Werner, B. M. and Souder, W. E. (1997) "Measuring R&D performance: state of the art," *Research Technology Management* **40** (2), pp. 34–43.

Wernerfelt, B. (1984) "A resource-based view of the firm," *Strategic Management Journal* **5** (2), pp 171–81.

Zack, M. H. (2001) "Developing a knowledge strategy," in A. A. Thompson and A. J. Strickland III (eds), *Crafting and Executing Strategy*, Boston, Mass.: McGraw-Hill Irwin.

INDEX

Aaker, D. A., 128, 129
ABB, 70
absorptive capacity, 158–9, 173–4
agglomerative economies, 171
agile, 205
  approaches, 206–11
  features, 207
  organization, 11
  success factors, 207–8
Agilent, 191–2
Ainscough, M., 204
Alcoa Laboratories, 240
alliances, 8, 141, 152, 186, 228, 271
  capabilities, 159
  conditions for success, 145–7
  constellations, 158–9, 161
  causes of failure, 146
  function, 160
  knowledge, 61
  networks, 158–9, 161
  risk management, 157–8
  role, 144
  trust, 155
  see also partnering
America's Cup, 150
Andriessen, D., 22
Angle, H. L., 70
Apple, 92
Arino, A., 155
Armstrong, M., 110, 228
Arthur D. Little, 71, 72–3, 77, 96,
  252–3
AT&T, 91
automotive tyre manufacture, 134

Bagel, 39–40
Bahrami, H., 11, 98
Bain & Company, 227
Balanced Score Card (BSC), 214,
  236, 252–3
Barbeschi, M., 50

Barney, J. B., 20
Barré, B., 112–13
Bean, A. S., 228
Bell Laboratories, 256
Bessant, J., 229
Biemans, W. G., 109
Bilderbeek, J., 235, 251–3
biotechnology in India, 5–6
Birchall, D. W., 22, 31, 36, 38, 71, 77,
  82, 110, 120, 228, 229, 230,
  231, 234, 242, 244, 263
Bognor, W. C., 28, 58
Borg-Warner, 240
Borgatti, S. P., 164
boundary spanning, 109
bounding box, 192
Bower, J. L., 74
Boyle, E., 71, 232–3
BP, 33, 59, 260
BP Amoco, 275–9
Braun, E., 167, 177
Brockhoff, K., 114
Browning, T. R., 203
Buckley, P. J., 165
Buckman Laboratories, 46–7
business intelligence, 128
  gathering, 129
business model, 83, 89, 223
  alignment, 14–15
business strategy, 20, 50, 72, 166,
  215, 242, 273
  integration of technology strategy,
  129
Bussiere, D., 144, 152, 156, 159
Butler, J. E., 21

Calato, R., 117
Calatone, R. J., 108
Canon, 33, 43
capabilities, 3–103, 158, 181, 261
  appropriability, 42

Index